TOXIC
NOURISHMENT

TOXIC NOURISHMENT

Michael Eigen

London
KARNAC BOOKS

Chapter 3: Miscarriages. In: *Mind-Body Problems: Psychotherapy with Psychosomatic Disorders* (pp. 333–351). Ed. J. Schumacher Finell. Northvale, NJ: Jason Aronson.

Chapter 4: A bug-free universe. *Contemporary Psychoanalysis, 33,* No. 1 (1997): 19–41. Copyright 1997 William Alanson White Institute.

Chapter 8: Empty and violent nourishment. *Journal of Melanie Klein and Object Relations, 16,* No. 2 (1998): 349–365. Copyright 1998 ESF Publishers, Binghamton, NY.

Chapter 10: Soundproof sanity and fear of madness. *Journal of Melanie Klein and Object Relations, 16,* No. 3 (1998): 411–423. Copyright 1998 ESF Publishers, Binghamton, NY.

First published in 1999 by
H. Karnac (Books) Ltd.
6 Pembroke Buildings
London NW10 6RE

Reprinted 2001

British Library Cataloguing in Publication Data

ISBN 1 85575 212 3

10 9 8 7 6 5 4 3 2 1

Edited, designed and produced by Communication Crafts

Printed and bound in Great Britain by Biddles Ltd, *www.biddles.co.uk*

To all who live through the unlivable.
To the Life no poison can kill.

CONTENTS

ACKNOWLEDGEMENTS

There are many influences that go into the making of the person who wrote this book. Most are not referred to in any specific passage. They contribute to background sensibility, the "feel" of the whole. I would like to list some of them in hope of conveying a little of the tone and texture that nourished the work.

Freud and Melanie Klein intuited the amazing conjunction of toxins and nourishment in every human act. Bion and Winnicott felt keenly how our very sense of aliveness has destructive properties and the reverse, the ghastly fact that destructive activities heighten our sense of aliveness. We find ourselves in positions where we nourish ourselves by the very things that poison us and poison ourselves by what nourishes.

Themes relevant to the main lines of this book run through Wilhelm Reich, Kohut, Jung, Lacan, Matte-Blanco, Searles, Grotstein, S. Keleman, McDougall, Green, Meltzer, Milner. Jewish mystical thinking, especially the Bible and Tanya, permeate my psychotherapy experience. I find incessant confirmation of transformations that go on in the depths of misery, the gold of illumination from the bitter cup. Psychotherapy plays a vital role in ensuring that those who struggle in the night do not do so in vain.

Hints of the great mysticisms of East and West are implicit in the work of many sessions. So are Bartok, Beethoven, Blake, Shakespeare, Jackson Pollock, Miles Davis, and hosts of poets, painters, and musicians too many to mention. I have told the story—really, parts of stories—of many people who opened themselves to what they most feared, and those who were unable to. There is music, colour, and mystery in both the opening and closing. We extend and deepen ourselves in attempting the work itself.

There are many colleagues who have, at some point, supported me with thoughts, experiences, or friendship, and these include: Marie Coleman Nelson, Marion Milner, Anthony Molino, Mark Epstein, Adam Phillips, Christopher Bollas, Jessica Benjamin, Nathan Schwartz-Salant, Art Robbins, Emmanuel Ghent, and Jerome Travers. I regret leaving out more than I include. I am indebted to my major analysts, Henry Elkin and Dorothy Bloch, who have made significant contributions to our awareness of the intertwining of good and evil in everyday life.

My thanks to Graham Sleight, who read the manuscript for Karnac Books and delighted me with informed associations to my themes. I incorporated what I could and have the bonus of a reading list I look forward to. It can be depressing to face what one might never get to, but it is rewarding to feel that one's own thread links up with others' in networks one just barely glimpses. My thanks, also, to Cesare Sacerdoti, who supported the publication of this book, and whose response was immediate and welcoming.

My weekly seminar on Bion, Winnicott, and Lacan has grown over the years. I am extremely grateful to my colleagues/students for our co-exploratory journey. It has been a persistent source of nourishment, with a minimum of toxins. I think this amazing, considering the depth of toxins exposed.

Most of all, this book is about lines of self that psychotherapy makes visible. The fact some of these lines intersect with explorations of religion, the arts, philosophy, literature, and science gives one a sense that we are busy learning what we can about what most concerns us. So often in therapy we try to look straight into ourselves or use each other as filters. My patients lead the way. We go where we must, sometimes to our mutual delight, sometimes to our chagrin. But we keep finding ways to go farther with ourselves, to appreciate what we are made of and what all this is about. I hope that what we touch together in some measure repays a portion of my debt to those who work with me.

So much of this book is concerned with what happens in therapy sessions that I need to note that care has been taken to protect the identities of those written about. For example, names, circumstances, and other details have been changed, while remaining true to the spirit of the work.

As always, my wife, Betty, and children, David and Jacob, provide not only balance and nourishment, but challenges in daily living that keep me forthright and real.

INTRODUCTION

E motional nourishment and poisons can be so interwoven that it is difficult, if not impossible, to tell the difference between them. The problem can be so extreme that nourishment one needs to support life is toxic or, worse, one learns to extract what nourishment one can from poisons at hand.

The problem is social as well as personal. We are flooded by cultural and political toxins. Emotional poisons pervade television, movies, the written word, political posturing, economic produce. We are used to foraging for bits of nourishment in abundant waste. The other side of plenty is that we are inundated by good things, too. We are, simultaneously, contaminated and uplifted by nourishing and toxic aspects in the stream of events.

Individuals seek psychotherapy when cumulative toxins threaten to overwhelm their sense of life's goodness. At one pole, there are individuals who perceive life's dangers and want help negotiating them. They have a clear-headed sense of poisons and goods of the world but are aware that destructive tendencies in themselves may lead to fatal miscalculation. At crucial junctures, they do something to damage themselves and begin to wonder if something is working against them from within. These individuals sometimes thrive on disasters they court.

At the other pole, individuals may be so poisoned by self-hate that their entire life feels like a prolonged disaster. Good elements are infiltrated by a toxic atmosphere that seems inescapable. These individuals may feel basically marred or crippled and succumb to depressive inertia or masochistic fatigue. They are entombed in worthlessness and feel that every pore of existence is poisoned.

The former individuals feel that they have a right to the good things life offers but are plagued by something inexplicable that works against them. The latter scarcely feel they have the right to be alive. In the first group, a seemingly confident person begins to glimpse, with horror and amazement, the possibility of a destructive force within. For the second, the destructive force is home—a ghastly home, to be sure, but business as usual. He is used to living in a medium that eats at his life and poisons it. He extracts from poisons what nourishment he can (chapters 1, 8, 11).

There are individuals who feel poisoned by love as well as by hate. Those poisoned by hate know what they are up against. They were unwanted, unloved, treated badly—their lack of self-worth makes sense. They may not feel good about themselves, but the battle lines are drawn. Even so, they cannot shake off the sense that being hated is normal (chapter 5). Decrease in emotional toxins makes them feel weird and unreal. They can bear some happy moments, not a happy life.

Those poisoned by love suffer unfathomable self-doubt. They cannot locate where the bad thing is coming from. It is impossible to believe that love can kill. The difficulty is more subtle than a double-bind. In the latter, self is stymied by a show of love that masks hatred. However, those poisoned by love are *really* loved. Parents feel that children are precious and thrill to their existence. In one scenario, the child is overestimated, and too much is expected. A child may be the parent's religion: parenthood sacred, children holy. Entry into the real world can be as troublesome for the chronically idolized as for the chronically maligned.

When love poisons, a parent who loves may pour limitless negative energy into the child. This is not necessarily the result of a hidden hatred towards the child. It is more an offshoot of the fact that the child is the spontaneous object of the parents' deepest feelings. The pent-up energies of the parent flow towards the child, an indiscriminate mixture of bad with good. All that is in the parent floods the child. Thus love is mixed with a variety of tendencies, including anxious control, worry, death dread, ambition, self-hate. Parental love is not pure—it is mixed with everything else.

Parents often view children as extensions of themselves, food for ego, stimulants for self. Parent–child boundaries are variable and fluid. The child must digest messianic expectations fused with everyday life. To an extent, we learn to use what psychic nutrients we can and avoid what is toxic. Often, we more or less succeed, but not without casualties. In different measures, no one escapes toxic elements in nourishment secured.

This book portrays a range of individuals who seek nourishment from poisons or, to variable extents, are poisoned by the nourishment they seek. In chapters 1, 4, and 11, I write of "Alice", who spent a lifetime coming alive, battling for life. She had grown up in an atmosphere of parental self-hate that poisoned her existence. At various times, she experienced life as a swamp, oozing with putrid and petrified emotions. Parental self-hate/self-pity was the air she breathed. What baffled her were moments of beauty arising from the pain. Redemptive moments were few and tended to get swallowed by a sense of futility, yet they meant all the more in contrast with daily agony. Especially dangerous was Alice's tendency to become ill or to collapse whenever she made a serious move to better herself. It was as if her system had adapted to the toxins she knew and could not survive without them.

Chapter 2 focuses on the relationship between toxic nourishment and suicide, with a special emphasis on the confusion between nourishment and achievement. Parental love mixed with pressure to succeed may boomerang, rip individuals apart, and lay bare the need for simple human contact. After a brief discussion of different kinds of suicide, including teenage suicide, a young woman's suicide attempt is explored in detail. "Doris" had enjoyed a privileged, idyllic upbringing, which, she discovered with horror, failed to support real growth of self. Stress had been placed on performance, and she developed expertise in many activities. Doris was so good at so many things that she became enamoured with being successful and lost contact with what she loved.

In time, her need to succeed spiralled into chronic self-deprivation that involved forcing herself into narrow moulds and demands. The cruelty of her workplace exacerbated latent aspects of stunted development and led to a serious attempt to kill herself. Doris did not understand what had happened. She was not prepared for such horrible feelings, such a collapse of self. She had always been on top of things and found the sickly agony that overwhelmed her incomprehensible. The gap between the fullness she imagined and the misery that overtook her was too much to bear. The need to re-establish her life on a sounder basis struggled to gain a hearing. Questions as to what constitutes a genuinely nourishing life became important.

At times the balance between emotional toxins and nourishment can play a role in whether life is possible—not only whether an individual lives or dies, but also whether an individual can succeed in having and parenting a baby. "Lucia" (chapter 3), who almost certainly would have had another miscarriage without therapy, was helped to complete a pregnancy and enjoy the travails of motherhood. Toxic elements that had characterized Lucia's upbringing and marriage became part of a therapy relationship that sustained her in the face of them. Therapy provided a place where Lucia could establish a freer relationship to painful mixtures of toxins and nourishment that stymied her. Chapter 3 explores factors that made this possible.

Alice, Doris, and Lucia (chapters 1–3) show ways that an overload of emotional toxins fused with nourishment can have dire somatic consequences, sour a person's life-feeling, and influence whether one wishes to live or die. One's experience of toxic nourishment may even, in certain instances, determine whether one is able to give birth to the next generation. In chapter 4, the consequences of toxic nourishment are traced beyond physical illness, suicide, and miscarriage, to silent agonies that pervade lives.

In some individuals, a war of spirit hangs in moment-to-moment balance. It is an awful thing to live with the feeling that nourishment is not really possible, that whatever nourishment appears must be blighted. There are individuals who have lived past their suicidal tendencies, only to have nowhere to go inside. Every moment is a crisis of faith, a battle for the possibility that goodness exists in spite of poisonous waves within. In one person, "Larry" (chapter 4), the torture was heightened by a certainty that there were good things in life (his wife, children, aspects of work), but he could not sustain a *feeling of goodness with conviction* in the face of the way that nourishment had poisoned him in the past and continued doing so deep within. Severe mistrust he could not control almost instantaneously reduced potential nourishment to toxic traces.

In contrast with Larry, there are people who feel that life should be free from toxins altogether and that it ought to be possible to live without disturbances. These people act as if the world should not have "bugs". For many individuals, children turn out to be the biggest bugs. Many parents resent the disturbance caused by children. They try to create lives that are relatively disturbance-free. The problems that children bring are first minimized, then mushroom amidst disbelief. Sometimes emotions are treated as if they were toxic, and then they become toxic.

In chapter 4, the attitudes of a very busy couple are studied, and a link is made between their incomprehending, dismissive styles and the difficulties (e.g. attention and behaviour problems) their children manifest. These parents seek a good life and want good things, but they are not prepared to slow down to deal with personal problems. They imagine that the mastery of emotional difficulties should conform to the same model as becoming financially successful. Chapter 4 studies variations in ways that not only children, but one's own sense of aliveness—emotional life itself—can be the "bug" that one tries to kill or get away from.

Chapter 5 focuses on issues suggested by D. W. Winnicott's remark, a "baby tends to assume that what is there is normal". It may take some time before a deformed infant realizes it is deformed. The baby may "feel normal" before it can view itself from the outside. What is the fate of the sense of normalcy? Do conflicting ways of feeling normal arise? What happens if the sense of normalcy is poisoned?

The struggles of a deformed child whose parents supported his élan are contrasted with those of a potentially gifted woman whose sense of self was poisoned, possibly from the outset. For the latter it was "normal" to feel poisoned–poisonous, for the former it was normal to struggle and shine. The "feeling normal" emotional nucleus of the crippled child helped him to use himself maximally. A poisoned core, on the other hand, made a physically well-endowed individual feel deformed and spoiled chances that life provided.

One wonders to what extent a poisoned self taken as normal affects social and political life. For example, a group pervaded by poisons may imagine itself healthy and wreak havoc among its members and other groups who do not share or assent to the same poisonous core.

Winnicott writes of a mysterious self-feeling that can be more or less embodied and warm or chill one's existence. There are so many variations in what can make one feel right or wrong to oneself. One's very sense of aliveness can feel "normal" or "abnormal". One might even wonder, what is normal about being alive? The detailed discussion of feeling normal–abnormal in chapter 5 attempts to enrich appreciation of how precious, fragile, yet persistent self-feeling can be.

Problems involving the association of aliveness with toxic nourishment and dread of loss are studied in chapter 6. A single case—"Penny"—explored in detail, brings out how frightening aliveness can be. Factors in Penny's background intensified a fear that too much aliveness might kill her. The really alive one in her family, her father, had died suddenly and prematurely. He had been a genuine source of nourishment and support, which she had lost at a crucial time. For Penny, nourishment, aliveness, and death were interwoven.

Penny was forced to get what nourishment she could from her depressed, chaotic, assaultive mother. She felt that her mother was deeply poisonous, yet she needed the nourishment the poisons offered. She nurtured herself in the depths of her mother's mental illness. If Penny learned from her father that nourishment is dangerous, she learned from her mother that poisons must be nourishing. If she learned from her father that aliveness kills, she learned from her mother that deadness can be life-preserving.

Lethal self-nulling processes are discussed in chapter 7. People cancel their lives, sometimes in part, sometimes massively, with-

out literally committing suicide. The ratio of toxins to nourishment may be lopsided, the balance in favour of toxins. Nevertheless, even in adverse circumstances, something positive often
comes through, if only as a promise or wish.

In one case, an individual wanted a love as perfect and as
good as the violation she had endured was evil. She would not,
could not, live if life would not right the injury. In another instance, association of nourishment with evacuation was so intense
that a person dreamt of nourishing food coming out of his anus,
akin to milk from a breast. He expected others to be nourished
by toxins he spewed, as he had partly swallowed his parents'
warped view of life and treatment of others. Some of the individuals in this chapter felt that they could not let themselves go
on if life was so malignant and unfair. Instead of committing suicide, they found ways of undoing life as they lived it. Little by
little, therapy worked with the bad feeling that poisoned life yet
provided nourishment—even if the nourishment was profoundly
self-cancelling.

What is offered as nourishment can be both empty and violent. Individuals forced to make do with empty and violent nourishment are trapped inside and outside themselves. In chapter 8,
fusions of trauma and nourishment—traumatizing nourishment—are discussed with reference to two individuals in danger
of disappearing into a vacuum at their centre while, simultaneously, expelling themselves beyond any exterior boundary. At the
same time as they are disappearing, they reach out for life. One
individual clings to a reduced sense of sanity and becomes ever
more rigid, the other breaks down and becomes more fluid. Aspects of their predicaments evoke respect for expanding–contracting and rigid–fluid rhythms in one's own life.

Chapters 9 and 10 explore Winnicott's formulation of madness
as an unconscious pole in human life that exerts a directional
pull. Winnicott associates unknowable agony with a core madness at one's origin that one tries to reach yet avoid. Therapy
provides a setting in which unknowable madness can be con-
tacted in semi-usable doses. Winnicott describes a dual pull towards normalcy and madness. This division is ambiguous, since
Winnicott associates madness with what is most personal in an
individual—an important part of what gives life flavour and

makes people feel alive. At the same time, madness is nursed by trauma when the personality is forming and remains a wound in one's makeup. One is in the predicament of being nourished by what deforms one and deformed by what nourishes one. Chapters 9 and 10 focus on individuals who needed to contact sources of hidden madness. Their struggle to taste themselves in deeper, often alarming ways conflicted with their need to run away. Their difficulties bring out how challenging letting oneself live more fully on many levels can be.

Chapter 11 begins with W. R. Bion's observation that there are cases in which a person's sense of "well-being and vitality spring from the same characteristics which give trouble" (Bion, 1965, p. 144). This remark takes us deeply into issues regarding the indistinguishability of nourishment and toxins (see also chapter 8 for Bionic formulations of this problem). What can a therapist do when attachment to toxic nourishment is life-threatening *and* when movement towards less toxic nourishment is life-threatening?

There are individuals whom we cannot help. But even in the most difficult cases, something often gets through, something changes. What combination of faith, sincerity, realism, wisdom, and cunning make this possible? A therapist may have a well-developed cynical, ironical, pessimistic side—that is part of living, of being a partly sophisticated, wounded being. Without bitter wounds, how empathic can a therapist be, how deep can a therapist reach? Nevertheless, it may also be the case that the deepest illness cannot be cured without a taste of heaven. There are miracles that occur in places hidden far from ordinary life. Therapy helps people find and believe in such places, so that, in time, heavenly, hellish, earthly selves become partners.

Chapter 12, the final chapter, is semi-autobiographical. I share some nourishing aspects of my life and difficulties that nourishment brings. One never undoes the tangles of real living. I am not sure that undoing knots is a good model for many problems we endure. More important is appreciative access to density, to navels of experience. Wave after wave of experience passes, if one notices, and one cannot with assurance tease nourishment from toxins. One has better and worse hunches at times. My work with patients has been an enormous source of nourishment for me. As is ever true, I work with myself as I work with them. I write of myself as I write of them. The book ends with a tribute to difficulties that relationships involve—the mixtures of damage and desire that await both the timid and the brave.

TOXIC
NOURISHMENT

—But you believe then in the existence of a paradise
in the earliest days of mankind?

—Even if it was a hell—and certainly that time to which
I can go back in historical thought was full of fury
and anguish and torment and cruelty—at any rate it was not
unreal."

Martin Buber, *I and Thou*

Breath infect breath,
That their society, as their friendship, may
Be merely poison!

William Shakespeare, *Timon*, Act IV, Scene 1

Feeding on that which doth preserve the ill,
The uncertain sickly appetite to please.

William Shakespeare, Sonnet 147

What! Are men mad? Hath nature given them eyes
To see this vaulted arch, and the rich crop
Of sea and land, which can distinguish 'twixt
The fiery orbs above and the twinn'd stones
Upon the number'd beach? And can we not
Partition make with spectacles so precious
'Twixt fair and foul?
It cannot be in the eye . . .
. . . nor in the judgment,
. . . nor in the appetite;
Sluttery to such neat excellence oppos'd
Should make desire vomit emptiness,
Not so allur'd to feed. The cloy'd will,—
That satiate yet unsatisfied desire, that tub
both fill'd and running,—ravening first the lamb,
Longs after for the garbage.

William Shakespeare, *Cymbeline*, Act I, Scene 6

O Rose thou art sick.
The invisible worm,
That flies in the night
In the howling storm:

Has found out thy bed
Of crimson joy:
And his dark scret love
Does thy life destroy.

William Blake, The Sick Rose

CHAPTER ONE

Toxic nourishment

Emotional toxins and nourishment often are so mixed as to be indistinguishable. Even if they can be distinguished, it may be impossible for an individual to get one without the other. In order to get emotional nourishment, one may have to take in emotional toxins.

A life can so sour, and a person so accommodate to high levels of toxins, that he or she may develop aversive reactions to less polluted opportunities for nourishment. Life may not feel real without large doses of emotional toxins. Some people cannot take nourishment that is not embedded in psychic poisons.

Alice

Alice grew up in an atmosphere of warm self-hate. Her parents hated themselves, each other, and Alice. Yet the hate was not cold or icy. It was mixed with love. Alice tried to be a good girl in order to get the love. As she grew into middle childhood, it began to dawn on her that she was the family scapegoat. As she saw it,

1

her older brother got all the support and advantages and idealizing. He could do no wrong. He was the family hero, destined for big things, the messiah. He would justify their existence.

She was worse than Cinderella, for she was no hidden princess, and no prince was looking for her. As she grew up, the men who courted her seemed so messed up that genuine consummation was impossible. She took her failures with men as confirmations of worthlessness, a worthlessness that went back as far as she could remember, a bottomless, timeless worthlessness. She clearly linked it with her parents' own bottomless worthlessness, which they could not process and dumped on her.

She, indeed, felt like the garbage heap of the family. Her mother put her down at will. Nothing Alice did met with maternal delight. When Alice accomplished something at school, and later at work, her mother reacted with incomprehending surprise. It was as if Alice's success must have been a freak occurrence, a lucky chance. Her mother anticipated failure with everything, even the simplest household chores. Alice was used to orgies of maternal rage, tempered by scorn and snide remarks. According to her mother, Alice could not do anything right.

Alice felt loved by her father, but he was too weak to support her. He would collapse after a day's work and look for comfort from her. There was deep warmth buried in his helplessness, and Alice felt nourished by it. But she also felt guilty for not being able to make him happy. She could feel his deep, muffled joy in her existence when he looked at her, yet it was somehow stillborn, ineffective. He was basically depressed, angry at life, and filled with self-pity, and she could not rescue him. She felt drawn in by his depression and feared sinking in it. The nourishment that she got from his stifled warmth was spoiled by the depressive anger and self-pity she drank in with it.

Yet Alice did not give up on herself. She persevered, went to school, became a talented psychotherapist, although she suffered many setbacks. For many years she could not sustain having her own apartment. She *had* to move back to her mother. She felt too guilty to separate and have her own life. Her mother exercised a pull on her that was irresistible.

Yet did her mother *really* want her home, or was the pull inside Alice? Her mother continued to be self-absorbed and to use

Alice as a psychic garbage dump. She buried Alice in the detritus of her own self-hate, putting her down for everything she did or did not do, scarcely aware of her daughter's actual existence. Alice would stay with her until it became more than unbearable, and then she would try living away again. When Alice was away just long enough to begin to feel a little like a human being, the pull would start again; she would fight the urge to go back to the hating mother until the pull simply overwhelmed her.

It was like a negative refuelling. She was addicted to toxic nourishment. She had to go back until she overdosed on indifference and disparagement. It was what she was used to—the emotional atmosphere that she grew (or failed to grow) up in. It was like having a seizure. We could see it coming, but there was nothing we could do to stop it.

Did Alice feel too empty and unreal without negative refuelling? Yes, to some extent, but the opposite seemed truer. Just as she began to feel more real, more alive, more herself, she gave way to the need to undo her movement into life. It was as if she lacked the ability to support movement into life, even with help. She lacked equipment to sustain less toxic living.

I think of a wonderful philosophy teacher who had emphysema. In his first semester of retirement, he decided to teach in Switzerland, after years in New York. He died soon after arriving in Switzerland. I imagined his lungs could not take fresh air, after years of adaptation to toxins.

Alice's psychic lungs could not take much fresh air. She collapsed under strain of supporting more life than she was used to. At first, I naively encouraged her attempts to separate and build a life. I tried to support her in face of the undertow. This worked for a time but was doomed to failure. In one of her first apartments, she actually began to smell her mother—an odour she could not bear. Just as she was about to make a break for it and escape the horror of her early life, her sensory equipment tricked her. She "hallucinated" her mother's odour in the place where she had begun to feel free. Her respiratory apparatus produced what it was used to, haunted air.

Alice looked haunted when I first met her. She was in her late 20s, thin and frightened, with anorexic tendencies. It was as though she was chronically cowering, as though something or someone were scaring her. I feared that a strong wind (e.g. a series of disappointments, failures, rejections) might blow her away. Yet she had quiet tenacity and surprising strength. Her life was reduced to a sliver of will that refused to give up, hard-bone persistence in the face of collapse. We worked once or twice a week.

Alice had friends. For the first years of our relationship, she fought with them. She and they were always disappointing and attacking one another. A lot of bitterness characterized her relationships. Although Alice spent much of her time alone (and felt very alone), she also spent a good deal of time with friends.

One in particular occupied her time and vexed her. This "friend" exercised a tyrannical hold over Alice. She complained that Alice did not do enough for her. Whatever time Alice spent with her, this friend wanted more. Any show of will on Alice's part met with biting exasperation. She accused Alice of every sort of failure in their relationship. Yet Alice did not stop seeing her—and for quite some time did not even think of stopping.

Alice contracted to an apparently indestructible and invulnerable sliver of self, a condensed point that did little but bite back. Alice and her friend spent most of their time verbally biting each other. I imagined each as a magnetic poisoned apple for the other. They bit into each other, yet poisoned each other, and the poison held them together, as if it were nourishing. As time went on, the situation worsened. The attacks became more venomous. It seemed as if her friend meant to break Alice's fortified position down.

It was painful for me to listen to Alice recount what seemed to me to be a tale of injury and helplessness week after week. Clearly, she managed to reconstitute with her friend some semblance of her relationship with her mother, in which the binding element was being put down by the other.

Meanwhile, in the background, I held some of the pain. It might be thought that, to some extent, Alice now was the mother who held together by putting pain into Alice–me. But, I think, more deeply, she finally found someone who sensed and shared how painful life can be. Her mother had been impervious to Alice's pain, had even been nourished by it. At this early phase of work, I felt Alice's pain without breaking down or inflicting damage. In time, we became far more permeable with each other.

With her friend (and eventually me), Alice was able to bite back more than with her mother. With her mother, Alice was relatively toothless. When she tried to bite her mother back, nothing happened. Alice had no power, force, or effect with regard to her mother. Her mother went on imperviously, as if Alice were invisible or existing only as a target of animosity and emotional waste. With her friend, it was like fighting mother once or twice removed. She visibly affected her friend, since her friend desperately increased her ire in response to Alice's attempts to protect herself. One often displaces on to friends what is impossible to work out within the family.

Eventually her friend succeeded in breaking Alice down—like Alice's mother, up to a point. After months of accelerated pounding, the dam broke, and Alice began to feel the pain that I was holding in safekeeping for her. As their relationship became unbearable, Alice saw her friend less, then not at all. It was her friend who broke off all contact, once Alice backed off a bit. Not long after, Alice heard that her friend had been hospitalized. Alice went into a spin of guilty self-recrimination: had her backing off driven her friend crazy? Apparently her friend needed Alice more than the reverse. As is often the case, the more active hater in a relationship turns out to be more ill than the hated one imagined.

The fact that her friend broke down while trying to break Alice down made quite a dramatic impression on Alice. What enabled Alice to survive, while her friend disintegrated? Alice was used to surviving bombardment. It was horrifying to see her friend drop off the edge. Her friend began a downward spiral, from medication to medication, doctor to doctor. She was never the same.

Her friend had much higher aspirations than Alice and demanded perfection. Her parents were wealthy and expected great things from her. They pushed her past what her inner resources could support. In the end, Alice's friend collapsed into the position that Alice most dreaded: she fell entirely into her parents' hands. Her parents dictated the terms of her life, including getting her the doctors and treatments *they* wanted for her, rather than letting her find someone she might want.

It took a while, but for the first time in Alice's life an amazing thought began to form. Could it be that in some way Alice was luckier than her friend? How could this be? If her friend's parents wanted too much, Alice's wanted too little. Their expectations for Alice were nil. They expected nothing from her therapy and did not even have a sense of what getting help might mean. Could their total lack of interest in Alice's life turn out to be a boon? At least they did not interfere with her choice of therapist. Alice was left to go her own way, since what she did meant so little to them.

Alice felt lucky to have found me. She had gone through several therapists, with poor results. Her last therapist helped her to some extent, but Alice felt that he lost interest in her. He began to talk on the telephone when she was there and showed other signs of not caring. She felt ashamed of seeing him in face of his lack of interest. With any helper, she might feel the bad feelings that characterized her relationship with her parents. Nevertheless, she refused to tolerate her doctor's impatience with her, and finally she left him.

Alice nearly left me many times. One especially important crisis occurred in group therapy. At this time, about two years into therapy, Alice was seeing me weekly in individual therapy, and once weekly in a group. Alice began raging at me for my insensitivity, and she started to leave. The group members stopped her and formed a psychic cushion for her. They consoled her yet insisted that I was not as uncaring about her as she thought. The group did not deny my faults but refused to let her destroy her life because of them, or, rather, refused to let her let my faults spoil what she could get out of working together.

Her rage, trying to leave, and staying was a turning point. It marked the possibility of going through the inevitable trials of a relationship that was not essentially mutually annihilating. Alice could scarcely believe that our relationship did not have to spiral downhill and remain horrible. Could our faults really be part of a larger, working relationship?

Eventually, our group broke up, and Alice and I were left alone with each other. I wondered whether we could survive one-to-one intensity without the buffer of the group. It did not take long for Alice to rage at me, threaten to break things in my office, and rush towards the door. I do not remember exactly what I did, but I remember standing up and shouting and holding her arms.

What I remember most vividly was how strong she felt. I was surprised by her strength and a sexual feeling in her skin. She seemed frail, but not to the touch. I was taken aback, as if an electric current had passed through me. Alice was high voltage. I was fearful and happy. She was *alive*.

We weathered many emotional storms. My appreciation of Alice grew over the years. I admired her persistence in the face of horrors and periodic depressive collapse. I cherished her hard-pressed aliveness that surfaced through difficulties. As time went on, our relationship was no longer endangered. Alice realized we had each other as long as she wished.

When she began to settle into our relationship and use it, she had the following dream:

A doctor removed what seemed like an infinity of micro tongue depressors from Alice's mouth. Like the sorcerer's apprentice, the more he took out, the more they multiplied. He persisted and, finally, they began to diminish.

We took this as an image of depression from an early age. The nipple was depressing instead of nourishing: perhaps depression *was* the nourishment. I pictured Alice's mouth filled with particles of glass, not simply tiny tongue depressors. What dreadful inhibitions she had to fight in order to function! Oral rape. A splintered mother stuffing her psychotic fragments into her daughter. Quite a feed! To use herself at all (to move her tongue, to taste life, to speak, to express feelings, to think and be), Alice had to oppose an enormous, destructive undertow.

As we went on together, Alice's relationships with friends changed. Her new friends were more in life, not mainly attacking and noxious. Whatever their problems, they mainly helped each other and had good times together. Alice still had a tendency to accuse her friends of neglecting her and not caring enough. The sense of being emotionally undernourished and fed bad things ran deep. She and her friends got through rough waters together without unduly damaging each other. They liked and respected each other and learned to absorb or work with destructive cross-currents.

Things went well for Alice with friends in general, but not with boyfriends. The men she went out with turned out to be self-absorbed, ungiving, and unable to create with Alice a relationship in which she felt good. She inevitably felt put down, used, put upon, and deprived of basic consideration. Her resentment would mount until she felt impelled to break off.

One man, in particular, refused to go away. He had an earthy warmth and acceptance that made Alice stay with him longer than usual. She wondered if they could work things out. She tried to stay in the ring and talk to him about what bothered her in their relationship. Perhaps if they communicated, resentment would not mount. But talking did not work. He needed to have things on his terms, constantly ignored her wishes, and did as he wished. No matter how she tried, Alice felt that she could not get him to realize that she might have wishes different from his, or that what she wished might matter. In time, Alice came to the conclusion, that, yes, he had a certain warmth, tolerance, accept-ance—but that he accepted her like a piece of furniture, a com-fortable object to use as needed.

Still, Alice tried to stay in the relationship, thinking it was not so bad. Her conscience told her that she should work on it if she wanted to be with a man. Alice was keenly aware that she had problems, that her bad feelings about herself could poison a rela-tionship. If she worked hard enough on her end of things, maybe the relationship would get better, or become tolerable. Perhaps she needed to build the capacity to tolerate a relationship with a man.

Eventually, Alice became very ill. Her physician believed that her immune system was compromised by a chemical substance to which she had been exposed over a long period of time. I could not help thinking that I was the foreign substance leaking into her system, exacerbating her difficulties. Life can be cruel indeed in its black logic, at times creating dreadful unities. Alice's immune system becoming poisoned objectifies poisoning processes going on in the psychic sphere. On the other hand, poisoning processes in one sphere may develop or increase, as health improves in an-other area. As Alice's life got better, her body became worse, at least for a time. Still, chemical processes were working, and it would be dangerous to over-psychologize them.

Alice stopped work and graduate school and spent the better part of a year nursing herself and seeking help. Alice had little energy, yet she maintained a relationship with her boyfriend against her inclination. He brought her to doctors and sometimes helped in other ways. Yet he, too, seemed indifferent or angry and impatient with her wasted state. He was sour and consuming and needed someone to nurse his own damaged self. He expected her to be there for him when she could not be there for herself.

His mixture of indifference, anger, and helpfulness tied her up. Alice did not really feel cared for or seen by him. He wanted her to get better so he could use her again. Finally, she reached a point where she could not continue with him. But each time she broke up, her conscience told her that she was unfair, that he cared, that she was too damaged to sustain a relationship with a real man. She feared never having a relationship if she threw this one away, so she would go back with him, then feel miserable. Once they were together, she again felt that he was unbearably self-centred, and that his warmth was his way of getting her to take care of him.

Conscience pecked at her. Stay with the relationship, give it more of a chance, maybe it will work. It was not his fault that she was ill. She should try harder. Must she be someone who cannot sustain a relationship with a man? She could not take much life. She could not take a man. Perhaps, too, she could not take doing well at work or school or with friends. Was having a better life killing her? Better to be nothing.

But no, she liked being with her friends. She got something from studies and work, even if she hated the degrading aspects of workplace and school. Not all her life was demoralizing. It was mainly her boyfriend's condescending expectations, disregard, and petty demands that wore her spirit. She found him less than uninspiring. Whether she went along with him or fought him, she felt that he brought life down to a level that was not worth the trouble.

Having a one-to-one relationship with a man provoked too many fears, too many dangers. It mobilized all the old terrors of family life: suffocation, loss of will and autonomy, a horrifying mixture of annihilation, longing, deprivation, and the sickening nourishment one takes in from the other's egocentric love. She was too damaged for love. Toxic love had damaged her.

Now her relationship with her boyfriend was poisoning her. She was paralysed by the toxic nourishment that it offered. He could not bear listening to her. He had no room for another person, except as an extension of himself or someone to buttress him. To be with him was a full time job. Alice could not be herself with him—worse, she could not even *be*. She hung on, because letting go of the relationship was a sign of failure.

When she was away from him, she felt better—but then she felt guilty for feeling better. Being with him drained her. At last she reached a point where she refused to apologize for herself. Right or wrong, failure or not, she felt better without him. She could breathe without him. If having a relationship would kill her, to hell with the relationship, and to hell with a so-called conscience that forced her to stay in situations that she would rather not be in. She sided with feeling better.

Giving him up felt like giving up hope of having a family. In the course of our years together, her parents died. Alice was a grown-up orphan. There was no one to go home to. Home now had to be where she was or nowhere. Our sessions were momentary homes, places to find and be herself. So were relationships with friends. And she made her own apartment more and more a nest. She became more and more a centre of life, her own life.

Still, leaving him was like saying goodbye to her family again. He embodied, in somewhat milder form, a mixture of traits that she had grown up with in family life. His sour disposition expressed a chronic sense of deprivation and anger at life. He looked down at her, yet needed her. He offered her his willingness to spend time with her in exchange for her willingness to be a receptacle for his emotional toxins. It was as if she should be satisfied with his just being there, while she relieved him of the hardships of existence, the hardships of his own personality. As with her family, she became an emotional latrine or garbage dump. There are creatures who thrive in such an environment, but it was breaking her down.

Perhaps it was a coincidence that she gradually regained her health after breaking up with him. Had she already begun to feel better, and that gave her strength enough to end it? Or did she feel better afterwards? Or both? It seems less likely that he was the cause of her condition than a barometric reading of it, a sign of spirit or energy or flow. His parasitic esconcement in her existence was a sign of collapse, as his departure was a sign of recovery. Through him she hoped to bring her family back to life, to reunite with them. With him (and them) gone, she had no choice but to go forward with existence, her new life, the life that she was building.

Alice felt that her new life was closer to the one she might have had if her family had been healthier. She became more herself, less eaten up by corrosive versions of herself. She was less miserable, at times even happy with herself. As she surveyed her life, she felt keenly how taking in her family's toxic nourishment undermined her immune system. She absorbed so much garbage in order to survive that the latter wreaked havoc with her psychobiological substratum.

Her ability to sustain living was undermined from the outset. Her very immune system was jeopardized by what nourished her. It was more than being addicted to emotional "shit" as self-violating sustenance. The very atmosphere that kept her alive throughout childhood and adolescence was toxic. She hated the atmosphere she had grown up in, but her psychobiological equipment and very sense of self were informed by it. It permeated her cells.

As much as she wanted to free herself, unconscious sensors sought out toxic situations outside the family (as it turns out, even chemical toxins), so that the atmosphere that she grew up in encased her life. Alice was caught between the impossibility of continuing to live on poisons and the impossibility of living on healthier nutriments, since she lacked ability to maintain use of the latter. Yet she felt propelled to better herself, even if her equipment could not support her. Thus she could fall ill from poisons, or from inability to support herself when seeking a healthier psychosocial atmosphere.

Therapy was a kind of mixed atmospheric chamber, where a somewhat healthier atmosphere could be provided in nearly tolerable doses, so that Alice could adapt to it and use it by degrees. She could gradually get used to exercising psychic lungs in alternative atmospheric conditions, so that the contrast between what she was used to, what she wanted, and what she got would not do her in. As years passed, she built more of the kind of life that she could say yes to.

Imagine a being that gets oxygen from water, then develops capacity to get oxygen from air, or *vice versa*. I feel that this describes Alice's condition, only in her case it had to do with developing capacity to sustain using less toxic emotional nutriments over time, or breathing better emotional air. I was deeply moved when, in a recent session, Alice brought to mind a far-reaching change in her condition. She reminded me that when we first met she could look into a mirror and see a devil (quite literally), or something horribly twisted, ugly, marred. Now she could look in a mirror and like who she saw. She had a nice look, somewhat fun, playful, ironical, caring, at times attractive—someone that interesting, searching, and good-hearted people might like to be with. People like herself.

CHAPTER TWO

Suicide

Is it possible to say why some people try to kill themselves, whereas others, with no fewer difficulties, are able to go on? This question may be unanswerable, yet pondering it enables one to dig more deeply into life. Thinking about violence that people do to themselves makes us appreciate more keenly our little chance at living. Tracing aspects of the urge to end it all helps sensitize us to what it means to stay alive.

We cannot ask people who succeeded in killing themselves what enabled them to do so. Those who speak about death—even those who believe that they died or nearly died—can only do so as alive persons. Had they completed the death process, we would not hear from them now. As much as they might tell us about death and the need to murder oneself, it is from the point of view of life.

Still, we see that suicides differ. A Judas Iscariot might kill himself because he could not bear betrayal of the Good. There are souls who, attached to goodness, yet attack it, and attack themselves for their evil ways. This differs from individuals who rely on violence to feel big and then become violent with themselves when violence against others fails to bring the desired results. If Hitler killed himself, it was not out of guilt, but because his grandiose aspirations met with failure. Even if he had the imaginative perspicacity to realize that he had paved the way for Germany's economic triumph, he could not endure the humiliation of being executed by those he should have beaten.

There are individuals who kill themselves when faced by another kind of unbeatable enemy: terminal disease. Here it is not a matter of violence against others turning against the self (or *vice versa*), but a matter of affirming a measure of personal dignity, integrity, quality of life. This is a choice that can be abused, since one can use disease as an excuse to prematurely end one's life for reasons masked by illness. The weakness, helplessness, disability, and anger exacerbated by illness can give focus to long-standing resentments related to a sense of insufficient power in one's life. Also, an aging or infirm person is vulnerable to pressures of caretakers. There are many reasons one may end one's misery before facing oneself.

Freud, on the other hand, suffered his lethal injection only when illness made productivity nearly impossible. His last papers and notes were remarkable. He opened new vistas and possibilities until the end (Eigen, 1996, Chapter 1). One could argue that had he allowed himself to live a bit longer, we would have had even more fertile suggestions, as pain permitted. But he reached the point where illness ate his days away. The cost of pain and disability became too high. One can hardly accuse this octogenarian, after more than a decade of living and working while ill, of taking the easy way out. He battled depressive tendencies, phobias, obsessions, and hypochondriacal anxieties all his life, yet squeezed out of his psychophysical frame whatever it could yield.

What a contrast this is with a recent news account of a teenager putting a bullet through his head while hanging himself. The teen was a star football player in high school and a top student always pushing himself to do better. He came from a broken home and shot himself with his father's gun, while hanging from a tree, the night before the first game of the season. It was incon-

ceivable that this hyper-perfectionist would try to kill himself and
fail. He succeeded with a vengeance, leaving nothing to chance. It
was as if he killed himself twice, to make sure that he did it right.

Did anyone know he was unhappy? Did he? Could anyone
have done anything?

Among his papers was a note saying that there was something
terribly wrong with him. This young man, who did everything
right, lacked the chance or resources to identify and deal with
what felt wrong. He felt helpless in the face of something he
feared irreparable, something he could not right. The newspaper
called this state depression and quoted counsellors who claimed
that medication and therapy would have helped. The fact that no
one connected with what was bothering him, that he could not
connect with it or share it—the fact that something wrong missed
contact with the community—all this became part of the community's mourning process.

The public face to the disaster was a kind of failed activism. If
only we had known, if only we had identified the signs, if only
the correct diagnosis had been made, a remedy would have been
possible. Of course, this is very often the private reaction to a
death as well. Still, treatment does not work with everyone.
People kill themselves with medication and therapy, too. Perhaps
no one could have done anything. As if acknowledging this, a
correlative public response placed responsibility on the victim—if
only he had been able to let down and reach out, if only he had
been able to go public with his under-side.

People differ enormously with regard to the perceived flexibil-
ity–rigidity of their worlds. Some milk their secret selves for private or public gain. Others are too ashamed, helpless or terrified
to own clay feet. Some cannot stop talking about themselves, and
others cannot begin. There are vast personal and cultural differences regarding what attention one gives to the hidden.

Attitudes towards people needing help can be very punishing,
even if many find rewards in the help they get. Too many individuals feel stigmatized asking for help. Can the president of the
United States be in therapy and acknowledge it? Being a patient
is more scandalous than being promiscuous. With all the acknowledgement that we are simply human, there is still the omi-

nous commandment: "Thou shalt not have anything wrong with you." Did this commandment make a top athlete–student in a small-town high school feel beyond help? Did he succumb to an ideology of rugged individualism and atomistic idealism ("Be your best") which left no room for what was really wrong?

We need room for what is wrong. We need to be able to feel how painful it all is. We need time and place to feel terrible, cry, grieve or scream (just as we need allowance to be silly or ridiculous). This is more than being able to take time off from ourselves and our lives, important as that is. The parts of society that we find ourselves in and that make our lives possible need to make space for the sense that something is wrong.

The sense that something is off or wrong or rotten has been voiced by literature and religion through the ages. Hamlet's utterance about something rotten in the state applies, in one or another context, to all levels of life, from individual soul to cosmos.

Hubris, original sin, evil inclination, a destructive power or force, economic, political, and social injustice—all these are among the ways people say that x is wrong. Elizabethan and romantic poets wrote of a worm in the rose. The worm might mean death or limitation, but also something malignant, evil, a flaw or fault within a system (mind, heart, nation, body, cosmos). Human beings have long been aware of psychological and political, as well as physical infections. Psychoanalysis continues a long line of meditations on envy, jealousy, omnipotence–omniscience, disastrous over/underestimations of vanity or power.

Perhaps from an evolutionary viewpoint there is nothing wrong at all. Life takes this form, that form. Why is one form better than another? People devour each other politically, economically, sexually, culturally, just as animals eat animals: the struggle for survival goes on psychologically, as well as physically. If nothing is wrong, anything is possible. If life is a struggle for survival, I am justified in putting my survival above yours, as you are justified in putting your survival above mine. The sense of something wrong may merely mean that I want more, perhaps what you have, perhaps not merely your possessions but your very self. Psychic cannibalism is prevalent, even if physical cannibalism is rare.

A possible outcome of soft-pedalling the value of individual torment is a national vision like the following. George Kennan (1948) writes (in one of the waves of early cold-world-war paranoia?): "We should cease to talk about vague and . . . unreal objectives such as human rights, the raising of the living standards, and democratization. The day is not far off when we are going to have to deal in straight power concepts. The less we are hampered by idealistic slogans, the better" (p. 10). Without national survival, where would we be? Survival easily slips into ideas of dominance: my nation over yours, me over you. The idea of reciprocity gives way to fear of losing advantage and the need to control the other, the need to control conditions that I consider necessary for my welfare (i.e. dominance).

Clinical work teaches that many teenagers cannot envision living in the political world that Kennan describes. Idealism is too real for them. Individual torment is real. If the world does not have an authentic place for idealism and personal torment, the world has no place for them. It is not a world in which they want to live. Depression is the under-side of power. Suicide is a mark of conscience.

The suicide of the tormented idealist is not the same as the suicide of those driven to the precipice by abject circumstances, or those so brutalized and maimed that they hold life empty and cheap. The idealist is tormented by his or her own achievements, which are always lacking. The materialist is more likely to be satisfied with whatever she or he can get, even while trying for more.

Why did the high-achieving student athlete kill himself? Did he recoil from achievement pressure? Did he get too big a dose of emptiness or achievement blues? Did he crash from a too tightly strung need to be best? Sometimes achievement kills the achiever. How bleak the hangover from incessant striving can be! One needs to learn how to pace oneself psychologically, as well as physically. What accounts for the failure in this boy's emotional education? Why did he organize himself around one strand of being and feel resourceless when other bits of self voiced unhappiness and discontent? Why was he unable to learn from the voice that told him that something was terribly wrong? Why did he hear a message of doom, rather than a sounding about the state of self?

Doris

Doris sought help after a serious suicide attempt. She was brought to the hospital while unconscious, and she woke up in an intensive care unit. It took her a while to realize that she was still alive. At first there was confusion: there are times when a person is not sure whether she is alive or dead. Things swirl in a numb kind of jumble, and eventually it begins to dawn, "My God, I'm alive!"

Then comes the horrible thought—"I did not die." It can take some time for this clarity to come. To the observer, the two thoughts are connected, but to the subject they are totally different. I am alive is one thing, I did not die another. When Doris realized that she had failed to die, she was filled with shame. She couldn't do anything right—not even kill herself.

All her life, Doris had done everything right. Failure was a stranger to her. But in recent years failure came her way. She did not know what to do with it, but she felt terribly ashamed. She now felt ashamed that she had failed to kill herself and ashamed she had tried. She had failed as an alive person and as a dead one.

"You can't know what I feel", she said. "You can't know."

I nodded. I could feel her agony keenly, but it would do no good to say so. If I knew Doris better, I might have wondered whether *she* knew what she felt, whether she could feel her feelings. At the moment, all I could do was stay with her as the room dissolved in waves of shame.

I was Doris's third therapist, so I did not see her at her worst. She worried that I would not know how bad she could get, I might not take her pain seriously enough, I would think her too well.

"I only know you as a success?", I ventured.

She laughed. She was an anxious wreck, a muddle, and there was a thin tissue separating her from the abyss. She had a sense of the black hole that she was falling into, and anything that deviated too far from it was dubious.

"I know I can make myself look put together. You'll think I am better than I am and I'll fall in again." She feared her breakdown would come to nothing. Her life would go on as before, on the same shaky foundations, in the same pretend way, with the same horrible results.

Her first two doctors got her from hospital to consulting-room, then passed her along to me for long-term work. She was uncomfortable with therapy. It was not something that she was supposed to be in. She was supposed to be able to do everything herself. Being in therapy meant that she was a failure as a person. It also meant that her parents were failures. Therapy was equivalent to failure.

All her life she was supposed to sparkle. She sparkled as a student, and for a while as an athlete and for a while as a musician. She went to top schools, got top grades, top scores on national tests. The first sign that something was wrong was in college. She had to return home for a year—an anxious and depressed mess. Her family physician got her over it with medication. She finished college brilliantly, her image nearly intact. The shining self triumphed.

She went to graduate-school in business and communication and was a star. She began her climb up the television production ladder. Competition became stiffer and stiffer, pressures mounted. At one point she was under a severe and demanding boss, who offered little support or warmth, just the demand to produce: "Be the best, beat the rest." She began calling friends and grabbing on to people in mindless, haphazard fashion, trying to hold self together. Friends could not stop the spin and diffusion. Terror and despair mounted. Fear of failure spiralled into a consuming sense of worthless and hopeless disability. She tried to end her fall with pills.

Common phrases such as "she took the easy way out" or "she tried to end it all" suggest that one kills oneself to end pain, to get out of hopelessness. The wish to end or get out implies the wish to end or get out of some state, whether a state of being, mind, or circumstances. Too often, ending or getting out of a state becomes confused with ending or getting out of life. One loses or never sufficiently develops the ability to experience oneself as more than the sum of one's states. Pain so expands as to blur the fact that there are undamaged aspects of self, or it renders undamaged elements irrelevant. Life contracts or collapses to pain points and for a time is unable to defend itself against the accusation that it is worthless.

Is life the villain, or is self? Are life and self the same? What is life, what is self? In Doris's case, an immense self-attack process went along with lack of external support. Self-attack mushroomed so that it became difficult to use what support came her way. In the first half-year that I knew her, Doris ran through a variety of men and then announced that she was ugly, undesirable, not one of the beautiful women whom men want. Despite evidence to the contrary, she felt that no one wanted sex with her and no one wanted to marry her. She worried, "Men can't show me off. They cannot be proud of me. They don't get a thrill walking down the street with me."

Bad feelings about herself got focused on her looks. She could not stop asking me if she was homely, if she repelled me or failed to be stunningly attractive. She had lots of sexual experiences, but they did not make her feel better about herself for long. She focused on men who treated her with obvious ambivalence and dismissed ones who really liked her. She was hypercritical of men, and I had the feeling that she damaged herself by damaging them, or vice versa. Could anyone survive the damaging process? Could I? If I were nice, I would not be dangerous enough. If I were helpful, she would have to cut me down, and hurt herself in the process.

I had urges to reassure her. She looked just fine. But such responses would be a drop in the bucket and dissolve nearly as soon as they were made. She was speaking of inner damage, and, unless that was addressed, surface compliments would go to waste. There were times when she was anxious that I could see a self with craters, pock-marks, blemishes, alive like an injured nerve—unlike her well-groomed outside, which, alive as it was, tried to undo traces of injury. "Your attacks on your looks must only be a small portion of your attacks on yourself" would be something I might say.

Just as she began to feel something for me and to let in some of the good feelings that I felt for her, a friend of hers told her she should see a more orthodox therapist, that I was too far out. We were still in our first half-year—still in the fairly early stages of getting to know each other. But something was happening. She was already getting better. Did she need to protect me from her attacks by shifting her doubts to her friend, attacking me once-removed?

It was our first crisis of faith. Her friend's criticism of me reinforced her own inner spoiler. What was right—the attacker, or the feeling that something good was happening? Both? The war was basic. Dare she trust her sense that therapy was helping, could help more? Would she listen to her friend and side with her self-doubt against a deeper self?

The fact that therapy was helping did not prove *my* value. She might make more progress with someone else. Would she leave me, just as she had left her boyfriends or they her? Would she leave me before I hurt her badly, before I rejected her or became critical of her, or before she had a chance to see how damaging she could be with me? "You mean, you would not be proud to walk into a room of therapists with me?" I mused. Now I was the pock-marked, blemished self.

Her friend's "supportive" attack on Doris's therapy was a mini-version of a life-long experience with her parents, especially her mother. Doris's parents loved her and invested great interest in her. Doris felt cared for. Yet Doris's parents had a way of making her feel anxious about herself. Much emphasis was placed on skills, training, learning to do things. As a child, Doris took swimming, tennis, art, music, riding lessons, and much else. Whatever she did, she did more than well. On the one hand, her skills gave her confidence. On the other, she cannot remember a time when she was not anxious about how she was doing or going to do in one or another activity.

She did not have much time for herself or time to do nothing or whatever she might feel like doing. If she seemed to be quiet or moping, one or the other parent would ask her how she was doing in one or another of her activities. If she was not busy making progress in something, her parents wondered what was wrong. She was the opposite of a latchkey child. Nearly all her time was

planned and productive, with a parent interested in nearly everything she did. She had every advantage and devoted her time
trying to make use of them.

It would not be fair to say that Doris's parents were not interested in her as a person. What complicates matters is that they
loved her but their very love seemed to fuel anxiety. They worried too much about how she was doing, although she always did
well. They incessantly compared her with her friends. Who did
what better? Did x do something Doris did not? They had anten-
nae for something Doris might miss, then poured their anxiety
onto the imaginary or perceived lack. It was as though they were
looking for signs that something was wrong, some inarticulate
and ineradicable disability, an inchoate, invisible deficiency at the
centre of Doris's being and in the heart of the family.

"Something was broken that could not be fixed", Doris said
near the end of our first year together. "It was there in the background. It was not even that they pretended it wasn't there. They
didn't seem to know. They didn't let on to themselves. I felt it and
didn't know what it was. I'm barely beginning to know now. I am
just beginning to talk about it. It never came out this far before.
They were always trying to fix it, make it better, without knowing
what they were fixing, or that anything was bad."

How could they not know something was wrong? Doris's
mother was depressed throughout Doris's early and middle
childhood. Doris's father was depressed now. Her sister led a
marginal existence, unable to hold a job or go to school. Yet they
tried to live as though nothing were wrong, as if they were not
depressed, as if the children were beautiful and brilliant and
wonderfully all right.

The family tended to act as if nothing were wrong, even
though Doris's mother was critical of everyone's faults. The "it"
that was broken remained nebulous—it was Doris's background
sense of self. She could not quite let on, but her mother's depression and criticism played a role in the sense of something wrong.
A support and pillar of her family also damaged it. Not until
therapy could Doris begin to let the cat out of the bag, or even let
herself connect with the sense of something wrong.

Doris recalls her early mother as overweight, poorly dressed,
unhappy. When Doris was about 8 years old, her mother's de-

pression started to lift. By the time that Doris neared adolescence, her mother was energetic and alive. Doris described her as bright, witty, fashionable, often caustic and satirical, and very active, with a host of cultural interests. Her mother prided herself in being intellectually up to date and knowing what was going on. As Doris got older, her mother made a good companion. Doris repeatedly told me: "I still feel my mother is my best friend."

Doris recalls her early father as stable and reliable, someone on whom she and mother could count. Nevertheless, her mother berated and belittled him. He was not the big man she had hoped for. He was neither successful nor powerful enough to satisfy her. He was successful, but not super-super successful. Perhaps she was angry at him for not being able to save her from depression.

Doris counted on his warmth, and in his way he was there for her. But she slyly mocked him for not being mercurial like her mother. From high school on, she laughed a lot with mother. They bantered wittily for hours. Still, she appreciated her father's calm, flat-footed goodness, even while making fun of him. It was with her mother she could fly, but she warmed herself with his non-verbal constancy and devotion.

As Doris grew older, it gradually dawned on her that, scratch the surface, and he was as worried as her mother. Deep down he felt badly for not being the super-success his wife wanted, and he feared that he might not be able to stay the course. He became severely depressed after Doris struck out on her own, but it was not until the second year of our work that she learned that he was seeing a psychiatrist for medication and occasional counsel. Doris felt sandwiched between her mother's early depression and her father's later one. His therapy was less a search than an attempt to regulate his mood and maintain himself in life. Her therapy gradually became more a gesture of self-transformation.

Doris worried about her sister and began to see her as the embodiment of family fears. She never had an acute breakdown like Doris, but her whole life was a semi-breakdown. Perhaps her sister complied less but was more dependent on her parents for daily help and financial support. Was she rebellious or so sunk by family pressures that she could not be compliant? Neither Doris's suicide attempt nor her sister's chronic semi-collapse fit parental images of their children. But Doris was on the road to finding herself, while her sister was sinking. Her sister was by far the greater disappointment and concern.

Even more than Doris, her sister stood as a sign that, in spite of the virtues of this devoted, caring, superior family, something was wrong. She threw into question what being a parent and person were about. Doris was getting on with things. Her mother's depression lifted long ago. Her father's was semi-controlled by medication. Nothing helped her sister so far. She became the greatest magnet for family worry and chagrin. Everything that her parents feared about Doris, her sister was: someone who could not make it, someone who failed. The worm in the heart of this family was most floridly objectified by Doris's sister, but her malaise was in them all.

Not that Doris did not worry about herself. She was far from in the clear. Life blew her feelings about like leaves in the wind. A bad look from a boss or an anxious scene with a boyfriend could send her reeling. However, she regrouped and came back. She was starting to have faith in her resiliency. Still, she dreaded falling into a hole that she could not climb out of.

Her mother could throw her off faster than anyone. Doris drew comfort and support from her mother, who was fun and easy to be with. Yet her mother incessantly threw her into doublethink. Whatever move Doris made, her mother asked if something else would be better. Whatever job, or project within a job, or man she dated—her mother second-guessed her. Perhaps the job or project or man she did not choose would have been better.

Whatever one did not do seemed to be better than what one did. Nothing was good enough for her daughter, nothing was the best. The best was always elsewhere or something else. "When I was young, the message was I should be best in school", said Doris. "I was, but then I needed to be the most popular too. Now she says I am not feminine enough, I spend too much time working, I should go out more, get married. She's worried I am not going to marry and have a family, that I'm going to miss something, that I'm not going to have what she did. Whatever I do, it's not the right thing at the right time or it doesn't have the right results. I became the successful person she wanted to be and now it's not what she wanted."

Nothing big or small escaped her mother's doublethink. Whatever Doris wore, her facial expressions, her hairdo—even the
movies and plays she went to—her mother had a second thought
about them. How easily blown away Doris was by her mother's
innuendoes. She was never quite the right self, always somewhat
the wrong person.

By our third year of work, Doris established a firm enough
beachhead with herself to be able to rehearse her mother's sec-
ond-guessing without being thrown off very long. She found her
mother's voice in her own whirring mind and its stream of
doubts, disappointments with self, elusive expectations, lacerating criticisms. If she did this, the voice said maybe that, and if she
did that, the voice said maybe this. The voice was always telling
her that she was not what she could or ought to be. It was the
voice of her mother speaking to her father, her sister, herself. It
dawned on Doris that she was hearing the stream of self-hate and
disappointment that stained her mother's core.

Her mother often talked about what she might have been. She
might have been an artist or professional person. She bragged
about jobs that she had, but in truth she did not go far and was
angry and unhappy about work she never did. When children
came, she folded up and became bitter about what she did not do.
She could have worked when the children were young, or after
they were grown, but she never found herself as a working person. It was not that she lacked opportunity or support. The problem was deeper, less tangible. It was as if she suffered an
equipment failure or breakdown when children came, but it was
a breakdown that was waiting to happen.

The grim thought was taking form in Doris that not only was
her mother disappointed with her own life, but she had been in
no shape to take on a real, live baby. Her shell of competence and
confidence collapsed in that face of a task that could not be intel-
lectualized or treated like a business deal or an aesthetic composi-
tion. She was thrown into a situation where nothing saved her
from the demand for being-to-being contact. A baby's raw self
seeks the other's self as nutrient. Fantasies of achievement could
not substitute for self-to-self living.

She tried to get through by emphasizing external necessities of
care-giving. She saw to it that her baby was cared for and com-

fortable and had the best physical and, later, educational and social environments. Yet she was covertly angry because she gave
to the baby at her own expense. She did not take care of her own
life and career. She resented motherhood, although she wanted to
be a mother. She could not bear sacrificing her longing to rise to
the top, and she resented her baby for holding her back. At the
same time, she felt guilty for being angry at the new-born that she
really wanted. Guilty anger added to her emotional holding-back
and inability just to be. She could not give freely without feeling
driven to make Doris into something.

After repeatedly going over this material, Doris began penetrating to a deeper level. The hard thought taking shape was that
Doris's mother used motherhood as an excuse to mask an underlying sense of personal incapacity. "I'm really seeing that she
couldn't do it", Doris said with surprise and angry sadness. "All
my life she told me what she did and would have done, but
I became the doer of the family. I'm the one really doing things. I
became the doer she wanted to be. It's not that she became a
mother and stopped doing. It's that she couldn't do and became
a mother. I know it's not that simple. She really wanted me.
There's love in her, love of me, love of life. But she hates her life,
hates herself, and put hate in me. I have caught it like a virus. I
have the self-hate too. Once it's there you don't get rid of it so
easily. Maybe you don't get rid of it at all. Maybe it's something
you have to contend with, work with."

"It sounds like you absorbed a lot of toxins with your mother's nourishment, a lot of self-hate mixed with love", I said. It was
important that Doris felt that someone heard her, that there really
was something to hear. She lived her life with love and toxins so
utterly fused that they often were indistinguishable. Love made
psychic poisons palatable, and toxins poisoned love. Love provided a nest for self-hate. Love blinded Doris to self-poisoning
processes.

"I didn't know where it was coming from. Everything she said
sounded reasonable. She only wanted what was good. She didn't
want me to get fat or stupid or ugly. She wanted me to look good
and be bright and get ahead. She wanted me to be everything she
wasn't. She wants to see me well and happy. Now that I tell her I

am happy enough, she worries that I'll never be a mother. I look at her and think she's lied to herself. She thinks she should have been more, and I used to feel it's my fault she's who she is. But I'm seeing now that she's who she is because she's who she is. If she hadn't had me, she would have found some other way not to be the 'more' that she can see in her mind, the 'more' that she now expects me to be.

"Maybe she didn't have the social support women have now. Not that we have so much, but we have more than she did. Maybe it wasn't her fault. Dad was always for her. But it was something in her, not in me, that stopped her. I didn't stop her. Her own personality stopped her, something faulty or flawed or disabled in herself. I didn't do that to her. I think I always felt that I did her in, that it was my fault she fell. Now I'm getting the opposite idea, that she wasn't able to support me as a person, wasn't able to be there fully for me. She wasn't able to support herself or find the support she needed. I was born to a woman who was semi-collapsing. I was born into an emotional world that was falling apart. She tried to use me to pull herself together, but for a long time I dragged her down."

"And she dragged you with her?", I asked.

"We dragged each other down? She made me feel special—for my brains, talents, abilities. I do feel loved. But in the heart of that love is a knot of self-hate, a congealed knot. It sickens what I do, what I am. I see now that it was there before I was born, before I was conceived, waiting for me. Perhaps waiting for her too. I have built myself around it—I have grown around it. All these years I pretended it wasn't there—I felt that it shouldn't be there. I thought it would go away. *I* almost went away instead."

This is not quite a split between good and bad. It is good and bad permeating each other, simultaneously feeding–poisoning the psychic bloodstream. Self-hate places itself in the very heart of love, like a parasite burrowing deeper, staining goodness. Wherever there is love, self-hate is at its centre. For most of her life, it was a self-hate that Doris could not name or locate or relate to. It did its damage in the hollow of love. To begin to notice it, taste it, feel its corrosive trickle was the start of genuine, long-term movement.

Doris recently reached another level in her profession. Things keep opening for her. She dates but has found no one special yet. She does not know whether she will, nor does she know what course she will take when her biological clock for having a baby starts running down. She is living day to day, enjoying work, going through the traumas of everyday life, having experiences, building friendships. There is no longer danger of suicide.

She is getting something from therapy which her family could not give her. She is learning to take life as it comes, get what she can out of it, let herself be. She is more able to do things for their own sake, because they interest her, not merely for where they might get her. She is a little more able to live from the inside, not merely from the outside. She is more able to immerse herself in what is at hand, without spoiling experiences with calculations about what they are not. She feels increasingly in sync with the unfolding of her being.

Suicide and toxic nourishment

Doris amazed herself by staying in therapy after her life stabilized and she was no longer in danger. She began therapy because there was nothing else. She grabbed onto it like a life-preserver, against contrary wishes, since she wished she were dead. Clinging to therapy was a kind of reflex reaction: as she was going under, she took the helping hand. That she could take help reaching out to her was a good prognostic sign.

She did not accept help wholeheartedly or unbegrudgingly. She was an iffy and skittish patient. As soon as she felt a little better, she skipped sessions. When she came it would take a good part of the session to work through suspiciousness, cynicism, and supercilious attacks on therapy and self. Doris felt ashamed of being in therapy. It was a sign of failure, something wrong with her, something irredeemable, beyond the pale, a black mark on her life. She should not need it if she were as she should be.

It began to dawn on both of us that Doris, in the back of her mind, expected therapy to fail. It was not just that she thought that therapy was something to tide her over in an emergency. It was more that she did not really think that anything could help her. All her life she had been living without hope of help, without realizing it. A school-teacher had once remarked that Doris was a terrific student but seemed a little too sour. Doris and her mother were very upset by this remark, but events marched on and it faded into the background. Still, Doris remembers her mother badgering her for quite some time about looking sour. To be successful, one ought to be and seem positive. It bothered her mother terribly when Doris did not seem positive. Her mother tried to argue the sourness out of her.

In truth, Doris's teacher's remark never left her. She saw and felt the "something sour" through and through. When she was older, she tied it to her mother's biting sarcasm and wry wit. The latter was something that she could understand and grab hold of and use as a hook for both bad and funny moments. In therapy she was able to reach the sense that something sour ran through her family—there was a sour taste to the emotional world that she grew up in.

In one outburst, Doris said: "I felt the sourness in me. It never dawned on me that it was part of the family. I never felt that my mother or father were sour. He was hard-working and she was always driving me places, to my next appointment. We were very busy. Everything was upbeat. I forgot how heavy and lethargic she used to be. She was like an amorphous lump lying around. I felt repulsed by her. My mouth is making a sour movement now, like I'm tasting something sour, something ugly. She was ugly then. She didn't take care of herself. She left a bad taste in my mouth. I didn't know it then—or maybe I knew, but there was nothing I could do about it. Knowing was useless, useless pain. Now she can't stop taking care of herself, and even a year ago I was telling people how great she was and I could never be as great as my mom.

"I feel that therapy is a sign of a black mark, but the black mark is already there. The sourness grows from it and is part of it. The black mark is in the family, but no one breathes a word about it. No one looks at it. My breakdown is the black mark, and now I'm looking at it and I see how far it goes. It goes as far as I can see. It's not something to whisk away and get over. Now that I'm getting better, my mother is ready to pretend that my breakdown never happened, or was an accident, an aberration, a mistake. Nothing can be further from the truth. My breakdown is integral, it *is* the truth. It expresses something broken in my whole family. It is not something to be buried, but to be looked at. It has something to say. It says something important about us."

Doris thought that therapy would not help her because to her there was no place in life for her black mark—her family's black mark. The sourness/blackness was to be buried, whisked away. It was too dangerous to take up. It meant collapse, madness, death. People lacked tools for it. It was not something that anyone could handle. It certainly was not something to look at or talk about.

Doris's suicidal breakdown occurred in a very particular situation. She had a tough assignment at work and a boss who could not care less about her. Not only was he unsupportive, he ridiculed and lampooned workers who were not fast or smart or strong enough. Any sign of dependency, weakness, or lack of confidence was pounced on. He alternately neglected and mocked his charges. He knew what he wanted and expected: fast, top-notch delivery.

The net result was that he produced top-notch work, and those who stayed with him were thick-skinned enough to take it. But Doris was thin-skinned enough to need warmth, interest, and support to sustain herself and produce over extended periods of time. Her boss caricatured the worst elements in her mother without the nourishment. Doris was paralysed, neither able to leave the situation nor succeed. He was the cold, hard world, and she could not bear it. She collapsed into a suicidal spin, swallowed by the black mark that no one wanted to acknowledge.

It did not take long to help Doris to see that she needed a work situation that offered enough support and nourishment for her to function well. However, it took a long time for her to begin accepting this fact. She attacked herself for needing support and nourishment. She castigated herself for being weak, a cry baby, someone too spoiled and pampered to take life as it really is. The notion that one ought to be nourished by work seemed a luxury, an indulgence. The very fact that she had a need for support and nourishment proved that something was wrong with her.

Her unsupportive, mocking boss seemed an exaggerated distillation of toxic elements in her family that she had learned to live with because they were mixed with real nourishment. It was as if her boss were some sort of evil magician whom fate had sent to pull out the worst aspects of her life and force her to see the unseeable. She tried to please him, but he was impossible to please. Being pleased was besides the point. He was only interested in whether the work was there. The kindly glance or good word Doris needed did not grace his repertoire. Those who produced were rewarded with the need to produce more.

Doris found herself in a world ruled by achievement. Affection did not matter. In her mother's world, affection, at least, could be channelled into achievement. Affection had uses in supporting and fuelling achievement. In the work world that Doris had stumbled into, achievement swallowed affection. Her boss had no use for the latter. It was superfluous, a hindrance, something to mock and transcend, nothing to make an issue of. If you have feelings—and why should you?—keep them to yourself. Only the work matters.

Once, when going over her breakdown, Doris said: "I'm a leaky person. My feelings spill out. I want to be liked. I need to feel some appreciation for what I do. I felt out of place with my boss, like I came from a different world. Now I think he's a creature from a different world, an alien, an experiment, part of a race of creatures oriented to achieve at any cost, people who can live without affection and make do with winning, people who thrive on ambition and to hell with everything else. All his ego is in his work and nothing and no one matters except to score at work.

"My mother made me into a person who needs to work and be the best but also be loved for what I do. That's what held me back, the need to be loved. I achieved to be appreciated. My boss saw through that. He knew I was a wimp. My whole family is wimpish, really. We're really cream-puffs. I thought my mother was such a giantess, a superwoman, so great. I didn't see or know what to do with everything she swept under the carpet. I couldn't see or it didn't matter what my boss swept under *his* carpet. He was a giant insect version of my mother. Working for him lanced a boil. I couldn't achieve at any cost. I can't do without feelings about what I do and needing a world where others have feelings too. Work is not just work. It's also everything one feels about working. You can live so that your work has something to do with your feelings about life, your work has something to do with who you are, your work adds to your feelings about life. I'm not just a work machine. My whole system finally protested and said enough's enough. Enough of this sham. If *I am* not going to be alive in my life, who is? I was ashamed to be a human being. I was going around apologizing for not being inhuman enough. My breakdown saved me from a becoming a work machine like my boss. It was a reaction against being inhuman. Of course, that's a rationalization too, isn't it? I couldn't have been like my boss even if I wanted to. I couldn't cut the mustard. Only now I'm realizing that's not necessarily a bad thing. Imagine what life would be like if everyone were like my boss."

"You had a crisis of values without knowing it", I underscored to make sure that what she was saying did not vanish in the void. "You were forced to feel your way through what it is to be human, what sort of being you are."

"Everything was thrown into question. I'm groping now", Doris mused.

"Thank God for groping!" I murmured affirmatively.

Groping was not encouraged in Doris's family. It definitely was not among the cherished virtues. It was not positive enough. What a price Doris paid for such emphasis on being positive! She had to come to therapy to make room for wishy-washyness and wiggling-woggling through life. She had to come to therapy to make room for uncertainty and not knowing.

The need to appear better than one is, keep a stiff upper lip, carry on as best one can, go it alone—in one or another form, such attitudes are encouraged by many cultures. In Doris's case, American "rugged individualism" may have played a role. But her parents come from immigrant families that struggled against odds to make a go of it. They needed to emphasize strengths, play down weakness. Such strivings, sometimes necessary for survival, can backfire—for individuals, cultures, humanity. The struggle to surpass ourselves stimulates marvellous achievements but can also provoke collapse.

Doris's suicidal collapse expressed a variety of factors. There was too great an emphasis on external achievement, not enough on personal nourishment. For many individuals, achievement and nourishment go together, more or less. But for many, the gap between achievement and nourishment can grow. One finds oneself achieving for the sake of achieving, even doing tasks that are poisonous to one's sense of self, perhaps even to society.

As the twists and turns of life would have it, Doris found herself in a position where her sense of self was given over to an exacting taskmaster who cared nothing for her. The split between inner and outer reality became unendurable. Her self-doubt and sense of worthlessness sky-rocketed in the face of escalating impersonal demands. Her inner, secret world became an abyss of shame, humiliation, dread, disability. She could not keep up with what she felt was expected of her. She was caught between a crossfire of forces that she could no longer mediate.

In therapy, she began putting together the bits and pieces of her life and her picture of her life. She was able to make sense out of fragments of awareness that she had collected through the years. The myth of her mother as supermom delayed processing the fact that the mother of her childhood was depressed, semi-collapsed, and bitter. Her nourishing mother had a sour and frightful taste.

Her mother somewhat put herself together by becoming achievement-driven for her children and husband, spurring them on and attacking them. Doris got what nourishment she could by becoming a high achiever, but her lack of deep internal support eventually caught up with her. As Doris got older, her mother's love of life pushed past depression and collapse, although she remained an anxious person with a self-centred, stinging wit. She enthralled Doris with nourishing aspects of her being, since she was also playful, high-minded, and interested in life.

Doris's family lacked ability or desire to focus on what was wrong for long. Something wrong in the background was part of the everyday atmosphere, part of everyone's daily bread. Perhaps it was dimly felt better to let sleeping dogs lie. Perhaps the ability to encompass what was wrong had not yet evolved. There were enough good things mixed with what was wrong to enable the latter to be tolerated.

Doris got used to taking in toxins with what nourishment came her way. She broke down under the strain of trying to detoxify potential nourishment in a situation where the latter reached a minimum, the former a maximum. A job that Doris

hoped would nourish her turned out to be nearly fatal. Her suicidal breakdown saved her from a situation in which the ratio of
toxins relative to nourishment threatened her sense of humanity.

Therapy gave Doris space and time and the wherewithal and
support to link up with bad feelings about self that her family
and perhaps society could not face. The sense that there was
"something wrong" with family and world was recognized as
very real. Whatever was wrong needed attention, not dismissal.
Therapy partly helps individuals pump out accumulated psychic
poisons and find less toxic ways of nourishing self. In life, nourishment can never be free of toxins. But there can come points
when the latter increases to such an extent that suicide may seem
the only option.

CHAPTER THREE

Miscarriages

To some it may seem odd or unreasonable to treat miscarriage as a psychosomatic problem, yet it is difficult to avoid this impression in certain instances. Sometimes women with repeated miscarriages seek psychotherapy for help in bringing a pregnancy to term. Nearly 30 years of work have convinced me that psychotherapy *can* help many women have successful pregnancies. I have seen this happen with women who almost certainly would have miscarried otherwise.

I do not know why different therapies–therapists succeed or fail with particular patients, but I would like to share some impressions of work with a particular woman, Lucia. No claim is being made that miscarriages, in general, have a psychological basis, although, certainly, nearly all have psychological consequences. I simply wish to portray what can and does happen with a good number of women and touch on some things that therapy offers. The story of every woman is different, but going into detail in one case brings to light factors that many share.

Lucia and Jan

Lucia was an engaging woman in her mid-30s who, following her marriage, had two miscarriages in as many years. She was a professional woman who scaled down her career to become a mother. Her husband's work demanded that he be away a lot, so she was alone for weeks, sometimes months, at a time.

She and her husband, Jan, loved each other, but they often fought about how their lives were to be lived. He was picky and needed an exceptionally neat environment and well-prepared food. She seemed more involved with feelings and moods and did not pay a great deal of attention (not as much as he would have liked) to material chores. Making a living was up to him, since she had pretty much stopped work to focus on motherhood. He expected more from her at home than she could deliver, since she had neither the experience nor the inclination to maintain the sort of household that he envisioned.

When I met Lucia, she was despondent and fearful, anxious lest this pregnancy also fail. Friends urged her to seek help. She had been in therapy when she was single, developing a career. She left therapy when she and Jan became a solid couple, a few years before their marriage. She and Jan got along well when they were single, absorbed in their careers. At that point, neither demanded more than the other wished to give. They enjoyed each other's company when together and needed long periods away from each other for work. Neither was prepared for the strains that living together and a marriage with children in mind would bring.

Traits that were not intensely bothersome and even were amusing (e.g. his supercilious neatness, her inadvertent sloppiness) when they were single became incendiary in marriage. She admired and enjoyed his brilliance, the way he shone when they were with friends, the way they talked for hours, and she was never bored. The cutting edge of his precocity had been aimed at objects other than herself, except in fun. She was not prepared to be sliced for being an ineffectual housewife. She expected to be accepted as she was.

What especially bothered her was that his way of cutting was so controlled. She wished that he would get angry, as she did. She would get furious with him for criticizing her with aloof, untouchable nastiness. Her rages appalled him. He had loved her greater access to feelings before the fights began. For years he felt nourished by her emotionality and earthy perceptions. They filled him out, amplified his world. He was not ready for her stormy refusal of his mild-mannered defensiveness. She screamed at him for being withdrawn, withholding, wanting perfection. Both felt perfectly innocent, maligned by the other.

For a time, I saw Lucia and Jan together as a couple, in addition to Lucia's twice-weekly individual sessions, and sometimes I saw Jan alone (it took several years before it reached the point where he would re-enter therapy). Jan was convinced that everything was Lucia's fault because she was angry at her father. Her father criticized her and made her feel bad about herself. Now all men (i.e. Jan) were fathers getting the retribution due the original. Jan had previously had a lot of therapy, much more than Lucia, but he quit after he met Lucia and his life stabilized. He could not believe that he needed therapy again—he felt that he had had enough for a lifetime. He felt on top of his problems (he was so controlled), whereas Lucia went wild with hers. Every time we met, he repeated his picture of what was wrong with Lucia.

When I saw Jan and Lucia together, I could imagine them in an old-fashioned photograph. He was thin, precise, straight, she fuller, rounder, softer, fuzzier. Yet she would not let him get away with his defensive superiority, and this galled him. If he pointed at her father, she pointed at his mother. His mother was extremely self-centred, cool, and controlling, and it was easy for Lucia to see a connection between the former's emotional stinginess and Jan's fear of feelings. He found a way of living with his mother's distance by distancing himself from her. A real, live woman like Lucia was water for parched land, but also a problem. He was used to the calm of little contact, but now he had to deal with upsetting emotional demands. Lucia wanted more from him than he ever got from his mother, and Jan was convinced that he was getting the anger due her father. They were good at finger pointing. Their relationship put more pressure on them than either could bear.

As therapist in this case, a great deal of pressure was dumped on me. Each looked to me to take her or his side against the other.

Each looked for signs of support, which meant agreement. I liked them both. They were articulate, alive, creative, caring, and doing their best. Was it their fault that society provides no adequate vehicle for emotional education? It is far from clear that the human race knows what to do with itself and the states it goes through. How can two people learn how to get along, if they want to? Do we have resources to get along in ways that we can say yes to?

When Lucia spoke, I felt life from her standpoint; when Jan spoke, I could feel life from his. Each spoke from wounded sensitivity, and I felt the reality of both. Zigzagging between them gave me some sense of what it must be like for them to be torn apart by each other.

It is important to note that Lucia and Jan were right about what each said about the other's family. Each had truth on her/his side. Lucia felt ashamed of her family, also proud. She had to deal with too much of the wrong kind of feelings, but at least she was used to a lot of feelings. Her parents fought all the time. She knew about people screaming at each other. Jan was all too right about her father's critical, wounded–wounding nature. Her mother's resources went into surviving and holding her own in a coarse, abusive atmosphere. The children received the spill-over of stormy self-absorbed adult children, alternately fighting for their lives and succumbing to dreary accommodations to each other.

Where Lucia's father spent his spare time watching television in a daze, Jan's father was an artist. Jan's parents were better educated, refined, more reserved and dignified, the father warmer and weaker than mother. His parents were used to each other, put up with each other. They went their own ways, pursued their own interests, without seeming to be close to each other. Jan was baffled as to what positive tie might hold them together. For Jan, they were a negative example of relationship, a model of what a relationship should not be: it should not be nonexistent. Hostile control was quiet, indirect, but devastating.

It was inconceivable and appalling that Jan should be repeating elements of a relationship that he abhorred, although he easily saw that Lucia did so. What was wrong with her family was so much more obvious, since her parents were together too much in a quasi-collapsed, explosive way. He felt that his family was better off than Lucia's, steps up on the evolutionary scale. Lucia was tempted to feel coarse in light of Jan's refined background. But she was not coarse, simply expressive. Both were accomplished persons in their own right.

It would be too great an exaggeration to say that Lucia suffered from overstimulation, Jan from understimulation, since the background of each was mixed and variegated. Yet each craved a level and style of interaction that frustrated the other. When Jan wanted more intimacy in a calm, quiet way, Lucia stirred things up. When Lucia wanted more closeness, Jan was busy, preoccupied, disdainful. Each spent a good deal of time licking wounds, nursing grudges. The rhythm of their dance went awry. They could not coordinate closeness–distance and emotional thermal (warm–cool) needs. Yet there was a deep bond between them, and now and then good moments.

I felt happy that Lucia had chosen me as her therapist. I liked being with her. I could feel her feelings, her emotional presence, her realness. Sometimes I felt so good being with her that it was difficult to realize that she was depressed. My good feelings could not delude me long. Lucia and Jan got sick a lot. Lucia suffered from terrible sinus attacks that could linger for months. She had hosts of minor ills that could be debilitating for a time. Jan tended to get respiratory illnesses that responded to medication. While neither had life-threatening problems, the intensity and frequency of physical problems suggested something amiss with psychosomatic integrity. Neither had enough emotional support to promote psychosomatic cohesion, although support was not completely lacking.

They felt let down by families and each other. Neither their relationship nor bodies could handle what they were going through. They were ripped apart by multiple crosscurrents that neither had the capacity to navigate without injury. My writing that neither had life-threatening problems was not quite correct, since no foetus survived their psychophysical tensions.

Choices

It was tempting to see Lucia and Jan as a couple and each individually, and I did when hostility between them became too awful and they locked into unremitting mutual laceration. But the weight of the couple's and Jan's problems would have sunk my relationship with Lucia, had it not been clear to all (me, Jan, Lucia) that she was my primary patient. Lucia wanted a baby more than Jan, and it was she who came to see me. I do not know whether Jan wanted a baby or therapy less, but he was reluctant about both: he wanted neither fatherhood nor patienthood. He felt pushed or pulled into both. Lucia was the driving force where therapy and pregnancy were concerned.

I felt badly for Jan when I saw him. He felt under so much pressure. He was terribly worried about making a go of it in his profession. He worried that he would go under if he had to support a family without financial help from Lucia. It did not dawn on him that he was talking more about emotional than material support, that he did not feel emotionally supported enough to emotionally support a family. He looked pinched and pained, straining at the bit. He got so tightly coiled that it was easy to see that some form of somatic semi-collapse was likely, if only to buy resting time.

Jan was sensitive and bright. I felt that he would make a good father (or patient) in spite of himself, if things got started. When I saw him, I could not help feeling that deep down he wanted to be a father (and patient), but needed help in taking the leap. In this regard, I suppose, I was on Lucia's side. I could see why she loved him. He was a goodhearted person who felt threatened by the tumult she brought, pushing him over the edge of what he was used to. I would have loved to help him over the hurdle. But I had more than enough with Lucia and confined myself to taking the edge off the worst of it for Jan, until he realized that he wanted more.

I felt a sense of loss that Jan could not be my patient in the long run, even though I was happy to be with Lucia. A therapist cannot have everything, and it is useful to note that tolerance of loss or not having is something that Lucia and Jan needed to make more room for in their relationship. It is one thing to know that a marriage takes work, but actually to work at it is something else. It is terribly frustrating to see that somebody needs help, but not be able to help sufficiently. I suspected that a sense of frustration was something that Lucia and Jan, also, needed to make more room for.

Pain, frustration, loss, fear, anger—yet also a good feeling. I had a good feeling when I looked at Lucia, a good feeling when I looked at Jan, and when I thought of them together, and when I thought of them with a baby growing into a child growing into a teen. There was a lot wrong between them, but there was, also, life.

Lucia and I quickly became a therapy couple, and that must have added pressure to the marriage, as well as relieved it. If one person improves more than the other, the boat gets rocked. But the boat was rocking anyway.

The good feeling: waves of feelings

The physical, familial, and marital agonies that Lucia portrayed did not long dampen the good feeling that seeing her aroused in me. I could get into her agonies and even be stymied or paralysed by them for a time. But the good feeling welled up. I just liked seeing her, it felt good.

At times my good feeling bothered her. She did not think that I was taking her pain seriously. "You must think I don't believe you're depressed", I said.

"Yes", she nodded. "It's irritating seeing you content, smiling. Don't you know how worried I am?" She listed her worries: another miscarriage, no support from Jan or her family or his family.

"And now a therapist who isn't worried enough", I added.

"I'm worried you're not worried, but it's relieving", she said. "I'm used to people being nervous or angry."

"Do you fear I'm uncaring if I'm not nervous and angry?"

"I like the good feeling too. It feels good being here, in spite of what I say."

"But it also scares you? I won't see *you* if I'm blinded by liking you?"

"How can you know what I'm going through, if you're happy?"

But I certainly was worried. Being worried and anxious is part of my nature, very like the background radiation of the universe, now and then bursting from special densities into universes of particular worries and joys. I very much felt her and Jan's compression. Why, then, this good feeling?

There are plenty of bad reasons to feel good. We often substitute good for bad feelings in order to avoid, shortcircuit, or postpone the latter (see Eigen, 1986, pp. 40–51, 365–370). This can be useful, as it helps us get through things more easily. Still, fear, anger, and sadness are useful too, since they contribute to an important part of ourselves: our capacity to experience a wide range of feelings in life-giving ways. Was I trying to wash away Lucia's apprehension and grief with my good feelings? Was I like a parent who cannot bear the child's despondency and requires the child to feel good for the parent's well-being?

The above conversation suggests that I did this to some extent. But there were many other moments when Lucia and I sat with her worried, despondent self and gave it its due. We went through a wide range of states together. She spoke about daily events, her life with Jan, what she gained and gave up in marriage. She spoke of ins and outs with her friends and parents and wondered about going back to work. Yet whatever crises past or present we went over, we reliably reached a point where I looked at her and felt good, whether or not she felt good.

Was I feeling something that her mother/father felt when she was little—pure delight in her being? Was I in touch with a nuclear goodness in her life (our lives) which came through whatever threatened to wreck it? I listened to everything Lucia had to say, including the worst. But sooner or later the smile in my heart returned, and waves of good feeling pulsated heart to heart.

Therapy involves cognitive work, going over behavioural and emotional patterns, letting thinking processes emerge, encountering eclipsed parts of self and others. A great deal of rehearsal and repetition goes into working on stubborn sets of problems. One sees oneself and others in new ways and tries new responses. Still, understanding is not enough and can even add further tensions to what one already is undergoing. Much goes on outside understanding. There is a mute sensing or psychic body language in the subsoil. Whatever Lucia and I said or failed to say, we felt our beings work on each other in ways that smiles, frowns, and elusive gestures express more than words.

Eventually, Lucia began to stain and stay in bed, as in past pregnancies. When she came to see me, her apprehension was palpable. Would this be another failure? I gave her plenty of room to talk herself out and encouraged her to do so. Her fears, resentments, history of past and present injuries spilled out. Was her inability to complete a pregnancy simply biological? Was it a good she dare not give herself? Did she fear that a baby would ruin her marriage? Was there too much hate in her system for a foetus to survive? Were there ways she did not survive her upbringing and marriage? Had she reached too far beyond her parents, too far beyond herself? Was failure a form of self-punishment? Had she deserved a baby? Were the pressures of existence, together with her real and imaginary fears, too much for her psychosomatic frame to support? Was the failure to bear a baby linked with incapacity to bear life? Did she dread what a baby might do to her? Would not a baby reshape her life, misshape it?

But beneath all apprehensions was positive desire and good vision. Lucia wanted a baby, and she imagined happiness deeper than misgivings. She *felt* happiness more pervasive and more basic than evil imaginings. It suddenly dawned on me that my good feeling—whatever else it might be—was akin to the happiness of a good pregnancy. When I was with Lucia, without realizing it, I felt a bit like a pregnant woman. I was resonating to and validating an affirmation at the core of Lucia's being. Her bliss/joy/ecstasy over being a mother was a Yes! from the centre of her existence, triggering the Yes! at the centre of my mine.

It was the deep faith of motherhood at the core of life that I was called on to experience and support. In Lucia, this faith was very real, but was subject to internal and external attack. Her faith in her capacity to bring life into the world was imperilled by a variety of worries, pressures, hardships, including past experience of failure. Could her faith in her creative capacity and life's **creativeness survive failure?**

So often the therapist becomes a proxy (for a time) for work that the patient must do.

One becomes a kind of laboratory or workshop for processes that the patient must undergo in his or her own fashion. The work that one does (or fails to do) *can* be a life-and-death matter. I was required to experience the anti-life tendencies bombarding Lucia. I needed to struggle with destructive forces that threatened to dissolve her faith and generativity. If I could not telescope, survive, and work with forces that weighed on her, she would be alone with them, at their mercy.

In this context, my seeing Jan at his worst made further sense. The pinched, tight, no-saying Jan represented, in part, Lucia's tendency to tighten in face of pressures. Jan's taut face mirrored Lucia's contracted muscles, nerves, and circulatory and respiratory systems. Lucia's exterior was softer and rounder than Jan's, but inside she was knotted. He looked like she felt, an external image of her internal contraction. Of course, Jan was more than this, and so was Lucia, but would the more win out?

Similarly, everything that I learned about his and her parents, Lucia's and Jan's past and present lives, her hopes and frustrations, their economic, professional, and social dilemmas, became part of a high-velocity psychic particle-collider. What happens to the psychosomatic self under these pressures? Add to this a baby's impact. For some people, a baby is a crashing meteor causing black winter. Not only growth in the womb stretches one—a child's effect on a mother's life and psyche far outweighs changes that her body goes through in pregnancy.

All pregnant women I have worked with dream of water, floods, ocean waves, and eventually Lucia did too. I wonder if such images are not a normal part of pregnancy. My impression is that they increase in the last trimester but can appear earlier. The reference to water and being overwhelmed is obvious, from both the mother's and the embryo's/foetus's standpoints. In the dreams, it is almost always the mother who is being inundated by waves. Over the years, my patients and I have covered this territory with many permutations. The mother-to-be identifies with the growing baby within her, is concerned for its safety, fears that her own inner processes and states—physical and emotional—can upset the growing life within. In reciprocal manner, she fears for her own physical and psychic being. She, as well as her unborn baby, is at the mercy of psychosomatic processes that unfold without her governance. She, like the baby, is in over her head.

The age-old association of gestation–birth waters with catastrophe informs the dream-life of pregnant women today. On the one hand, fluids are life-giving. There is joy in bathing in the waters of life. Cleansing, baptism, birth and rebirth: psychospiritually as well as somatically. Waves also refer to waves of sensation–feeling, heightened intensity of emotional and mental aliveness, an increase in the capacity to generate and bear experiencing. But there is ever lurking the possibility that something will go wrong. Baby or mother may die or be ill or impaired. The peril may be psychological as well as somatic, as in a deepening maternal depression that blights existence, or violence aimed at life one cannot bear.

The story of Oedipus involves not only patricide, matricide, and incest but child abuse, including infanticide barely averted (see Young, 1994, and Bloch, 1984, for variations on this theme). It is useful to note that our cultural heritage is informed by stories of violence in high places (including violence aimed at babies), not simply the result of crippling socioeconomic impoverishment or disenfranchisement. Violence at the top sets standards for violence at the bottom, although both make special contributions. In literature, the association between birth and murder (partly a reversal, a mastery attempt, making the passive active, controlling the uncontrollable) has a noble lineage.

Does violence originate partly in the womb? Imagine, if an embryo could feel, what upheavals it goes through in so short a time. Is it fanciful to think of these changes as violent? How much imaginary/real violence a pregnant woman must contain, ride out, and even try to process! A young child complains of growing pains. What would a foetus complain of? I believe that the pregnant mother-to-be is sensitive to these complaints. She (unconsciously?) registers, experiences, and responds to violence happening to her baby and herself, of which signs are plentiful (including weight gain, change of shape, fatigue, forgetfulness, nausea, dizziness, emotional upheavals, perspectival shifts, pressure shifts, varieties of ecstasies–agonies, worries, intimations and presentiments, new desires, demands, and preoccupations).

Noah in his ark and Jonah in his whale dramatize, in part, what a mother and her baby come through: captured by a whale of a body, drawn through oceans of changes beyond individual control, floods of changes, life starting over. Mother may be less familiar to herself than her baby is to her. She may wonder who and where she is, since baby brings her to new places that are fresh, odd, challenging, redemptive/destructive. Columbus's discovery of America pales in comparison with the territory that opens with pregnancy.

Is it any wonder that psychophysical systems might short-circuit the process and recoil, with a sense, "I can't go through with it. Let's stop here!"? Excess of ecstasy wells up and floods excess agony, one infinity offsetting another. Which is the greater infinity? It depends on the moment. With Lucia and me (and, I believe, Jan), the infinite yes was more the home base and climactic movement of self. Not easily, not always.

Factors we worked with

Why did therapy enable Lucia to have a baby? The sceptic argues that she would have had it anyway: it is only an illusion that therapy made a difference. We cannot know with certainty what would have happened *if*. Yet I have little doubt that without help, Lucia would have had another miscarriage. Within weeks of her starting therapy, I could see a difference. Her face and body were visibly more open, less tight and strained. The difference was palpable. The way that she carried herself was changing, and so must have been her way of carrying a baby.

Therapy is not only a talking cure, although, with Lucia, talking certainly helped. Throughout this chapter, I mixed images that suggest different ingredients in the therapy stew. I wrote of pressure, bottled-up feeling, impacts of events and affects, injury, porousness–rigidity of personality, conflicts between/within individuals, openness, flow, faith, depression, ecstasy–agony, learning, evolving, the basic good feeling that sustains therapy. I would like to list and comment on some of the factors that played a role in helping Lucia's pregnancy come to term. Other factors could be chosen, along with other ways of writing about them.

Similarly, the factors noted are not unique to therapy seeking to avoid miscarriage: they are almost certainly facets of many therapeutic undertakings or, at least, part of ways we speak about therapy.

1. *Talking oneself out and hydraulic/eliminative images*

Therapy provided Lucia a place where she could say whatever was on her mind without retaliation. This took some pressure off her. In hydraulic and eliminative terms, she let off steam, cleaned herself out, lessened blocks and dams. Common speech associates talking oneself out with getting a load or weight off one's mind and, consequently, feeling lighter, carrying less baggage. When Lucia first sought help, she "felt like shit, clogged up". She looked low and tight. After she had some chance to talk herself out, she began to lighten. I could see tension in her upper and lower back (and, presumably, anal sphincter) ease. Her movements became more graceful and fluid. One wonders what pressure was placed on her body by holding herself in, tightening her muscles so. The tightening had become chronic, scarcely in awareness. As she spoke herself out, her energy-meaning flow became easier.

2. *Psychosomatic poisons*

At various points in sessions, Lucia feared that she was poisoning her baby, and, less consciously, that her baby would poison her. At times she felt poisoned–poisonous within. It is probable that such feelings represented aspects of physical processes that are part of gestation, birth, and development. Normal processes often have toxic elements. However, careful exploration suggested dread of poisonous insides was, also, associated with congealed hate.

It was easy to tap Lucia's hate through grudges she bore Jan. Marriage is a daily source of injustices. Jan was too remote, critical, ungiving, not *there* enough physically and emotionally. The rage one chokes on in daily living takes a toll. Even though Lucia got furious at Jan, the anger she expressed was a token of what she felt. One's psychophysical frame cannot possibly express the infinity of what one feels. A lot of what one feels becomes stagnant, hardens.

Also, Jan was right in linking Lucia's rage to her father. Lucia also tied her *injury rage* to her mother. The rage in one's life is cumulative. It sediments in the belly of one's being and corrupts muscles, nerves, veins. It not only stiffens one's body, it poisons one's thoughts. One bears grudges from early childhood on, so that one is ready to jump on others for not giving enough or, correlatively, be overly grateful for pittances. Cumulative rage helps nourish a pessimistic, depressive, semi-malevolent counterpart or undertow to one's official, happier self. In some people, bitterness/sourness is closer to the surface. In others it works more silently. One may recoil with surprise at the rage that a "nice" person harbours at the secret bad taste of things. In either case, more overtly or covertly, chronic outrage over injury can eat at life like an acid and corrode psychosomatic integrity.

Hate as a poison can be linked with hydraulic and eliminative notions. Hate builds up, explodes. One tries to get rid of pressures it exerts. However, the sense of poisoning and corroding the personality does not quite fit hydraulic/eliminative concerns, or perhaps is a special case of the latter. Insofar as hate eats away at personality, it may be said to get rid of or eliminate or kill aspects of personality functioning (Bion, 1967). Explosive hate obliterates the self. Poisonous hate corrupts the self. One's efforts to rid oneself of explosive/poisonous hate backfire, so that the latter deforms the self that fights it, and the evolution of one's personality and life may miscarry.

3.   *Equipment failure*

An important source of shame is the sense that one's psychosomatic equipment cannot support real living. Whether in professional, social, aesthetic, familial, or sexual realms, there is a dreadful presentiment or conviction that, at crucial moments, one's body–mind will let one down. The most dramatic instances of this in Lucia's case were her two miscarriages, but it is a theme that ran through her life. By the time I saw her, her marriage was becoming a mess and her faith in her professional self was shaky. Not only did she doubt her body's ability to support a baby, she doubted her personal ability to support a marriage and profession. She was getting ill a lot and felt more and more like a "basket case".

Lucia felt ashamed of her inability to support life. She and Jan tore each other down. She tore herself down. Her sense of shame spiralled as her life threatened to go downhill. Her ability to process what was happening to her jammed. Her responses to her situation become more constricted. She seemed to feel that her inadequacy to handle what was happening was her fault, even as she blamed others. Shame and blame were like viruses taking advantage of a general weakening of her condition, and they contributed to her feeling overwhelmed and flooded.

My sense was that Lucia's capacity to process affects had, in certain ways, been compromised early. She had done extremely well working around the rage–injury–shame that were part of the background of her existence. For much of her life, she had been able to maintain a more or less positive, upbeat tone and make use of her abilities. She pushed on in spite of the undertow, and she even made use of the latter in her aesthetic sensitivity. Still, a shame-filled sense of injury/rage remained unmetabolized and became more pressing as life placed her into situations that she could not "solve" and that no one could solve for her.

Therapy took the edge off Lucia's shame by enabling her to let down and acknowledge that she was in over her head. It gave her room to realize she was spinning her wheels, flailing, collapsing in on herself. There was no place in her life where she could admit she did not know what to do, that whatever she did made things worse. Jan was defensive with her, and all her parents wanted was for her to be happy. Her friends supported her but had their picture of what her life should be like, and they tried to bolster her will and ability to function. Therapy made fewer demands on her than anything else in her life. It gave her a chance to thaw out and experience the one true demand: it gave her a chance to link up with herself and see what it might feel like to be alive.

One can be alive with inadequate equipment. One can never adequately keep up with all that happens to one—and why would one want to? Therapy may help a person process injury/rage somewhat and help broaden one's response repertoire to the latter. Evolution in processing ability and response capability is a real achievement. But so is evolution of ability to live decently with the vast unprocessable, including wounds that never heal.

Therapy practices the art of making room for what another person can and cannot experience, can and cannot process, and so to some extent it models possibilities of making room for oneself and for others. To what extent can we become partners with the capacities that constitute us? Even a little familiarity with the packages that we have been given can bring enormous relief and enrichment. As Lucia reset herself and dared to dip in, she remembered/discovered how delicious being herself could be, with new appreciation for difficulties. Opening a little at a time in sessions went a long way. Just a bit of opening, with all its psychic chills, makes a difference. As faulty as our equipment is, it supplies us with more than enough for many lifetimes.

4.   Cognitive–behavioural insight and rehearsal

Lucia felt criticized, put down, and unsupported by her parents, yet also felt loved by them. How could this be? There were many good moments. She could remember her father smiling at her, kissing her. She remembers that many times her mother comforted and encouraged her. How, if they were bad to her, could she love them? How, if they were good to her, could she hate them?

The mixture of bad and good parenting can confuse a child, so that it is difficult to tell bad from good. One never knows whether one is hating or loving the good or bad parent. Often one lashes out at the good one and loves the bad. Such confusions carry over into adult relationships, especially when one tries to get close to another person. To a significant extent, Jan became a target for Lucia's confusions. At one moment, he was a wonderfully, sensitive, open, bright Jan, whom Lucia felt lucky to be with. At another moment, he was remote, self-preoccupied, critical, a source of pain. At times she beat up on him when he was good, and doubted herself when he was bad. She rarely felt that she got things right.

Over the years, Lucia went through these confusions with me. She was able to say what bothered her about me, say what she liked, and experience any number of reversals of attitudes and affect. We survived myriad changes of state together. She even got to enjoy liking me when I was bad and disliking me when I was good. It was possible to have varieties of feelings without regard to "goody–goody" or "baddy–baddy" fits. This was in marked contrast with her upbringing. Often as not, she would be punished for strong feelings by parental anger or incomprehension, and she would withdraw or make a stronger display of emotions in order to feel her impact.

She was not used to being listened to easily, and she felt it odd to impact on a man (me) just by speaking. She was used to having her feelings thrown back at her in some twisted way, and getting her own back by withdrawing (making the other sweat it out) or becoming furious (provoking hurt withdrawal and further retaliation). She mimicked ways her parents reacted to her.

In our first weeks and months, it was enough to convey a sense that a journey lay ahead, that we would get to know each other over time, and that, as time went on, perceptions/emotions/words would link in ways that would make her a better partner for herself. It did not take her very long to get ready for the undertaking.

5.   *How much aliveness can we take?*

The traumatic impact of "bad" aspects of parenting struck me, in Lucia's case, to be exaggerated instances of "normal" tendencies. It is not so unusual for parents to be critical of their children and of each other. Parents and children strike out and withdraw from each other in countless ways. Parents also idolize their children, as well as tear them down. Various forms of destruction and love commingle throughout a day. Shifting, variegated mixtures of love/anger/injury/recovery are a normal part of aliveness.

Nevertheless, some mixtures are more devastating than others. One ought not to underrate the damage that we do to ourselves and to each other. With luck, we learn to modulate viral tendencies and find comfortable enough ways of protecting others from ourselves, ourselves from others, ourselves from ourselves. It is important to find forms of protective modulations that fit and extend our sense of self, so that real growth is possible. In therapy, such a desirable outcome is often possible only after an individual thoroughly satiates herself or himself with first-hand knowledge of feelings one needs to modulate.

There is a vast difference between acting on a hint of feeling, and staying with the feeling, bathing in it. Lucia had fallen into the habit of lashing out at Jan or grinding herself into the ground in response to frustrating moments and rise of negative feeling.

As difficulties in marriage mounted, her emotionality became as much a liability as virtue. Her feelings followed gradients of least resistance, compressed into ruts, congealed around fault lines of her personality, became more stereotypical. She gradually collapsed to the worst she could be, rather than the best, and the former became more and more the everyday baseline.

The intensity of her depressive complaints, angry outbursts, begrudging silences became as unbearable to her as to Jan. She was becoming the sort of person she did not like, a person she never wanted to be and had fought against being. By the time she sought help, she was ready for it, since she was reaching the point of not being able to stand herself, as well as not being able to stand Jan.

Her pride in being the emotional one (next to Jan's remoteness) stood in her way somewhat, but she was also glad to move past this bit of marital mythology. It brought some relief, paradoxically, to realize how difficult it was for her to stay with feelings and situations and let them build, rather than cut herself off with rage and self-hate (which were becoming her specialities). Realizing how hard it was to stay with her feeling flow (and how unflowing her feelings had become) made Lucia hopeful that there was something more to her than the reduced her she was hating, that there was more to reach for.

She was too depressed, hurt, afraid, and angry to open to the larger sea within, but there was a larger sea to open to.

With help and encouragement, Lucia experienced how she short-circuited her states, her capacity to be. She was caught up pinning the tail on the donkey, blaming self or other. With support and hard work, she could stay with a feeling a little longer, so that her capacity to *experience* who she was and what she felt grew. Once she had located a feeling and focused on it, we could see where it would go and what it turned into, follow tributaries, guess sources. Sometimes it seemed important to investigate it, get ideas about it, map a history. But there was also a need simply to feel it, drink it in, get the most of it. Just soaking up feeling states can be nourishing, especially if one has been deprived of space and atmosphere to let feelings be.

Experiencing a feeling takes time. One needs time to follow its waves and pulsations as it builds, climaxes, subsides. This is as true of shame, for example, as joy. With practice and courage, Lucia bathed fully in streams of shame, seas of shame. There seemed no end to it. Once she started, it seemed like something that she needed to do, long wanted to do. What a relief to drink deeply and undefensively of the vast reservoir of shame that consumed her! She was used to fighting or evading it. She was not supposed to give in to unending shame. She was ashamed of shame.

Arrays of feelings came and went: shame, guilt, fears, furies, doubts, accusations, pleasures, joys. She had her fill of them, got to know them. She was becoming a little more familiar with herself, learning about feelings without having to rush. Her fear of getting lost forever was followed by disappointment in not being able to get lost forever, since feelings flowed along, one state limiting another.

How much could she take? How much would she need to take? It occurred to her that this was the best possible training she could have for being a mother. Yes, there would be practical problems of child management, daily chores, fatigue, and survival. But the simple ability to let feelings be, to tolerate build-up and flow—there would be times when all that mattered was how infant and mother felt together.

Without quite realizing it, she had been afraid of what she might do to a baby, with her fury or shame. She feared that she would inundate her baby with shame, make it as ashamed of itself as she was. She would make it ashamed of being a baby. Or she would be unable to break her addiction to lashing out/in. Instead of herself or Jan or her parents being objects or rage, she would rage at her baby. Suddenly, she saw herself and Jan as raging babies—screaming like mad with no parent to hear. Rage meets rage. Baby infant . . . baby parent. Where was the other to break this cycle, where was the other who could respond, not simply react?

In therapy, Lucia was learning to respond, to appreciate baby aliveness in herself and others, to give baby life its due. Life is more than baby life—but what damage results from fear of baby life and inability to respond!

6. *Faith in basic goodness*

A primacy of faith in the basic goodness of our time together provided a background context for everything that we went through. I cannot pretend to know where this faith comes from, but it is there. Without it, I doubt that our work would have been as successful. It would have had a different tone.

The faith in basic goodness that made our work possible spanned many levels and dimensions. First of all, it was an immediate experience. I felt *core goodness* in Lucia and myself. It felt good to be together. We increased each other just by being. This is on a level of sheer presence. Images of tuning-forks, resonance, positive reverberating circuits are among those that come to me. Perhaps the bare fact that such experience is possible is a good prognostic sign.

There were many semi-visionary experiences that I kept private. There were times I imagined Lucia's insides bathed in golden light. At times, it seemed more than imaginary: I *saw* her embryo/foetus-support system in radiant gold. I could move this golden radiance throughout her body and emotions and hoped it had some healing use. Such images seemed part of an overflow of the goodness circulating between Lucia and me, a core-to-core goodness.

Although we stimulated good feeling in each other, the latter belonged to neither of us, or to both. While it occurred within us/ between us, it was part of a good-feeling flow that went beyond our relationship. It was part of the basic goodness that supports the world and makes life possible.

The concrete clinical effects of basic goodness were many. It provided a tone and atmosphere ("spirit") that could absorb psychic toxins and a wide range of impacts. All the pressures of her life, everything that went wrong between Jan and her, the pressures she put on herself—the good feeling housed them. Similarly, goodness provided a frame for poisonous and stagnant rage and for all the feeling states that had no useful place to go and miscarried. All inadequacies, incapacities, disabilities—goodness bathed them all.

The pressures, toxins, impacts, fears, and unhappiness of her life strangled basic goodness, rendering it less effectual. The spontaneous, basic good feeling that makes life worthwhile was being suffocated. It could not do the work it needs to do. It was not getting sufficient support and education. It was too much under attack and too burdened. It could not offset the unhappiness and helplessness flooding Lucia.

Psychoanalytic faith did more than bolster Lucia's core good feeling, although this was essential. Psychoanalytic therapy is more than a shot of psychic vitamins, although affective infusion is a crucial element. Psychoanalytic faith stimulates cognitive-behavioural work that enables basic goodness to circulate more freely in the psychic body. Better circulation of basic goodness supports more adequate (always partial) metabolization of emotional trauma and toxins (which are inevitable parts of every life). Where a sense of life's goodness is too weak to support processing of trauma/toxins, the latter spiral and life itself may be threatened.

In Lucia's case, the baby growing within her raised the question of whether life was possible. Was it worth getting born? One cannot answer this question for another living soul. But sometimes one can affect conditions that form the background of a reply. Psychoanalytic faith and work provided a clearing that enabled Lucia to respond to life rather than merely react. One wonders whether the baby growing within her could sense the difference.

CHAPTER FOUR

A bug-free universe

Why are there bugs in the universe? This is an ego-centric question. Human beings are latecomers in this world, compared to bugs. But in our eyes and especially on our skin, bugs are a nuisance and at times a menace. They disturb us with buzz, bite, itch, swellings, disease. We learn, too, that our world and bodies are populated by invisible as well as visible bugs, and we are unwilling hosts at their mercy.

Many years ago, as a counsellor at the Henry Street Settlement House camp, I was forced to do unpleasant things, like put worms on hooks, so that disadvantaged children could have a nice time. One day in the woods we were having an especially nice time. We had gone fishing and were putting up tents for the night. Soon we would be roasting marshmallows over a fire. One of the boys, a Jehovah's Witness, broke my absorption by blurting out, "It's great. But I hate the bugs. Why do there have to be bugs?" It was an in-your-face question, and I had to answer it. The boy was serious. The rest of the night hung in the balance. I shrugged, then found myself saying, "To make sure you know you're not in heaven yet." He nodded, and we went on with our camping out.

In recent years more and more patients have come in wishing for a bug-free universe. In one form or another, it is an ancient wish. Religions promise a bug-free state someday, only not now. At times, it seems, religions treat the universe as a bug to be free of—life is the bug. Some promise freedom from suffering (a bug) by practising their path. My patients do not want the bug-free life later—they want it now. They do not want freedom from suffering through discipline. They expect it just by being. They wish to wish suffering away. Deep down, they feel they can will bugs out of the universe. They live by an unconscious imperative that there ought not be pain in their lives.

This contrasts with patients who are willing to suffer for the promise of getting better. There are tormented souls who laugh at painlessness. For them, agony is a necessary part of existence, of any life process. In their dreams, bugs refer to madness, and life is stamped by madness. In an earlier work, I wrote about different kinds of bugs and variations of madness that they express (Eigen, 1986, pp. 357–362). We say that someone is "bugs" or "buggy" when we mean crazy in a loose way ("he's got bugs in his bonnet"). We also refer to bugs when an error is made (a computer bug, for example). For the individual who expects a buggy universe, killing bugs in a dream may suggest becoming a little less mad or gaining a bit of freedom with regard to his or her madness.

For the individual who demands a pain-free universe, killing bugs in dreams is simply an extension of the wish for a disturbance-free universe.

In the case of the patient willing to suffer, killing bugs in a dream represents an achievement. It is not easy for this patient to have fewer bugs in life. Standing up to bugs—killing what is killing one—takes psychic work. For the individual who wills painlessness, killing bugs represents no work at all. It merely mirrors the desire to get rid of what is bugging one, to do away with sources of annoyance. It is less a symbol of psychic achievement than a signal of collapse or disabled development.

The imperative that pain ought not to exist acts as a judge. Experience is judged bad insofar as it is painful, good insofar as it is pain-free or filled with pleasure, joy, bliss, ecstasy, success, triumph. The results of this simple calculus can be bloodcurdling.

If I feel *you* are the cause of my pain, I may find ways of justifying my wish to be rid of you, to treat you as an annoying bug and stamp you out. I imagine that if I make you vanish, I will achieve my pain-free universe or be closer to it. If I should notice that pain is with me no matter where I go, I may conclude that the source of my pain is me, and try to eradicate myself. The urge to make the irritating or tormenting other or self disappear can be lethal. An individual or group may surrender to the idea that annihilation is the way to get rid of what is bugging one.

In clinical practice, we are used to people who have more or less collapsed under the pressure of self-hate and worthlessness, who feel like bugs, or shit, or garbage. Much clinical work deals with low self-esteem, bad self-image. We try to bring people out, support them, help them make advances in living. There are those who fail in life and seek help in becoming more successful or coping better with failure. We try to convince them that they are not merely bugs deserving to be squashed. They are precious beings who deserve a chance at living.

At the other end of the spectrum there are apparently successful individuals who have little capacity for sustaining meaningful emotional contact with others or themselves. They treat others as strategic objects, levers to push–pull for career or ego enhancement, targets to manipulate for sexual, aggressive, and socioeconomic gain. They seem impervious to the damage they cause others but are keenly aware of what others can and cannot do for them. These power and control freaks become anxious and depressed because of the incessant pressure to be on top of things and because reality, by its nature, eludes secure control.

Today's chemical technology encourages such people to use medication to get rid of anxiety and depression. This fits in with their ideology of power and control. One ought to be able to master anxiety and depression, as one master's demographics and competitors. Pills become adjuncts to the rush for success. They regulate mood and function and so help to keep on top and avoid falling down—emotionally, socioeconomically, personally, creatively.

So much effort in our society goes into avoiding the threat of collapse, as if the latter were an omnipresent danger. Suicide and drug abuse in high places exerts such fascination partly because it shocks us into awareness that needy beings stifle their screams behind effort, image, and achievement. As the gap between over- and underachievers in our society widens, hidden screams of the former unite with audible screams of the latter to form a haunting abyss that subtends the velocity of publicized events. The rush of television shows, hit movies and music, top stars in politics, sports, and other pop entertainment forms becomes a ghastly buzz—swarms of flashy bugs inundating psychic arteries. In this atmosphere, to be an author (once a proud calling) is to be part of the problem, another buzz adding to the noise.

Psychotherapy as a field has its problems, abuses, deceptions, its share of power and control freaks, its sexual, social, and finan- cial exploiters. But most therapists I know are loyal to their pa- tients and practice. They really try, to the best of their ability. I believe we offer something unique in our society. We try to listen and stay open to the impact listening has on us. We live at the creative edge of listening. We stay open to the impact another human being has on us moment to moment, week after week, month after month, year after year. We abandon neither the pa- tient nor ourselves but support our mutual attempts to live. We experiment in human relations, to see whether it is possible for two people to be alive at the same time, or whether one must thrive at the expense of the other.

We grow through creative listening. What pops out of our mouths surprises us. We deepen, become seasoned, as we turn the patient's impact over, as the patient bakes in us for long peri- ods of time. Speaking grows and changes through gestation. I know of no other place dedicated to enabling human beings to explore every nuance of what they feel in an atmosphere dedi- cated to growing the equipment to support such exploration.

Therapists are bugs too. The first time I met W. R. Bion, I thought, "My God—he looks like a bug." Something was bugging him, and he bugged others. Something bugged him to keep at the edge of his psychic universe, and his presence bugged others to keep at it too. My experience with Bion was paradoxical. I felt quite accepted or tolerated for what I was, while at the same time being urged to go farther. Our spirit gives us an invitation to join it in a movement that never stops. Dare we turn down the adventures of a lifetime?

The first real therapist I met was Socrates—the most famous, gentle bug in Western cultural history. He called himself a gadfly, as well as a midwife. Socrates asked questions that deconstructed beliefs and showed that thinking was no easy or usual business. What passed for knowledge was usually opinion. He knew he was annoying and that thinking was an irritant. It was thrilling to watch houses of cards he blew on collapse. What is left standing in Plato's dialogues apart from a taste for questioning and faith in the good that remains when falsehood disintegrates? Was Socrates guilty of corrupting the morals of youth? Only in the sense that he raised their ethical sense beyond conventional corrupt morality. He shared a taste of the vision of the good, so that the thrill that is the heart of life becomes something worth having.

Jesus, also, was executed, suggesting how easy it is to confuse the mystic—like the questioner—with criminality. Faith is at least as buggy as the questioning mind. Heart or head—both are ever-challenging. Faith does more than move mountains—it opens a heart and goes on opening it. The open heart, the open hand, the open mind: how far dare one go—how far *can* one go?

Cynicism bugs idealism and idealism bugs cynicism. One capacity bugs and/or nourishes another. The bug keeps changing forms. Bugs never go away for long.

A never-ending day

John

John is a university professor. He has been telling me for years that his colleagues are conspiring against him. They are trying to push him out of the department, out of university life. He is tenured, has seniority, is a full professor, is well published. He has made it impossible for them to get rid of him. Still, with my help, they might finally succeed. He feels I direct their attempts.

John is a complex, creative person and delightfully paranoid. He lives in a world where people are always thinking of bad things to do to him. He loves his research, his search for knowledge, but he constantly doubts himself. His self-doubt can be paralysing but, in the end, spurs productivity. He has to stay on his toes if he is to weave his way through the minefields set by others.

After many years, we reach the point where we can joke about his paranoia. He develops a lighter touch and lets in people who like him. I found John likeable from the outset, but it was a long time before that made a difference. It is beyond the scope of this chapter to do John and our work justice, but I want to portray a very moving moment.

John was feeling that he could not continue a moment longer in the university. How could he show his face? He was disliked by students and colleagues. Everyone laughed at him, thought him a joke. He was utterly wrong to think he should have gone into university life. He should have become a Madison Avenue shark, a Wall Street ace, the president of the United States. But he hated thinking about money and would surely hate politics. He probably would be lucky to end up a waiter or an usher in a theatre. He could not imagine what he might do outside the university—he just felt that he should have tried *something*.

The feeling mushroomed to crisis proportions. John was beginning to have difficulties with getting to work, as the intensity of self-attacks mounted. Then one day I sensed a sadness tinged with rage, which he readily heard when I pointed it out. Almost as soon as he recognized it, he virtually became a little boy on his first day of school:

"I was crying. My mother wanted me to cross the street and go into the school by myself. I wanted her to bring me to the class-room. I cried and cried. I cried through the entire first day. I learned to get through it. I learned to stop crying. But now I wonder if I ever stopped crying.

"I hated myself for being so weak. Why couldn't I be a big boy, like most of the other kids? Why did I have to be one of the cry-babies? I never stopped attacking myself for being weak. All through school I put myself down. Hating myself was a way to hold back tears. Self-hate is the great sealer.

"When I was older, I remember going to the blackboard to answer a question. I scribbled something, drew something, wrote something. Whatever it was, the teacher put it down. She thought I was scribbling nonsense. I was furious. I did something a bit spirited and got crushed. Now I'm angry I didn't do something different—strike out at her, strike out somehow. I don't know if I was scribbling, but if I was, it's something I was trying to do, something that meant something, something that meant *me*.

"Now I feel I ought to strike out on my own, do something different. I hear myself saying: 'strike out, strike out'. I struck out. Zero, nothing, out. But I feel the fury, the sadness. I always get sick every winter. I think it's a reaction to being in school. I'm still in school in the winter. I'm still a schoolboy.

"I'm still trying to get through my first day of school without crying. I've spent my life in a classroom trying not to cry."

John went on to think about his life as a whole. It was as if he had a "near-life" rather than "near-death" experience. His life flashed before him, together with the basic feeling tone that marked his existence. He concluded that it was not so bad being who he was, not so bad being a professor. He really loved learning, studying, exploring, communicating. He was a dedicated person who was bugged by stifled emotions and a sense of being squelched. The sense of being squashed as a child rendered him ever critical of himself. He expected horrible things to happen to him and could not digest the fact that he was liked and relatively successful.

In John's case, it was his mother who wanted a bug-free universe. She wanted her child to have a painless life and, especially, not to cause her pain. John's childhood task was to convince his mother he was OK, not in agony, not wincing inside. She wanted an imaginary superchild, an image of a child who is confident, at ease, able, brave. She did not want the actual child she had, the one who could not stop crying when he went to school. John's emotionality bugged her. She did not want him to feel the traumas she and life put him through. He had to learn to protect her from himself, at the same time doing the best he could with what was left over for himself.

His teachers picked up where his mother left off, putting him down for being buggy (e.g. scribbling nonsense). He learned to get by at great expense. Deep down he did not feel liked, either by others or himself. He felt put down for being himself, and his excluded self gnawed from within. In later life he could not believe that he was likeable because he had learned to be likeable as a ploy, a shield. He expected to be squashed if he came out of hiding.

As a way of forestalling further disaster, he imagined that others were against him. If they *really* knew him, they *would* be against him. His paranoia kept others focused on the wrong person, the wrong him, a proxy rejection of a self manqué. He hid behind the others' imaginary hatred. They could not *really* annihilate him, because he could not be found. He spent a great deal of time walking between raindrops that never fell.

John lived in dread of a universe frightened by (and mean to) babies. He put much of himself into aesthetic and intellectual labour, which reflected vital interests. He recognized his deepest self in the work he chose, that chose him. Work mediated contact with others. At times, work was asked to do to much. It could not always contain the emotional forces poured into it and wobbled under the strain.

Yet John aged well. He looked younger as he grew older. The throttled baby–child bloomed late, as John luxuriated in unhurried, timeless work he did on himself. One begins in a world frightened of babies and becomes frightened of oneself. Therapy enabled John's fear to become a little less greedy for the space it never had. Above all, moments of liking and being liked became possible.

Inner and outer circles:
the knotted core and defensive perimeter

Milton

Milton's self-hate was as thick and intense as any I have met. It gave him no peace. He was sophisticated, elegant, handsome, yet he hated himself for wanting to be admired. He was charitable, helpful, good to others, yet he hated himself for wanting love. He felt that everything that he was and did was secretly geared to being the centre of attention. He hated himself for wanting to be centre of attention. He was a good man living a good life, but no amount of goodness modified his self-hating core, which co-opted everything.

Milton's mother was a beautiful woman who had been drugged out of her mind throughout his infancy. She was an addict who spent many days in bed. Yet there were moments when she would envelop her baby, fill him with the bounty of her beauty, with flickers of radiance. She gave him moments of intense gratification which were more than he could bear—superfuellings to make up for wastelands.

His father rescued him in middle childhood, but the damage had been done. He had already spent years living in a vacuum, trying to reach someone who was out of touch much of the time. His largely unsupported emotional life collapsed into a dense knot of self-hate. A more normal, active life with his father lifted him somewhat. But living with his father had drawbacks too. His father was absorbed in building his business and exploiting women. He had some time for extroverted activities with Milton, but no time for a child's damaged feelings and problems. His father dismissed feelings that made him uncomfortable. At best, he tried to talk Milton out of his difficulties, but he could not hear them. Milton was caught between a steamroller and a vacuum.

Neither his mother nor his father could be bothered with a real child. Neither had any idea what a child might require. His mother treated him as if he were not there, or only sometimes there. In fact, *she* was not there, or at most only sometimes there. His father treated him as someone who *should* be glad to be alive, someone who *should* feel good, someone who should *only* be happy to be rescued. His father had an insatiable need to be centre of attention, admired, loved. Milton hated himself for being like his father—a bulldozer needing admiration. And he hated himself for being like his mother—a dead centre within a sea of promise.

Milton came to therapy to be heard. His great secret was that he was not alive, that he was a monster. People liked, admired, loved him. He was a successful professional, a good family man, an active community man. But he could not feel the goodness of his life. Inwardly he felt dead, self-hating, and contemptuous, and he was critical of others.

As the years passed, his wife began to catch on. He hoped to shield her from his unmitigated, lacerating barrenness. At first she supported him. She felt that he was good and wished he could feel his goodness. Even she had no inkling how eaten away by self-hate he was. Yet she had glimpses. She began giving ultimatums. She could not bear the ungivingness in his giving. She began to realize that nothing came from him. The closer she drew to his centre, the more punished she felt. Her own need for aliveness was getting no real support. She began to feel with him the way he must have felt with his mother as a baby and with his father as a child. She did not think she could live this way much longer.

I felt Milton a semi-heroic figure. He nursed a lifelong sensitivity to trauma. This might seem like self-pity and self-absorption, and perhaps it was. But it was also uncompromising dedication to what was most real to him: pain, injury, emptiness. It was as if he became hyperconscious to offset his mother's drugged self-absorption. It was as if, as a baby, he had woken up and stayed awake through the most agonizing unmet scream. He became an unmet scream going on endlessly, fading into oblivion, dying out, going on in the deadness. Painful deadness became an acute and permanently heightened state of consciousness. Milton found no relief in sleep or stupor. When he awoke, agony–deadness continued.

Whether or not I could help Milton was scarcely the issue. The first question was whether I could bear him. To bear something of what he was bearing seemed crucial. Milton was attempting to bear the unbearable. He was asking someone to stand what he was unable, yet forced, to stand. He was asking someone to stand with him. His wife tried but could not take it. By the time we met, Milton had given up hope that his pain could be mitigated. Attempts to ameliorate it seemed false. He was merely wondering whether it were possible for his agony to be seen, met, witnessed.

He felt that past therapists became better versions of his parents. They would reach a point where they subtly tried to talk him out of pain or try to lessen it. This was human, but it was not what Milton wanted. He could not bear deviating from the horror of his inner reality. He would rather die than give up the truth of his suffering.

Now and then I would venture remarks to explore whether there was any match between what I could say and what Milton felt. Most of the time my attempts were thrown back at me for some false note I was barely aware of. Once Milton pointed out the falseness in my truth or compassion or vain gropings, I could see it. He was terrific at finding the pea under the mattress, the fly in ointment. Milton was adept at keeping me close to what was off in me. One would think that I would give up on making any formulations at all, but this was not the case. Sooner or later I would regroup, back to square 1 or 0, and try again. It was a thrill, really, never to let go of—or be let go of—by the serpent in the garden. For years, the serpent *was* the garden, the only show in town.

You can imagine our surprise when one day, seemingly out of the blue, a picture of Milton's suffering that he could say yes to arose. The picture was embarrassingly simple and obvious, and in one form or another had flitted across my mind at one or another time. Now suddenly it popped out with compelling clarity. Milton was talking about his wife's love—his inability to let it in or to give to her. He envied her ability to love, but nothing threatened him more. His spoke, too, about his contempt for people who tried to give him something.

I pictured old cowboy-and-Indian movies, the cowboys defending the camp at the perimeter as the Indians circled around. The outer defensive perimeter was Milton's contempt aimed at the circling others (including me, if I stupidly tried to help him). At the perimeter were the guards, with weapons set to attack attackers. Anyone who threatened Milton's inner truth was an attacker.

Inside the circle is—nothing. The hostile perimeter guards nothing: Camp Nothing. "You'd think you'd be used to it [the nothing] by now, yet, oddly, you dread it. You dread the nothing you're used to." Normally I would be floored if Milton agreed to a match between my words and his being, but this time we shared a sense of something (nothing) unfolding, and I continued speaking with him, more than I ever could. "Outside the perimeter of the circle is Father Force, inside is Mother Emptiness. You contract to a hard knot in the middle, a knot/core that tends to disappear, a knot harder to locate than the plane that disappeared in the Florida swamp. Your wife wants to heal you with love. You fear that if the core dissolves, it'll explode, like many shells shattering. So you guard against the force coming from outside the circle, yet fear the imploding core within."

After a silence, Milton added his own image. "I've often conceived of anti-matter as the centre my being, with matter surrounding it. I've spent my life containing this tension. If the two meet, they'd be mutually explosive. I've been trying to keep them from meeting."

For the first time since we met, I felt that Milton really looked at me. I saw *me* coming into focus in his eyes. His face was warmer, more open, coming together naturally, not a composite of patches. I felt him coming into focus within me without hurting me—without needing to hurt me.

Of course, between sessions the bug came back, as it always does. Milton began his next session by saying: "You know you missed something last session. It's not just nothing I fear. There's something really destructive. I *want* to, *need* to, destroy whatever anyone hopes to give me. I can't help it. It's a destructive force—not simply nothing."

The life bug:
what do we do with babies?

A loose equation tends to hold in dreams: bugs = babies = madness = destruction. The cases above indicate that babies are born into a world that does not know what to do with them. The very aliveness of a baby stresses adult care-taking capacities. Dread of aliveness (and the destructiveness of aliveness)—whether one's own or another's—may well have played a significant role in Doris's miscarriages (chapter 2).

Babies bug adults, as well as vice versa. My examples are extreme, but not as atypical as may be thought. It is not so unusual, one way or another, for babies to be too much for adults. The traditional caricature of a father who feels uncomfortable holding a baby is only the tip of the iceberg. The adult world, in general, is somewhat at a loss in the face of the pressures babies exert.

Babies demand time

The time a baby demands can be overwhelming. Fatigue is a chronic liability of parenthood. Many adults are simply unable or unwilling to give a baby the time it needs. Some feel quite threatened, as if the demands of the baby menace their own life. There are mothers who cannot tear themselves away from their children, who overdo it. But there are many who feel too resentful about "giving up their lives" to support a child's. This can be so extreme that virtually any time with a baby is felt to be a strain and drain. Finding a workable balance between supporting one's own life and supporting the child's life is one of the most important and difficult challenges facing parenting today.

Many well-meaning parents seek help because of a failure to find a good-enough balance. Some express bewilderment over the most basic difficulties.

A fairly typical case involves families in which parents are too busy to give children enough time. Often very real busyness masks a deeper incapacity to be with children, an inability to mould one's personality so as to be able to respond to children as they are. Vicious circles spiral, in which the inability to be with children leads to more external busyness, which, in turn, exacerbates the underlying disability. Parental busyness can be an unconscious response to the baby, a way of (mis)regulating the baby's demand for time. Parental busyness saves the parent from drowning in the swamp of child-care.

A busy parent may say, "If only I had more time to spend with my child—I'd give anything for more time." Anything that does not take away from her or his own life—as if the child were necessarily a source of deprivation, as if child and parent were in a life-and-death struggle for time. Too often when parents find time, they discover how difficult being with a child is, and things go badly. They would like to wish away friction, miscommunications, power struggles, near-calamities, furiously painful tears.

Jim and Andrea

In one case, the father, Jim, was busy at work and the mother, Andrea, with social and athletic activities. Jim and Andrea came to see me for couple therapy. They hoped to better their communication, in the hope of helping their children as well. Neither wanted to make time for individual therapy, although Andrea seemed more receptive than Jim to the idea. They just managed to eke out an hour to come together, with the idea that therapy should be a short-lived problem-solving endeavour. When they got together, they were angry at each other. She was angry at him for not being around much. He was angry at her for not spending more time with the children and not taking better care of the house.

Andrea hired a stream of babysitters to fill the gap in parenting. She wanted to be the mother and could not hire a reliable homemaker to bind things together. She could not bring herself to put in the time the children needed, but she also could not risk having her felt centrality threatened. She diffused the coverage among many, and this diffused the children as well.

When Jim came home, he disciplined the children and played with them and expected them to shape up. Then he would leave. As the children grew older, Jim blamed Andrea for the children's difficulties in school. They could not concentrate and got into trouble, although they were nice kids in a spoiled–neglected sort of way. Jim was a workaholic, and the children expected to go through life without working. He could not stomach their expectation that everything should be easy. He also complained that things were too easy for his wife.

Andrea spent a good deal of time entertaining Jim's business colleagues and their wives and going to social events with him, which she enjoyed. But being with the children was a trial. It was a battle getting them to listen to her. Even when they tried to listen, things rarely went well. Home-life was disheartening. Why should she sink in daily impotence and exasperation while her husband was enjoying the thrill of success? Her beautiful house became an aversive stimulus. Being at home was intolerable. Increasing envy and resentment of her husband went along with a sense that her own centre of aliveness was atrophying. She became socially and athletically hyperactive in order to stay alive.

In my office Jim and Andrea quickly became contracted caricatures of themselves. Their emotional repertoire seemed reduced to blaming each other for whatever was wrong. Blame took the place of exploration and self-questioning: two real people in the real world, financially and socially successful, living such an impoverished slice of emotional possibilities.

They loved their children but could not deal with the reality of children. They did not come close to grasping their children's situation and were out of touch with the full range of their own needs as well. They lacked the equipment to bear experiencing how they affected their children and how their children affected them.

It is hard to bear knowing how we harm each other and ourselves.

Aliveness is disturbing

To be alive is amazing, but it is often also disturbing. A child's aliveness may be gratifying but upsetting. Destruction and messiness follow a child's lively interests. Children push adult buttons and boundaries. Adults try to teach children to control themselves. Sometimes control goes too far.

Larry

Larry came for help when an upsurge of aliveness nearly toppled him. He was happily married, had a fine job, then conceived a passion for his secretary. After simmering for months, he shared his feelings with the lovely woman, and she freaked out. She was furious that he had spoiled their happy working relationship. She

gave him the silent treatment, except for communications absolutely necessary for work. She applied for other jobs and enter-
tained the idea of suing him, but he was not abusive and did not
exploit her. He simply was crazy about her.

For months Larry savoured the rush of lively feelings that
came to him, a treasure of emotions. He did not feel this way for
his wife. His wife was his best friend, and he loved her. They
loved doing things together. But the excitement he now felt
eluded them. He had never felt such a thrill before. It seemed like
his chance to live.

Larry described himself as an onlooker. He loved to read and
was a physical fitness addict, but he lacked immediate and strong
feelings for people. He was thoughtful and kindly and often put
others first. He ruefully remarked that he could afford to be
pleasantly benevolent because he was not overly involved emotionally. His personality was something of an achievement. He
was a good Christian and wanted to convey good will. He would
not wilfully hurt anyone. He made others feel good but regretted
his lack of emotional intensity.

He felt that his personality lacked force. He was given the
toughest assignments and spent an enormous time at work because he could not fight for the jobs and helpers he wanted. He
valued being a good person, but he wished he could muster more
of a commanding presence when needed. His mild emotionality
resulted in mild behaviour. What intensity he had went into reveries while reading, physical activities, and the endurance required by countless hours of nearly meaningless work.

All his life he had been this way. He remembers being more
self-controlled than other children. He enjoyed rich experiences as
a child but recognized a difference between the more immediate
way many children played and his own ability to take others into
account. Other children tended to go after what they wanted and
do as they pleased without much thought. Larry was aware of
possessing a consciousness that filtered the totality of situations.
He watched his consciousness automatically evaluate who was
where and wanted what, so that he could insert himself into the
scene in ways that would not be jarring. He had a knack for finding niches that minimized frictions. To an extent, he found ways
of slipping between what other people wanted.

Larry liked being who he was, even if he wished he could be more assertive at times. Being an observer had varied, reflective pleasures. His temperate nature dampened pain as well as passion. Nevertheless, as time went on, the hours put into work that was devoid of intrinsic value took a toll. He was able to reconfigure corporate structures and took pleasure in his ability to work well. He was an extremely competent person. But he was locked into observing himself pour year after year into work that had no real meaning for him. He was locked into watching his competence. The little time left for reading and reverie scarcely compensated for the sense of waste that grew over the years.

As the logic of unconscious processes would have it, Larry's falling in love happened to coincide with his mounting discontent with his years of paperwork. Suddenly disaster bells and tumult sounded in the workplace. The first time in his life that he reached for someone he wanted with all the emotional aliveness he could muster a mess resulted—potentially the biggest mess of his life.

In a way, a real mess would be welcome. It might get him out of the wasteland of meaningless work. His marriage was more complicated, but he was willing to risk it for romance. The hope of breaking through his tepid self-sufficiency transfigured him. But as suddenly as the dramatic promise arose, it subsided. His secretary began speaking with him again, cautiously and remotely at first, but wanting to make peace. The old unselfconscious friendliness was no longer possible, but she wanted to continue working for him. No other prospect in her search proved as congenial. He would have to find a way to swallow his feelings and accommodate her. The hope for heaven or hell was over. It was back to the wasteland and quiet longing.

Instead of a marvellous, transforming romance, Larry had therapy—a poor substitute for the thrill of life, but for the moment he had nothing better. Therapy holds the promise of transformation too, but it is pale compared to what Larry had felt close to having. I guessed that Larry would leave me as the crisis subsided and life returned to business as usual. He looked down at therapy. He thought he was smarter than most therapists. What could they tell him that he could not tell himself? His own powers of observation were greater than most he knew. If he was an observer *par excellence*, a good therapist should be a super-ob-server. All his life he had handled problems himself. By exten-sion, a therapist should be a model of super-self-sufficiency. It did not occur to him that his model of therapy was lacking.

What surprised me was that Larry stayed with me. We really liked each other. I tried to give him a decent work-out in my psychic gymnasium, although a time must come when working out reaches diminishing returns and something more must hap-pen. We "played for time" in the hope that Larry could build enough psychic capacity to take something more. He went through life a supercontroller, but supercontrol masks needs be-yond control.

As we sat together, a vision unfolded of a child who had to do it himself or go under. He had learned early on that emotional aliveness was destructive or irrelevant. Mother could not take much of it. Optimally, a child's aliveness makes the mother more alive—a virtuous circle. Aliveness stimulates aliveness. Larry's mother could not be bothered. She tended to turn off when he was expressive, as if too much feeling threatened her.

Larry recalls being brushed off repeatedly as she turned from him to housework. She would tell him to go out and play with other kids, but often there were no other kids. He learned to make do on his own. His model for relatedness was she going her way, he his. Intense feeling failed to become a flowing link be-tween them. She was not up to a high level of emotional stimula-tion. She was most at ease when working on her own with her chores, a model for life Larry unwittingly absorbed. In fact, he did her one better, becoming brilliant at his chores in a larger financial community.

His model for community was a variant of parallel play, with each person pleasurably pursuing their own track, contributing to the whole, keeping things nice. Upsetting emotional surges and outbursts should be subdued, mute, confined to low-level back-ground noise. It was as if Larry went through life trying not to bother mother, since it would do no good if he did. He was afraid to create a disturbance or perhaps more afraid to learn that he could not be disturbing enough, even if he tried.

With guidance, Larry was gradually able to turn his capacity for reverie to the formation of self in childhood. For the purpose of communication, I am compressing bits of vision extended over many visits. A number of mothers or sides to mother emerged:

(1) An unresponsive or minimally responsive mother, she kept the level of emotional flow low. She felt best working on her own instead of interacting. She did not seem upset by Larry, because she did not let emotional impact get that far. Her tone and glance, let alone words, provided cues to keep things down. Larry slid off her. He could not strike terror in her face nor fury in her voice. It was as if she had an unconscious missile-defence system, so that any attempt to find her missed its mark.

(2) She became impatient if he could not handle her lack of presence well. It was more than not wanting to be bothered by a pesky child, although this was part of it. She seemed to lack the capacity to deal with being bothered in a way that would make it worthwhile bothering her. If Larry threatened to be demanding, her inner flame automatically burned as low as possible, with impatience substituting for concerned concentration. She was the result of a minimally responsive upbringing herself and passed it on. Impatience covered deficiencies. Larry lived in a larger world than his mother. He found sources of stimulation outside the home—nature, library, sports—that somewhat filled the need for emotional contact. He became better educated than his mother.

(3) Mother had good words for him only when he did not need her. If he was sick or injured, she provided the necessary care. She was not a physically absent or neglectful parent. She saw to his daily needs. She was a model of operational efficiency, which rubbed off on him. But he felt some sort of implicit approval only when he did things without her. From his earliest childhood, he remembers *feeling* disapproved of if he wanted or needed her, and approved of if he did not. This feeling of approval–disapproval was installed within him. It monitored his actions and urges. An inner yes came when he could do things on his own, and a sense of banishment when he wished something from the other. It was precisely when he needed the other that he felt rejected, and when he did not need anyone, he felt accepted.

(4) All his life Larry had a sense of something missing, very much like Doris (chapter 2) sensing something wrong or broken. A favourite way of putting it, was that he was missing something "wild". Much of what he had was good enough, but he also

wished he had the wild thing. At times he sensed his mother would go wild if he pushed hard enough. But there was no real evidence of this. It never seemed to him that he pushed hard enough, because no matter how hard he pushed, the wild thing did not happen. The more he pushed, the more she vanished or muted things. He banged on her and his emotional equipment as hard as he could and was shrugged off like a little bug—a harmless bug you do not kill but flick away by shaking a bit. Nevertheless, he feared she would go wild one day and told himself that he had better not press the issue. The dreadful truth was that he could press 'til kingdom come, and the wild moment would be postponed. Larry learned to live around the wish for something wild someday. In effect, he learned to live without the wild feeling in his heart.

(5) Where was Larry's father? Being nice to Larry's mother. An odd thing was that even though Larry's mother rarely got upset, Larry's father seemed always to be trying not to upset her. "Don't upset your mother" was his motto. This added to Larry's bewilderment, since mother was difficult to upset. Without quite realizing it, this gave Larry the uncanny feeling that his father could read his mind, since he *would* upset his mother if he could. His father addressed a wish Larry could not fulfil, at least not to his heart's desire. His father told Larry not to do what he could not do anyway. It seemed they were living with an imaginary mother—one who could get easily upset—when, in fact, it was maddening one could not get to her. Was an easily upset, hyper-responsive woman fabricated in order to maintain a feeling of alive sensitivity at the centre of a non-effusive family? Or was there really a madness that ran quietly through the family without being identified? Larry's father was a sort of failed bug. He seemed always to be protecting his wife from a sting or itch he could not inflict. He devoted himself to making his wife feel good, pulling punches that did not need to be pulled, so that his efforts seemed nice but somewhat superfluous—a lesson Larry learned well.

Aborted aliveness

At last came the moment in Larry's life when the wild thing raised its head and was chopped down. His life was a kind of aborted aliveness stretched over time. How could the upsurge of aliveness at work turn out well without practice? Larry lacked a background of successful bursts of shared aliveness with real people. Can one jump-start this capacity out of the blue? How does one get practice, if one never begins? Aliveness needs a life-time of practice if one is to learn to navigate its destructive aspects. But one has to start somewhere.

The woman at work gave Larry the sort of explosion he could not get from his mother. She was highly distressed, agonized, appalled. The little bug was, for a moment, a big bug, triggering a horrified reaction. Larry managed to upset a woman terribly. It was not the response he had hoped for. Instead of mad love, she just got mad. But at least it was strong feeling. Almost any kind of strong feeling was water in a desert.

As with his mother, the feeling he tried to ignite came to nothing—worse than nothing. First came the helpless distress and rage he feared his mother hid. At last he smoked it out, only for it to fizz. The woman withdrew into an angry shell. She accused him of harming their good business relationship. It seemed to Larry now that his mother treated motherhood like a business. She went about dealing with Larry as if stresses of emotional life were somehow secondary, illusory, easily brushed aside. He had to collude with the way she conducted business or be left out of the deal. What Larry had unconsciously most dreaded happened. The woman at work became a strangulated version of his mother, conducting business as usual, minimizing emotions and their meaning. Larry would have to cooperate in maintaining a world without emotional colour or bang himself against unfeeling walls.

As often happens in therapy and life, one repeats the past with a twist, a slight variation, a nuance that can make a difference. While growing up, Larry had had little choice but find pleasure in self-sufficiency. Now a similar adjustment began to form with a somewhat new feeling tone. The failure of love at work forced Larry back to himself. He had to regroup and find his own centre once more, but not simply as a cut-off work machine. In reaching out to therapy, he was reaching out to himself in a new way, not content with business as usual.

For one thing, it dawned on Larry that the mess at work was not all his fault. Yes, his imaginary sweetheart blamed him for upsetting things. It was, after all, the expression of his feelings that broke office peace. But there were other ways to handle him, not just angry withdrawal. She could not stop punishing him with accusatory looks and a sarcastic tone. She could not help recoiling and striking back. At first her reactions seemed reasonable, but when they became a permanent mood, he began to wonder whether the punishment fit the crime.

Her distress was more serious than he initially realized, and he felt that he needed to find a way to let her know that he knew that. He wanted to find some way of letting her know that he appreciated her work, that he could take her no, that they could continue working together, if she liked, that what happened need not be catastrophic. He spoke with her, but months went by, and her tone was still punishing, hostile, accusatory. Larry had to admit that he did not know who she was or what he had unleashed. He could not assume full responsibility for the extent and persistence of her contracted state.

That he did not know who she was constituted a therapeutic breakthrough. It meant, in reality, that he did not know who anyone was, including himself—and including his mother. Without quite realizing it, all his life he had taken responsibility for his mother's personality—or, rather, he had somehow assumed the rightness of things as they were, that things were as they had to be, as they should be, the best of all possible worlds. He muted himself emotionally in order to fit in and almost took having to do this for granted. He was born into a world that required the persistent and pervasive use of self-dampening capacities if he was to have what psychic nourishment and air was possible. What would he have been like had his mother been a little more spontaneous, expressive, enlivening?

He reached for spontaneity, aliveness, expressiveness in what he imagined his fantasy sweetheart to be, only to find that he reached beyond what her universe could bear. Reality was not what he had hoped or imagined, but what he dreaded. He was outside, beyond, excluded from inner promise. Whatever the real was, it was something that could not make use of his feelings. It was something that could not take him as he was. This must be what he had learned as a baby and what motivated his reflective quietude. And now he saw in his imaginary love a mirror image of what he went through—her contraction in the face of his promise: a promise to one is famine to another.

At last, a sigh of freedom: Larry drew back into himself, detached again, but with a feeling for the unknown, wounded–wounding other. His sense that more was unknown than known (and that the unknown about a person was at least as important as the known) gave the real-life other the room she needed. Her contracted fear–hostility no longer had fertile soil in him. He breathed easier. He had loved, lost, and was open to whatever. The next move, also, was unknown. He had done what he could to try to heal the situation and let it evolve. Whatever would happen would happen. This was a new feeling for Larry. For the first time, he began to be open to the great unknown he was. His life was no longer on hold.

Psyche: bugs and music

To have a psyche means to be uncomfortable. Any sensitive being is subject to discomfort, irritability, pain. Our psyche, in addition, is subject to ghastly agonies. Imagination is an infinity machine (Eigen, 1986; Matte-Blanco, 1975). Fear becomes nameless dread. Rage becomes boundless or coagulates into relentless, unforgiving hatred. Pleasure becomes ancillary to ecstasy. If we fulfil one wish, others appear. There is no end to anticipating dangers, no end to the stream of discontents. We are ever subject to being bugged by our own psyches.

The only way to be free of horror, agony, and the demands of fluctuating ecstasies would be not to have a psyche. In one way or another, people try to do just that.

People play down or attempt to get rid of psychic sensitivity in many ways. As implied above, the very "urge to exist" may be experienced as foreign, threatening, invasive (Bion, 1994, pp. 169, 175).

Alice

Alice (chapter 1) described herself as squashed from an early age. She had dreams of bugs assailing her from outside and inside her body. Most of her life she took the bugs to be herself—a bug her mother squashed. Her identity model was a squashed bug. It was what she most felt herself to be. Any urge to be other or more than that was menacing. If she came alive, she would be squashed again. But her mother, also, was buggy and bugged her. She was relentlessly and appallingly assailed by her mother's madness and self-hate.

When she was a child, it had never dawned on Alice that her mother hated herself and that she was the main recipient of her mother's self-hate. She just felt herself the target of her mother's rage and tried to numb herself until it passed. Alice became expert at waiting out storms, psychically vanishing until the tirade was over. Noah's flood seemed nothing compared with loss of life Alice underwent, submerged in mother's wrath.

Therapy stimulated Alice's potential rainbow. Whenever her urge to exist surfaced, it wrought havoc. She lacked the equipment to support it. Any surge of aliveness fell flat, since there was too little psyche to make use of it. In therapy, she felt emboldened to try to live, but it was too much for her. Her system recoiled and developed an autoimmune illness, signalling she could not take too much of herself. While chemical poisoning over a long period appeared to cause the immune-system breakdown, it was very fruitful to see what meaning lay in her illness. Alice's very urge to exist became a danger signal, for attempts to live imperilled her. If Alice wanted to survive, she needed to jettison her urge to exist.

Alice and I latched on to each other deep below the death roots. It took years to realize how deeply entwined we were. It was a silent feeling each of us had of the other that made the difference in the long run. We found each other below a crushed or non-existent psyche, in ways that allowed and enabled a life-supporting psyche to grow. I do not know why this is possible with some severely damaged individuals and not with others. It is a mystery how a life-begetting connection forms in the midst of savage devastation and enables help to evolve over years.

To outflank the damage caused by coming alive, we had to build a psyche to support the growing aliveness as we went, never without mishaps and ghastly setbacks.

It is dangerous when aliveness outstrips the capacity to support it, but heartening when it stimulates growth of the needed capacity.

For many years, Alice was in a world made of nothing but bugs. She was a squashed bug, bugged by a hopeless urge to live, assailed by poisonous internal and external persecutors, mired in a psyche-less psyche, a psyche unable to support anything but its own crushed state, ever sliding into non-existence. Her urge to exist was perhaps her biggest tormentor, since it responded to promise, which led to disaster. Neither death nor life offered solace—both were enemies. The urge to live was an irritant—indeed, deeply wounding.

Why did the invisible inner connection between us take? Dare I say it? I felt something musical in our mute sense of each other. It was highly compressed, nearly impossible to hear, virtually useless, very buried. It was something like a tuning fork in her resonating with a tuning fork in me, but the tuning forks had a lot of dirt on them, a lot of waste, clutter, crushed soul fragments, so they did not give much sound. You would not have to be tone-deaf not to hear it—it would be easy not to hear. But we felt it. Our crushed souls saw and heard each other. In some highly compressed bit of our beings, we were transparent.

In reality, I did not know whether Alice would stay with me or whether we would succeed. There are Alices who leave me in bitter frustration. Yet this Alice and I stuck it out for decades, bugging each other, hearing music intermittently growing clearer. Sometimes I think music saved my life. I wonder if unheard melodies, ravaged "spirit ditties of no tone", saved Alice's. Sometimes bugs make sounds a little like violins or woodwinds. The sounds bugs make do not really come close to truly beautiful music. But they make one sit up and take notice, as if listening for something they cannot quite supply. Alice and I are still listening to each other and occasionally hear more than a drone. How is it possible to be squashed bugs yet upheld in life by soul music, music of the spheres?

Music permeates the self. Visual art and literature can do this
too, especially the musical element in each. Words and colours
make music too. Sound envelops, passes through defences more
readily. It is invisible like wind yet moves emotions deeply. It
is intangible like thoughts and feelings but real in impact. Very
often deeply damaged people reach for something musical in
the therapist, and hope that the latter will respond to something
deeply musical in themselves. At such moments, how we sound
to each other is a gateway to how we taste emotionally.

Ben

I find it appalling that some people are brought up in a world
without music, if that is possible. A patient, Ben, recently painted
a picture of being brought up by parents who emphasized material success. Any attempt to bring music into his life was put
down. Ben's interest in theatre, playing guitar, listening to music
were mocked. His parents made fun of him as an actor or musician or when he seemed to feel anything deeply. "Don't get excited", said his mother. "Where will it get you?" asked his father.
His father's energies went into looking for ways to make money.
Nothing else mattered very much.

Against such a background, I felt it a gift from God when
Ben's wish to play guitar or listen to music surfaced in therapy.
Ben was wired tightly. The possibility of not making enough
money drove him crazy. He made more than enough, but he
lived in terror that he would not. Although he had left home
young in order to be free of his parents, they never left him inwardly. His inner parents bugged him mercilessly. They drove
him to be obsessed with money, to the point where his health and
well-being were threatened. At a particular crux in therapy, if Ben
did not make room for music in his life, he would fall ill.

It was not easy to support his need for music against his consuming obsession with making money. All the things he had
heard in childhood and hated then came out of him now. "What
good will music do? Who needs it! Go for what's really important." Ben needed a great deal of encouragement to begin indulg-

ing his wish to bathe in sounds. Music terrified him as well as nourished him. It stimulated annihilation dread as well as love. Ben was so used to splitting off a part of himself and making the world an object of schemes that bathing in sound made him afraid of falling apart. His practical self could not conceive of surviving in a musical universe. His internal parents dominated him, but music did not give up.

What if music is not an adjunct to life, a hobby, but part of life's basic ingredients? Music is no guarantee of health. There were Nazis who loved music while gassing or shooting or beating or stabbing people. Musicians kill themselves. But life without music? Ben was terrified of music lest it make him less effective, less practical, less driven. He dreaded that more music would make him less hungry. He had enormous energy and buzzed from task to task with no evidence of fatigue. Music threatened to drown the successful, hyperactive self he had developed over the years.

Therapy often must work both ends against the middle. Sometimes therapy helps monomanic individuals soften their focus. Sometimes it helps dispersed individuals pull together. Often it does both together. There are individuals who treat psychic life as a foreign invader and so live in terror of invading themselves. Individuals may try to eliminate the psyche in order to achieve a bug-free universe and/or become a kind of bug to get along. Enlightenment and helping traditions notwithstanding, we are novices learning what to do with musical, buggy selves and worlds.

CHAPTER FIVE

Feeling normal

"Normal is what is there", writes Winnicott (1989, p. 270) of the baby at the beginning of life. "The baby tends to assume that what is there is normal." A deformed baby or child may not experience deformity for some time. It may have a more or less prolonged period before awareness of deformity sets in (and this is so whether deformity resides in self or in the parents). Eventually, the baby or child makes comparisons or reads itself through the eyes of others who see deformity. It begins to feel the impact of attitudes towards deformity (especially, at first, the attitudes of loved ones and care-takers) and feels the gap between inner self and external standards.

Thus Winnicott posits a period of feeling normal prior to an awareness of deformity, a "primary normalcy" (my term) subject to "slings and arrows of outrageous fortune". For Winnicott, the sense of primary normalcy is contingent on being met by parental acceptance and love without sanctions. Winnicott even suggests that primary, unconditional love is expressed physiologically through the care the foetus receives in the womb. He posits a link between how the new-born is held by the emotional life of the

parents and the support and acceptance that pervade the womb
before birth. Emotional and somatic living are interwoven from
the outset.

There is a difference between the mother who feels she must
cure her child of deformity and one who loves the child as is.
Winnicott (1989, p. 263) describes a boy who needed to be certain
he was loved as he was born before he could go forward. Even
though he *knew* he was deformed, he had to reach a sense that it
was normal to be he. Deep in his own body was his own aliveness, which needed room and support. He would have to join his
mother and medical practitioners in work with his deformity, but
only if he could first feel the primary normalcy of being alive, his
alive being—and this included, especially, the body that contributed to feeling alive. Without the body he was born with, there
would be no aliveness at all.

"At the beginning the child has a blueprint for normality
which is largely a matter of the shape and functioning of his or
her own body" (1989, p. 264). The child will feel derailed from
nearly the outset if this blueprint is not joined by the mother's
"emotional involvement, which is originally physical and physiological" (1989, p. 264). More lethal than physical deformity, perhaps, is the psychic deformity resulting from spontaneous
aliveness having no place to go or suffering mutation by parental
anxiety, coldness, fury, or incomprehension.

A *caveat* might be added to the effect that infant and mother
adapt to one another. Interpersonal adaptation is not merely onesided. Bodies spontaneously mould to and resist each other. The
fact that baby and mother exert pressure on each other ultimately
enriches the sense of self of both. Winnicott emphasizes an area of
trauma, especially when adaptive flow aborts because of maternal difficulties. He is concerned with the fate of aliveness in a
milieu that cannot support it. We follow his view to the extreme
juxtaposition: What happens when the sense of self of a physically deformed child is supported *vis-à-vis* the case of a child born
physically well but whose sense of self becomes deformed by psychological toxins?

Winnicott's physically deformed child becomes the centre of
two seemingly opposite tasks or tendencies. On the one hand, the
child must feel (and in some way actually be) accepted and val-

ued for the self (including, especially, the deformed body self) that is. The mother's womb, the birth, and the child's post-birth world must be imbued with this acceptance. On the other hand, the child must develop awareness of how he appears to a range of others, experience the specific disabilities he is heir to, and learn to make the most of the materials he has to work with. In other words, Winnicott's deformed child provides a parable or paradigm for cross-currents of self and developmental tasks we must all face.

Winnicott stresses that there is a period of experiencing aliveness and going on being before developing a picture of life and body from the outside. The spontaneous sense of going on being provides the home-base feeling of self, a basis of normal feeling and feeling normal that subtends later ideas and images of normality based on external standards.

We have multiple roots and branches, since we draw from the primordial pulse or raw feeling of aliveness and the many forms aliveness takes, including standards that feel extrinsic to one's natural flow. In clinical work we find people living too much from their intrinsic flow, without regard to external standards, and others who see themselves so much from the outside that they feel little or no flow at all. The task of going back and forth and evolving as we go is paramount today.

Depersonalization–personalization

Many of Winnicott's most memorable clinical explorations throughout his *oeuvre* revolve around the problem of depersonalization. In a broad sense, depersonalization has to do with not feeling real to oneself, and not feeling real can take many forms, with many nuances. Winnicott tends to associate not feeling real with loss of contact with one's body and body functioning (1989, p. 261). He introduces the term "personalization" as a positive counterpart to depersonalization in order to explore the way contact with the body develops and thrives, so that one feels real and alive.

If personalization or dwelling in one's body is a developmental achievement, then how much more of an issue can it be when one's body is deformed. A mother "is constantly introducing and re-introducing the baby's body and psyche to each other", a task increasing in difficulty if an abnormality "makes the mother feel ashamed, guilty, frightened, excited, hopeless" (1989, p. 271).

A mother dealing with her child's physical deformity brings out with special clarity the fact that in the best of circumstances a mother's feelings towards motherhood and her child are mixed. Her attitude can contain a nucleus of loving acceptance, while at the same time she is besieged by doubts, misgivings, fear, shame or guilt. The child's attitude, too, is mixed. Since there is a period of being a living self before outside criticism sets in, primordial self-feeling may be intact, in spite of the fight against negativity at some later point.

Clinical optimism may be naive, but clinical pessimism is unwarranted. An early sense of feeling normal that is part of primordial self-feeling may be available for therapeutic work, if it can be reached.

In and out of the body: some other part of personality

When Winnicott writes of loss or gain of body contact he notes the existence of "some other aspect of personality" (1992, p. 261) that can be more or less in contact. In health "this other part of the personality" (1989, p. 261) dwells in the body—it is a gradual developmental achievement. We cannot be sure from Winnicott's text what "this other part of the personality" is.

Does he mean psyche—since it is the mother's function to introduce and keep introducing body and psyche to one another? He seems to suggest that the indwelling of "this other part" has something to do with establishing a firm link between "whatever is there which we call psyche" and body.

Whatever this part—which can be more or less in or out of the body—can be, it is part of the personality, which suggests that the body is also part of the personality. The personality is the larger field that the body and what goes in and out of it are parts of. Whatever psyche and body may be, they are parts of a larger field called "personality".

On the one hand, the body contributes alive impulse, emotions, sensations to personality. Kinaesthetic–proprioceptive swirls of sensation and impetus are part of what make one feel alive. There are outer and inner skin sensations. There are background undulating sensation seas with shifting subcurrents, eddies, interoceptive delights—all manner of surface–depth delicacies, intimations, premonitions, squooshiness: Freud's polymorphous streamings, fountains of youth, body juiciness, along with more tightly organized impulse–action arcs, the press towards climax and discharge, ebbing into background, supporting, rising–falling seas. Is it odd to say that raw sensation has personality, as well as being part of personality? It is precisely the personality of sensations that lends colouring and tone to our more developed personalities.

Does the I grow out of sensation fields? Is the I already implicit in them? Do successive waves of sensation give rise to the I? Is the I part of sensation and a part of personality aware of sensation? What is the part that is aware of other parts—body parts, like sensations? A distinction between a part that is aware and parts that are objects of awareness cannot be maintained in any clear and systematic way. Terms of experience keep shifting into and between one another. Is personality more than psyche, as psyche is more than self, as self is more than I, as I am both more and less than body? We can create all sorts of circles and flows of energy and meaning with such terms and still be happy jugglers with more and more colourful balls to juggle.

Winnicott describes a healthy movement between personalization–depersonalization. The child who personalizes existence also needs to be able to disintegrate, depersonalize, and "even for a moment abandon the almost fundamental urge to exist, and to feel existent" (1989, p. 261). It is as if personal existence and embodiment is a strain, and one needs to let go of everything intermittently, even of one's need to live. Unimpeded movement in and out of existence, personalization, and body is facilitated by relationships in which maximal trust plays a role. Emotional tone and quality of relationships inform how going in and out of body and existence feels and how this capacity is used.

In health the I or self or psyche that goes out of body does not simply stay aloof or become a detached observer. In Winnicott's work, healthy depersonalization tends towards unintegration or letting go of firm boundaries and personality organization, simply floating, drifting, relaxing one's tight hold on self, others, things. What a relief it is not to have to be in life or even *be* all the time, a blessing to relax one's grip on life. And what a warm surprise one is to oneself when life returns, brings one back, and one begins to form again or re-form.

Winnicott's emphasis is less on studying oneself than on letting oneself come and go, relaxing into being-and-not being in the context of a relationship that can support coming and going. It is not always possible to be part of a relationship that can tolerate going in and out of existence. Too often a parent's need to be affirmed breaks the flow between aliveness and the fading of aliveness. The parent needs the child to mirror life, possibly to fan the parent's weak and insecure self-flame. If the parent's need is chronic and inordinate, the child's own rhythm may abort or go underground, the very sense of self may be poisoned. As with everything in life, there is endless variability, infinite gradations.

Nevertheless, one can become interested in consciousness for its own sake. One can explore more disembodied and embodied moments and the transitions between them. Wherever one finds oneself, there is plenty to work on and play with. Wherever one turns one's hand, there are more regions of being. Pluralism is inside as well as outside ourselves. Are we invited to enter a new age of tolerance? Must spiritual, intellectual, or embodied souls mistrust, envy, scoff, even fight each other to gain advantages? Is there not more than enough everything for everyone? If not, why not? In principle and possible fact, there certainly is. Let us end being right at someone's expense, or at least recognize the functions and uses of this drive.

Winnicott comes down on the side of greater embodiment but implies the fragility of this achievement. It is always possible to give up or diminish or be unable to initiate embodiment in the face of traumas such as physical illness, deformity, abuse, exploitation, loss. Winnicott's warm formulations cover vast mysteries. What is the self or psyche that warms the body, personalizes body, personalizes existence? For Winnicott, self and psyche are warmed by the warmth of other embodied, percipient psyches. Cold psyches depersonalize body and existence.

Consciousness suffuses body, body suffuses consciousness. Which personalizes–depersonalizes which? Either may be more or less personal or impersonal. Where does personal, warm me-feeling come from? Winnicott values the personal me as an innate part or potential of the psyche and personality dependent on good conditions for development. But the personal me is co-extensive neither with consciousness nor with body. It needs to establish toeholds in both.

Personal feeling needs to spread through consciousness as well as body. Consciousness can be as alien, inimical, and frightening a place or no-place as the body. Personal feeling is a special part of being, which can spread–contract through various regions of being, including consciousness and body. The personal warming of consciousness can be as much an achievement as the personalization of the body. Both consciousness and body are anonymous as well as potentially, if variably, personal. Personal me can lose or never gain contact with vast areas of consciousness, as well as body. Depersonalization is not simply the loss of body contact. It can involve trauma so massive or noxious that the personalization of anything, including consciousness, can go awry or run amok.

We are at a loss to say what this "other part of the personality" that goes in and out of body is, if it is not psyche (which is conscious–unconscious). Is it self?—not anonymous, impersonal self, but, for Winnicott, personal self-feeling, me-ness. If so, it goes in and out of psyche and consciousness and self as well as body. It may be easier to become aware of variable links between personalization and body, but body holds no monopoly on issues of personalization. There are people for whom personalization and me-ness (the me-ness of me-ness), embodied or not, is the strangest thing of all.

What goes in and out of what shifts meaning in different contexts. Spirit, mind, I, self, consciousness, unconscious, psyche, breath, energy, meaning, personality, body aliveness, variable fields of being—what mysterious x comes and goes through all of these and whatever one experiences and formulates? *Ruach Elohim*—breath of God? We do not exactly know what in and out are or what may be going in and out. Whatever mysterious x comes and goes and maintains us in and out of life at every moment—we are that and share that and so, in some respect, share sameness. Nothing is less personal or exclusive than personal me. We are the same personal–impersonal me in our very special ways. Nothing is more special or unique than the same breath of life and spirit that gives us to ourselves.

Jack

There are disadvantaged and deformed people who push the edge of the possible. They challenge limits most of us dread. Jack was one of those indefatigable children who never give up. He was born with legs deformed and useless, yet he became a dynamo of energy. He made himself part of whatever activity he jumped into. He took dance classes, played in the school band, writhed around the floor in gym in an inconquerable fury, doing what he could in games he loved. He refused to be beaten by himself.

Most people are taken aback the first time they see Jack in a school performance. What is that little bug twisting and turning dervish-like under the feet of the other children? He is never still. After a while, the blur of movement that evoked twinges of horror, even revulsion, leaves one uplifted, inspired, with a renewed sense of beauty.

We mirror life for each other. Sometimes the mirrors are horrible, sometimes they are beautiful, and often neither one nor the other but something more differentiated and subtle. Jack's real achievement is stepping out of the mirror. Whatever he seems at a distance to adults who do not really know him—to his peers he is just Jack. Other kids like him and he likes them. He is fun to be with. He enjoys life—the whole roller-coaster. To his classmates he is not mainly a symbol, a being who means something, but someone to be with, someone to feel enlivened with. It is not a matter of being accepted as he is—acceptance and non-acceptance are beside the point, not relevant terms. He simply is. He and his classmates simply *are* together.

What made this remarkable achievement possible? A lot of work by parents and school went into it. But even with a lot of work, such inclusiveness does not always work out. One ingredient in the mix was the unswerving support Jack felt from his parents. They gave him every advantage, including the right to test his ability, the right to see what he could do for himself. He was accepted the day he was born. Love was waiting for him even before conception. Birth ratified the love that warms existence. Jack's deformity intensified parental love and efforts. He lucked out in his choice of parents and his parents choice of him.

At the core of Jack's being was the good feeling that was, also, at the core of his parents' being, a reciprocity of goodness kindling and answering goodness. He thus had an early period of "primary normalcy", in which his own being and the emotional nourishment he received from the surrounding world established a sense that aliveness was good, going on being was wondrous, and the soul sparkle of his body, the shivers and tingles that make movement yummy, were part of a never-ending abundance nothing could exhaust.

What is crucial is that Jack's core aliveness, the aliveness of aliveness, was affirmed. In interactions with parents and others, aliveness spoke to aliveness, aliveness met aliveness. Affirmation includes respect, not only reverence, awe, and love. Jack's parents recognized from the beginning that his life must be different, that they would need to learn to create an environment that enabled him to learn what would be useful for his growth. They did not pretend omniscience. They sought help. They respected and created the possibility for Jack to respect the materials he had to work with. But the joy in his own existence was in place from day one. One appreciates this simple fact upon meeting individuals whose very sense of aliveness was poisoned by parental self-hate and angry or aloof critical dispositions. For such individuals, the precious foundational period of primary normalcy was seriously threatened, besieged, and possibly compromised.

It may be cruel to think that Jack was better off than many psychically deformed individuals. Who can say? His was no painless life, but he had a concrete focus for his difficulties. Feelings of inadequacy and inferiority were organized by his battle to live successfully in spite of being crippled. He had something specific and clear and limited to feel inadequate about, something to organize his efforts around.

There are many individuals who are not so lucky. There are psychically maimed people who cannot locate an effective "cause" for their problems. The amorphous self-hate that devastates them seems to come from nowhere, eats everything in its path, leaves nothing untainted. For them, agony feeds on agony. Little is left for them but to display their wounds in oblique ways, often receiving little help. More often than not, they are out of contact with the wounds they need to show. They have become giant wounds or systems of wounds coated by layers of imaginings, rendering them difficult to find or to touch. Indeed, the wound systems themselves have turned into abysses and labyrinths in which one wanders aimlessly, if one stumbles on them.

Jack's life was cleaner and stronger. He mobilized resources against an obstacle everyone could see. It was as if his disability stimulated the energy to transcend it. He had something to pit himself against, to define himself against. There was a strong and obvious negative in his life to be positive about. He was determined not to define himself as a crippled person. He wanted acceptance on his own terms, as the person he felt himself to be, as the person he was. This was possible because he had a basic experience of primary normalcy—his core aliveness embraced by the core aliveness of others. He had time for an intact, wholesome sense of self to incubate before externalizing himself as disabled. Once core aliveness is established, it gathers momentum if given favourable-enough conditions.

As Jack grew, he wanted to be accepted for himself and for his achievements, like everyone else. He did not want to be judged as a crippled person. He wanted acknowledgement because he was a shining part of life. Yet his negative shaped his positive outside full of awareness. Although he wanted to be judged on his merits and not as a disabled person, this "not" played an important role in defining the active and assertive person he became. His inability to use his legs triggered almost a reflex response against dropping into areas of helplessness. It was less denial than refusal to give in. He refused to be cowed. He mobilized himself as a pocket of energy in whatever situation interested him.

Jack did not have the brittleness of denial, but his incessant self-mobilization could seem forced and overdone—an overkill, at times. He was not someone to sit still with. If you wanted to rest or be quietly peaceful with someone, Jack was not the one. If you wanted to be active, have fun, do things, you could count on Jack. Chances are he would wear you out and go on to his next partner while you recuperated. He was active with a vengeance. Jack would be fun to go body-surfing with but not to watch a sunset with.

For Jack, passivity was associated with a fear of dropping into bottomless helplessness. The need *not to be helpless* overgeneralized, so passivity was avoided. He was not exactly manic, although sometimes he might be. Even so, Jack's manic tendencies were not so much defences against depression as part of more general attempts to ward off helplessness. He so built himself around not feeling helpless that average expectable helplessness was experienced as dangerous. Intimations of helplessness acted as a signal to trigger further surges of the mastery drive.

Many individuals who suffer from an obvious abnormality persecute themselves with an over-idealized idea of normality. They imagine that if only they could be normal, their problems would be solved, or they would only have normal problems. A young woman who suffered from a muscular disease wished with all her heart she could, just once in her life, dance like a normal person. In particular, she pictured a popular friend who danced often and wonderfully. Her friend was on top of the world—she seemed to have life made—she had everything.

My young woman patient swam, worked out—did the best she could with herself. One night she magically achieved something approaching her dream. She danced the night away at a party. For once in her life, her body was not something to drag around. It became liquid, colour, sound. How happy she was! Yet how surprised she was when the aftermath subsided, and she had to struggle with problems as usual. Being more nearly "normal" for a night was truly wonderful, but it solved nothing.

How mystified she was when she visited her friend in a mental hospital a month later. Her friend had fallen apart—she heard messages in obscure sounds, everything was saying things about her, giving messages of personal and cosmic import. Her friend was terrified, paralysed; she feared that she would never be herself again. My patient had a great deal to digest. Life did not fit her picture. The magic of dancing resolved neither mental nor physical illness. Normal was not what she imagined it to be. Still, it is wonderful to have truly wonderful moments.

Jack grew up in a milieu that placed a great deal of emphasis on creativity, so his consciousness was never totally dominated by the idea of normality. No one around him pretended to be very normal or, for that matter, even to know what normal was. "Energy" was an important term in the discourse of Jack's world. People around him spoke of good and bad energy and more or less of it. This gave Jack a somewhat expanded world, yet not without his own way of narrowing consciousness. His push was towards more good energy. Negative states acted like signals to reach more positive states. Thus his need to avoid helplessness was reinforced, adding a somewhat compulsive, driven feel to his high-energy life.

That Jack could live as well as he did was partly made possible by an early period of primary normalcy in which his sense of aliveness was affirmed. The bare fact of being alive was supported with all its mixes of emotions, feelings, sensations—the whole natural flow. In this foundational period the baby does not have to keep itself in life artificially. It does not have to hold on to itself unduly. Consciousness comes and goes, waxes and wanes. Whatever we call ego or self is subtended by larger fields of sensation–feeling ebbs and flows, which contribute to a background sense of depth beyond sums of later, more compressed and tightly organized identity formations.

The basic feeling flow includes how one's body feels before one knows one has a body. One's body is a normal source and part of how it feels to be alive. To speak of knowing one has a body is already using too hyperconscious a language, distinguishing knower from known, I from an object I can know. The body has not yet been objectified, mapped as a body. The body of primary normalcy is the lived body or body subject contributing to how it feels to be alive, how aliveness feels. The I–self–body–feeling–sensation blend comes and goes, an undulating aliveness more or less fading in and out of being.

Insofar as the early flow of undulating aliveness has breathing room, one implicitly feels the right to be alive, and being alive is right, a feeling pervading one's very sense of being. To feel the right to be alive and the rightness of aliveness stamped in every pore of one's psychosomatic being is a glorious thing. The right to be alive may have cellular counterparts. Religious terms like "justification" or "salvation" are partly rooted in the struggle to feel alive, envisioned as eternal aliveness.

The right to be alive is challenged over time by many countertendencies. It comes and goes with the natural flow of aliveness. But it may also be attacked and maligned by anti-life forces, elements of personality that are afraid of or hostile to life. Or it may not find conditions that can support life or support life well. Even if conditions are favourable, one needs to learn how to filter the primordial emotional flow and funnel it into forms communities can digest. One finds ways of turning oneself into some viable type of cultural currency. Some funnels and currencies are better than others. Too many individuals are pinched, even suffocated or poisoned by theirs.

To put it another way, primary normalcy gets filtered–funnelled through secondary, tertiary (and so on) normalcies, with better and worse fits. As cognition develops, one makes more discriminating comparisons, measuring self and other on many different scales. One learns where and how to compete, lie low, feign cooperation, bond, break bonds, use skills, develop relationships of many degrees and qualities. To some degree it may be normal to feign normalcy as one passes from one situation to another, level to level. "Normal" changes its meaning and assumes different values as one develops and contexts and conditions shift.

A good-enough phase of primary normalcy provided a positive foundation for the filter–funnel systems Jack's personality adopted. A positive outlook tied to energic imagery yielded a congenial mould for placing himself in life. If anything, the secondary–tertiary forms of normality were a little too successful. Jack's image of himself as a positive energic force was a bit too onesided, even cramped, if not desperate. It rendered his personality somewhat monotonic. Jack did not need therapy to get him into life or to make him more active. Therapy was useful because it helped him dip into the feared helplessness in tolerable doses.

Primary normalcy includes periods of helplessness as part of its flow. Primordial awareness spontaneously goes through

moments of might and weakness, greater and lesser aliveness–
deadness, bliss–agony, power–powerlessness. A kaleidoscopic
range of experiencing is its norm. As Jack developed, the sense of
helplessness became more than usually alarming—too real and
overwhelming in light of actual physical defect.

To compensate for real inability, he had to push himself past
helplessness. This led to a barely visible skew in development. As
time went on, he became more of a specialist in active pleasures
and was deprived of passive ones. His well-meaning milieu contributed to this nearly invisible skew by rewarding Jack's active
efforts, playing down the helpless side of life. They naturally
feared that he might not be able to do what others did, and they
emphasized the doing side of his nature.

Thus several attitudes became superimposed on each other.
His parents rejoiced in his existence, providing a core or substratum of primary normalcy. They saw to it that he would live as
normal a life as possible, developing skills and potentials. Neither
he nor they surrendered to deficiency. They encouraged him to
maximize his strengths. The flow of primary aliveness was filtered through an ideology emphasizing energy and activity. The
strand of development having to do with weakness, helplessness,
passivity, surrender received scant attention. To some degree, it
remained as undeveloped as the legs he was born with. Therapy
helped to reconnect primary and secondary normalcy in fuller
ways, increasing tolerance for fear of weakness and eventually for
fear of stillness.

Can primary normalcy be tainted?

Insofar as babies go through free-flowing sensation–feeling states,
prior to seeing themselves from the outside, would not all or most
individuals have a period of primary normalcy? Would it not be
"normal" for babies to have no criteria outside their own experiencing to judge themselves by? There would be no mental judge
or critic outside the infant's experiential flow—shifting sensations–feelings, bliss, agony, relief, ease, well-being, turbulence,
pleasure, distress, joy, empty or placid or calm eternity gazing,

streams of perceptual delights, sensory, motor and emotional shocks, and so on.

Yet there appear to be individuals for whom the emotional flow itself, including body sensations, is compromised, spoiled, tainted. Being and self taste sour. In extreme instances there is little or no relief: nothing tastes good. Life is indigestible, unliveable. Aliveness is repudiated and repugnant, through and through.

In many individuals, self-attack processes play a role in spoiling life. Aggression turned against the self can paralyse, maim, or otherwise poison one's attitude and ruin one's chance to live. Self-hate can destroy the capacity for thinking, feeling, and acting and attack emotional links between people. Self-attack processes can gather such momentum as to seem irreversible. They are capable of devouring whatever comes their way, leaving nothing free of malignancy. Such processes can have vast consequences in sociopolitical as well as familial groups and play a role in the social–individual psychology of oppression on many levels.

There are some individuals for whom the spoiling appears so thorough, early, and pervasive that terms implying the work of active self-hate pale in view of the enormity of suffering and degradation. The obliteration of human potential can be so massive and shocking that it is hard to imagine that self-attack had a chance to get off the ground or, if present, could account for such chronic devastation. In such cases aggression against the self appears part of a broader, more extensive and insistent destructive mass. It is difficult not to think of Winnicott's (1992, p. 264) suggestion that a child needs to be accepted at the beginning, even before birth. The quality of parental emotional involvement may have consequences in the womb and impact on how aliveness feels for the foetus.

The mother's ability to "join up her emotional involvement" (1992, p. 264) and the tone and atmosphere of her emotional involvement may affect the "feel" of life in a very physical way. It is not only a matter of the body becoming a place one can dwell in. Whether or not or how or to what extent one can live in or with one's aliveness can be an issue. One's inability to inhabit or even tolerate aliveness can be a problem in any experiential dimension—physical, emotional, mental, aesthetic, political, spiritual. How aliveness feels or the feeling of aliveness may not merely be threatening but ruined, so that one may not want to dwell in aliveness or make aliveness a home. If this is so, feeling alive may never have a chance to enjoy a period of primary normalcy.

A wide spectrum

Josh

Without a period of primary normalcy, life may never feel right. One's very sense of self and aliveness feels off. This may vary from a nagging sense that something needs correction to a heavy conviction that what is wrong is so fundamental that nothing can make it better. One may feel that one is living the wrong life or that one is the wrong person for the life one is living. A person told me: "I kept expecting something to right itself. Maybe next year the x will feel better—in five years, in ten. But as I got older, life didn't right itself. I never righted myself. It never happened."

As it happened, Josh did very well in therapy. The sense of something wrong never left him entirely, but more of life felt right. In therapy, Josh let himself discover or admit that as long as he could remember or envision, something in life, his home, himself had been wrong. The "wrong" feeling never left for long. By the time he was 4 or 5 years old, he remembers telling himself, "Something is wrong." Now and then a moment would escape the wrongness and life felt bright and right, and he could tell, by comparison, that most of his life was blighted.

In kindergarten Josh had felt a yawning gulf between those who felt right and those who felt wrong. What complicated things more was that sometimes those who felt wrong could be right about something the right ones were wrong about. Life puzzled him, and he developed talents in a kind of haze.

One finds all manner of combinations of feeling off–on, right–wrong in one's sense of aliveness. One may dimly feel a mixture of rightness–wrongness without knowing why. For many years Josh felt more wrong than right without being able to locate where the wrongness was coming from. It never occurred to him that it was coming from aliveness itself—that something felt wrong in his primary sense of aliveness.

Josh's case was severe, but not as severe as many. He discovered talents he could use to mine pockets of life with some satisfaction and give creative expression to the x that felt off. As time went on, he was able to trace some of the ingredients in the emotional atmosphere that stymied him. His father was an angry, controlling, anxious hard-working man who was not around enough. But even the little he was around felt too much. His love was an engulfing, needy love that left little room for Josh. This father's love was fused with all the insufficiencies, hopes, needs, longings, fears, hatreds of his life. The enormity of love filled his father with a feeling of wholeness.

Josh pictured his father's love as an overpowering wind or flood, sweeping him up, dissolving him. Josh was food for his father's love, wine for his father's spirit to get drunk on. His father had no idea who Josh was, other than a divine essence he could unite with. The immensity and irregularity of his father's emotionality and the saviour role Josh played contributed to a sense that something was wrong with life, his life, his aliveness. For many years, Josh could not locate the wrongness because it was part of the atmosphere he lived in.

Josh also came to sense that his mother was afraid of his aliveness. She loved him and was warm-hearted. But an infant's inconsiderate aliveness threatened her. Perhaps she also feared her own aliveness. Many years later Josh learned that she had feared injuring him, which led to uncertainty and insecurity in her handling of him, mixed with a loving touch. It was no specifically bad thing she did to him, just a defect in the emotional atmosphere he lived in.

The combination of his father's suffocating love and his mother's frightened love coloured Josh's sense of aliveness from his first moments. Suffocating and frightened love permeated his pores. His primary sense of aliveness was supported and compromised by this love. As his consciousness grew from his earliest years, he felt something off in his being and eventually located some of it in the way he was loved. His parents' way of loving poisoned as it nourished him. Their love debilitated and drained as it supported him. He felt inflated, misused, and worn down by parental love.

Parental love is a confusing mixture of extreme selfishness and sacrifice. Josh's parents used him to hold themselves together. In a profound sense, they set their inner lives by him. He was their compass, their peak experience. They would do anything for him. They sacrificed everything for their children—Josh first and foremost. Family was the glue of life. Josh felt bound and repulsed by the parental warning, justification, supplication: "Wait 'til you have children. You'll see."

Josh felt enormous pressure to do what his parents wanted, since they wanted what was good. But this was only the tip. More deeply, Josh felt an *osmotic pressure*, a pressure to absorb and be absorbed by them, agglutinated, sponge-like beings, a clotted parental mass that kept extending its boundaries, a boundless osmotic mass. Their goodness made him feel that things would right themselves someday, that there would be a happy ending. Yet he was sinking, drowning, suffocating, and knew he had to get away.

Josh never felt more acutely lonely and in pain than when he left his parents' home. He established intense, osmotic, obsessively controlling loving relationships with girlfriends as quickly as possible. He kept asking them, "Do you love me? Do you love me?" When these relationships crashed, he sought therapy. He kept asking me, "Am I changing? Am I changing?" Can there be life outside osmosis?

Josh and I have been together a long time. He still wonders to what extent change is possible, but he has the conviction and resonance that comes from grappling with self and life and growing. I learned from Josh and people like him, and from myself, that growth is not a matter of breaking or indulging in osmotic tendencies that have been exploited, abused, or overused in upbringing. It is more a matter of tolerating osmotic tendencies and letting them evolve. One gets a lot by becoming partners with permeability and learning to use and cultivate this valuable capacity. Josh was crippled by parental osmotic needs and paralysed by his own hyperpermeability. Therapy helped him to learn how to mine permeability, develop it, and develop with it, whereas his parents simply milked it for self-support. Permeability can be a valuable part of the sense of aliveness, but misuse of it can be numbing, suffocating, frightening, and noxious.

Jeri

Jeri was bombarded with relentless criticism and disparagement. Her parents were frustrated, angry people who put everything down, especially Jeri. Her sense of aliveness was under attack, not infiltration. Josh was crippled by a love that stole him away as it filled and supported him, a kind of annihilating love. Jeri kept getting her psychic legs crushed by obvious assaults and insults.

The result was a weakening of personality not only or mainly maintained by bad inner parents attacking aspects of self. Jeri's very sense of aliveness was maimed, smashed, compromised. This is not the same as attributing the persistence of bad feelings to superego attacks or to bad object attacks against attachment, although these and similar tendencies may be present. Jeri's very sense of aliveness became used to being partly crushed, so that its crash or collapse or hurt was part of its rhythm, part of its surge.

At times one's sense of aliveness seems a blind uprising, pulsing, but often it carries a sense of direction, an evaluative feeling, a yes–no closely related to off–on or right–wrong. The mute aliveness feeling, so precious because it is wordless, speaks to us, intimates whether we are on the right or the wrong track, whether what we are doing takes us closer or further from ourselves, more or less into life. The feeling of being off or on may be an implicit part of the sense of aliveness, rich with inherent expectations shaping experience.

Life-giving yet toxic love seeped into Josh, poisoning as it nourished him. Jeri's aliveness was battered, cut down. Josh knew something was off from an early age but he could not pin it down. He could point to parental fear, fury, overprotectiveness— but all this was chronically drowned in love. It took years of self-doubt before he traced toxic aspects of love and discovered that his sense of aliveness was affected. Jeri also knew that things were not as they should be, not as she wanted, but she had a clearer picture of what was wrong. She could not miss noting elephants landing on her, stabbing her with cutting words.

Jeri had good moments too. She felt close to her mother, even if the latter put her down. There was a porridgy warmth between them that her mother's scathing aspect intensified. Relentless criticism and warmth were so interwoven as to form an indistinguishable blend. In sessions Jeri could be ruthlessly cutting. No fault of mine escaped her. Moments later a warm smile spread, neck and face reddening slightly, filling out. A soupy warmth enveloped us, and I could feel a throbbing, sticky pain, a bloody warmth.

Jeri had no idea how cutting she could be, although she knew how cutting her parents were. Her relentless picking me apart seemed to her a natural act of self-defence. She was just responding to bad things I did or ways I failed. She was justified by her victim status. She had been relentlessly criticized, so she became a relentless critic.

She especially picked on me because I did not do enough to help her. She felt that I ought to be able to say things that would fix her, make the pain less, reset her sense of self, give her the health she yearned for. Blocks in my personality or ability to reach out or in or find the right word or tone impeded her growth, kept her fastened to her own inner pain and horror. Somehow I was to make up for all that had failed her. This left us in an intractable bind—she once more haplessly, malignantly passive (although an active accuser), and I impotent and dumbfounded, getting a taste of the poisons that immobilized her.

She seemed to expect my hurt feelings to be washed away by a swell of warmth, as if the former did not count. Yet *her* injured feelings mattered to her and she very much needed them to matter to me. Perhaps her parents controlled her rage at them by inundating her with warmth. They could be as nasty as they liked, then sweep it under the rug with love. One hand washed the other. The constant conjunction of criticism and warmth had telling consequences on how it felt to be alive for Jeri. The cutting and warmth melded into Jeri's sense of aliveness. Cutting warmth or warm cutting became part of her aliveness feeling.

The cutting in the warmth made her twist and turn and gyrate every which way to try to get rid of the cutting. But the two had become one with being alive. To get rid of the warmth, the cutting, or their union would be to get out of life. The result was a vicious circle. To feel less cut or cutting, she would have to feel less warm and alive.

It is barely imaginable that Jeri may have enjoyed some period of primary normalcy when parental warmth was ascendant and subdued parental critical nastiness. This may have occurred in early and perhaps most of infancy, although it is hard to think that Jeri's infancy could be free of parental mockery. The parental need to make fun of, shame, and humiliate Jeri must have been in place from the outset and could not be checked for long.

Still, let us assume moments of raw rapture in the presence of a baby celebrated the new life and dominated destruction. Celebration of life would alternate and be indelibly mixed with spoiling tendencies and, vice versa, spoiling tendencies would be indistinguishable from the celebration of life. From the outset, or nearly so, a sense of something off-and-on, right-and-wrong would have permeated existence.

Jeri's sense of aliveness contained a joyous core fused with cutting closeness (mother) and lack of sustained interest (father). This aliveness-feeling formed the nucleus of her personal relationships. She would begin warmly, seek closeness, become cutting–cut. Our relationship, too, was close and cutting, and inevitably rocky. She could not know from session to session whether or not she would continue seeing me. She had no other way of being alive than dropping off the end of the universe into fathomless depression.

How normal is feeling normal?

Feeling normal is somewhat free-floating. What feels normal changes. Some people need solitude to feel normal. Others need many friends to feel normal. Feeling off-on or right–wrong changes too. What feels right now may feel wrong later, and vice versa. To try to live only by what feels off or on now can be quite maddening and, possibly, destructive.

A person may hear God's voice telling him to kill his mother. Only murder feels real and true. Not to kill is to live a lie. Another individual may need to have a woman representing mother defecate on him in order to climax. Nothing else brings peace. To murder mother or have mother shit on one may be psychically interchangeable. Yet particular individuals may be more or less organized along one or the other pole.

In one case, murder and aliveness are fused. In the other, aliveness is faecalized. A person with murder in his soul may sleep through life and quicken at the thought of killing someone. A person who is a murderer without knowing it may feel dislocated much of the time, not knowing why. Life may be drab, meaningless, empty, yet blood rushes at news reports of violence and murder movies. Most people do not have to kill to feel alive, but some do. And there are many who feel less alive for failing to access the murderer within.

On the other side of the coin are people who need to feel like shit to maintain a balance. A certain amount of depression is needed for self-regulation. For some individuals, depression functions as an anchor, to offset jumping out of their skins. Feeling too good makes some giddy, dizzy, out of contact. The Icarus complex is more than a matter of flying too close to the sun with wax wings, then falling. It can involve an attachment to the fall itself, a need to fall (otherwise, why wax wings or why fly too close to the sun?). There are people for whom falling is more important than flying. They go up in order to go down. On a roller-coaster, going up is only an excuse to go down—the real thrill is the drop down.

Some try to hold on to and prolong the downward movement by making their entire lives a downward slide. Others are content to confine the downward spin to cycles or phases of larger rhythms. In one way or another, the drop down is part of our sense of aliveness, and for some it exerts a pre-eminent and abiding fascination. In extreme cases, one sinks to a lower level of existence in order to stretch the downside out, to make it last as long as possible. A shitty life may feel all too normal. One realizes, too late, that shit hardens into a death monument before one is ready.

Almost any way of being alive can feel normal or abnormal to an individual, depending on a variety of inner and outer conditions. We tend to think of normal in terms of statistics, averages, what most people do and feel, or what we are used to. We judge normal by making comparisons. We see each other through each other's eyes and construct sets of collective, superordinate evaluative eyes and minds outside our particular situations. But we also have a feeling of normalcy built into our sense of aliveness, and the emotional world we live in infiltrates and influences the way aliveness feels.

Someone like Jeri has so much hurt built into feeling alive that the advent of good feeling almost acts as a signal that something very bad is about to happen. It is difficult to maintain much good in life when good means that bad is on the way. This is akin to Fairbairn's (1954) formulation that, for the schizophrenic, love is destructive. The schizophrenic feels that his love is bad, even evil. The situation is not confined to overt psychotics. The sense that there is something wrong with one's aliveness is more widespread than may be imagined.

Jeri continued to struggle with her confusion over aliveness. She gradually got some sense of the crash built into any attempt she made to feel alive or build a life. She felt deeply that a fall was built into every moment of her existence, into everything she tried to do. It was more than an existential structure—for Jeri it was the breath of life. She was addicted to an experience that made life impossible for her, yet it felt right because it was built into her aliveness feeling, yet it felt wrong because it stole life from her.

Some people simplify the situation by embracing the life that feels wrong as the only life possible. Milton's (1667) Satan tries to make the most of hell—"evil be my good". Lautreamont's (1868) Maldoror represents a fairly pure slide of embracing evil consciousness as the only "good" possible. Someone like Jeri is caught in oscillation between what feels right-and-wrong in the sense of aliveness. Aliveness itself feels off-and-on in variable ways. No matter how Jeri tries, she keeps sliding off the "on" feeling. But she does keep trying, although she cannot catch up to herself.

It is not simply a matter of trying to be or do something different. One needs to be able to taste emotional worlds that affect one's sense of aliveness for the better. This may require finding a therapist who can sustain the struggle necessary to create an atmosphere that permits one's sense of aliveness to evolve. The ironic and often ghastly paradox is that the patient must develop the capacity to make use of the difficulties that the therapist's personality offers. The bottom line is that both individuals are charged with the task of growing the equipment needed to be with each other in ways that will help such equipment to grow.

It can take a long time for a person to realize how confused and confusing her or his very sense of aliveness may be. Therapy is an experiment in different ways of being alive together, both people discovering ways that work for each other. Therapist and patient grow in complexity and sophistication with regard to how it feels to be alive and how aliveness changes or stays the same.

It may never feel normal to be alive. How normal is aliveness in the universe? How normal is the universe? To be a universe is something very special, and to be alive in it even more special. It is not a chance given to everything everywhere.

To be amazed by aliveness can make us passive admirers. We may appreciate the bare fact of aliveness without doing much with it. On the other hand, we may do too much with our chance at life, with variable results. Some who cannot get enough life lose their taste for it by their hyperactivity. Others manage to intensify it. Some of our tinkering brings very beneficial results, while some mystifies us with destructiveness.

To some extent, we can focus on the sense of aliveness itself and learn to modulate its volume, colour, intensity. We develop an aesthetics and ethics of aliveness. We learn to regulate aliveness somewhat so as to maximize what we get from it and to minimize destruction. How much aliveness can we take, and in what ways? What is normal about feeling alive? What makes aliveness right, and what makes it right to be alive? Such questions are far from being the luxuries of a philosophical elite.

CHAPTER SIX

Unconscious learnings:
beyond the lines

Penny

Everything happens at once in therapy, but it takes a long time to unfold—so it sometimes feels. Penelope's (Penny's) impact was immediate: shock waves, quivering densities in my chest, tendrils of many changing colours spreading through my shoulders, in my skin, mixing joy with fear. It was an impact I could draw on, return to, find new things in, a Penny spark lighting life—fighting for life. Could she feel it? It was, I came to know, her very own spark searching for her. There are so many wandering sparks searching for lives to ignite. How lucky we are when we help the right spark and life find each other.

Penny was beautiful and expressive, yet lips pursed, somewhat twisted with tension. The room brightened–darkened, reflecting expansive feeling, hemmed by contraction that dimmed, but did not extinguish it. She was warmly expressive but also held in, as if fearing her impact. On the one hand, she knew she was a magnificent woman. On the other, she did not know what to do with it, at once openly contactful and gripping herself.

I felt the pressure inside her, a force moving from the periphery towards the centre, from out → in, more precisely, from the under-side of her skin → deeper into her interior. Although self is not localizable, my sense was of a contracting force exerting enormous pressure from the under-side of her skin towards interior layers of self.

Concomitantly, I felt the contracting force exert pressure from the insides of her breasts, scooping them out, creating concave pressure waves, leaving concave cavities in their wake, hollowing out her insides as they whooshed into the self, carrying self-materials through a vanishing point. She feared her breasts' impact, not only as nourishing but as penetrating (and, indeed, does not nourishment penetrate, and penetration nourish?).

My mind runs away, and I imagine her fear of her nipples against my chest, pressing into me, through my chest, deeper, deeper, into my heart, my soul, where they could find and feed my substance, my very essence, and draw nourishment, like a bee. Later I would realize how true it was, that she needed to feel she could give something to someone, to the world, with all her might, and that she could get something from someone, from the world, with all her being.

Yes, Penny was penetrating—brilliant and beautiful. Her beauty and brilliance scorched me, ripped me, pierced me. I felt her brilliance from the moment I saw her. Later I would hear of her professors' amazement at her papers and hear at first-hand her way with words. She *could* make fine contributions to her chosen profession, if she ever *could* let herself get that far. What I want to convey is that in that first flash there was immediate transmission of intense mental activity, a brilliant mind. I could feel her brilliance—mind to mind—as immediately as I could see her beauty—a passionate, brilliant, beautiful woman.

What was she doing with me? Surely, she was too much for me. She would leave me. I was not enough for her. I knew these feelings of insufficiency well. So did she. She drew back from herself, protecting me from the fullness of her powers. She somewhat shielded me from her splendour, showing enough to engage me, not so much as to strike me dumb. Penny was nothing if not intensely penetrating, totally fearful of her penetrating power.

She was adept at dosing herself out, especially playing herself down, so that she and the other could go along.

Sexuality, expressive beauty, brilliant mind—what is a poor male therapist going to do?—Feel it all, keep on feeling it, stay with everything, keep opening, let God work? Being a therapist has lacerating aspects, among them suffering the pain of someone one would love to be with in other ways. At the same time, something clicks into gear, one can feel it in the depths. We are already working, calling something new into being, interpenetrating in ways we scarcely knew we needed. As soon as Penny enters the room, we begin to be with each other, see each other, feel each other, journeying towards mutual recognition and beyond.

Layers of loss

One evening, Penny spoke about how badly she felt over not taking a course taught by a particular nice teacher. This teacher extended himself, made himself available to her inquiries, let her sample his classes, was friendly, encouraging. But her schedule was crowded, and his course turned out not to be what she wanted. She wanted others more. She was surprised how terrible she felt not taking this man's course. She knew she would not take it just because he was good to her, or to avoid bad feelings. She would go her way, in spite of inner turmoil. But why so much turmoil? Why so hard? Almost everything she did to better herself cost so much.

She felt a deep sense of loss—piercing, ripping loss. Not taking his course *hurt*. Was she identified with the injury she imagined she inflicted on him? She knew he was all right, he was understanding about her not taking his course. Perhaps it was precisely because he was all right about whatever she wanted to do that she could experience her pain more acutely. The pain she felt was her own sense of loss, with very deep echoes, a loss of something, someone good, a loss of goodness itself.

Now, Penny *knew* she was not losing all the goodness in the world by not taking this man's course. But inside herself the sun darkened. To be herself, she had to lose some of the goodness the world offered. Her inner sun underwent a partial eclipse, which, for the moment, felt total. "It feels like I'm losing the good object", she offered. "I felt this with my father. With my mother, it's a problem of guilt separating from a bad object. With my father, it's loss of the good object."

"I wonder if that wasn't Winnicott's problem, the problem he tried answering with his 'use of object' as antidote?" I remarked. "Being oneself finds the good object vs. being oneself loses the good object." Penny was a therapist-in-training who read Winnicott and my writings on Winnicott, and it was natural to speak this way (Winnicott, 1989, pp. 217–246; see also Benjamin, 1995, 1988; Eigen, 1993, 1996).

"Yes", Penny responded. "But the good object here is a fantasy. Loss of the fantasy object. The fantasy gets destroyed in Winnicott's account, projective–introjective fantasy."

The above was a brief, shorthand exchange, but very real, in spite of sounding intellectual. Very real emotions were packed in this shorthand. Penny was summarizing her basic dilemma, and it drew on all the work she did.

Penny's father had been a warm light in her life. He had a temper that could flare, but it was situational, coming and going with specific events. Penny had treasured his love and closeness. He had truly enjoyed being with his children, engaging them, doing things together. He had played a very active role in their upbringing. He was also a bright, articulate man who took pleasure in his daughter's mental aliveness. Penny felt affirmed by him—physically, emotionally, mentally. He died abruptly in her early teens, the shock of her life, leaving her emotionally stranded.

Penny's mother suffered severe depression when Penny was growing up. She made Penny feel responsible for taking care of her, although no amount of care-taking helped. She was tyrannical, clinging, helpless—so much so that Penny felt enormous guilt for any attempt to get away from her. Penny felt criticized, never good enough, always failing. The concavity I felt exerting force towards collapse (going from behind her breasts into her chest) must be linked to her mother's depressive collapse sucking out Penny's aliveness.

The emotions aroused by both parents indelibly commingled, a nearly indistinguishable mixture of affirmation and shame, swirls of enabling–disabling cross-currents. This bit of history provides some background for the turmoil she goes through when affirming herself. She must push past loss of the good and dread of leaving the bad. Even what may seem like a little thing—taking one course and not another—is fraught with momentous undertones. Every loss of goodness is associated with loss of father, every negation of badness is associated with loss of mother.

Such matters are unbearably complicated, since mother has good moments, father bad. But the overall atmosphere contrasted her father's light with her mother's lacerating darkness. The former uplifted, the latter scarred, depleted her. Father showered her with treasures in the face of maternal neglect. Not only did her mother fail to support Penny, she chronically accused her of not providing enough support, not being there enough for her. Penny drowned in guilt for not giving what she was not getting. When Penny lost her father, the danger of going under in the face of mother's demands became overwhelming. But she had enough taste of life to lure her on, with undertow.

In love relationships, Penny had a pronounced tendency to subjugate herself to the man. Her natural tendency was to defer. But once romance kicked in, she was in danger of giving up her life for the other. When I met her, she was almost totally submerged in her lover's projects, helping him get ahead. They shared common ideals and goals, and she put her energies into his social causes, which she believed in. Her own life was on hold. She followed her "sometimes" lover around the country, working for him day and night. I say "sometimes" lover because he rarely spent time with her alone. They were rarely intimate. He gave her tasks, and she did them, using characteristic initiative and resourcefulness.

When they did get together, he made it seem as if he was doing her a favour. The implication was that she would be bereft without him, no one would want her. She was not able to absorb the reality that she was bereft *with* him, that he wanted her mainly for what she could do for him, he did not really want *her*—at least not in a way that he would *be* with her and share life together.

In our early sessions, I listened to her ripped feelings over his rare nights with her, her admiration for him, her wish to follow him, help him, the poor returns for her self-giving. She realized he was having affairs, that he preferred others, but she could not digest this reality. She kept making excuses for him. According to Penny, it was not that he did not *want* to be with her, but that he *could not*. He came from a terrible background, too devastated by his mother to get close to a woman. He poured himself into the public arena, crippled in intimacy. He needed women to give to him, as he kept his distance, tantalizing and disappointing them.

Penny felt that her problem had to do with her father dying before she could work out her idealization of him. He died before she went through adolescent rebellion and secured more freedom. Penny felt that the mixture of mutual idealization and realism would have evolved in a natural way if they had had more time. She was stuck loving him, looking up to him, feeling close to him (he was a fun companion as well as an admirable man). She was stuck in teenage love when the bottom fell out.

At the same time, her father had been a limit-setter. His angry flare-ups frightened her but also brought relief, because they announced that a limit had been reached. Her mother's depression, chaotic helplessness, demands for care-taking were boundless. Her father brought fun and order into a household that would otherwise have been lost. Penny felt that she repeated her idealization and loss of him with men in her life. Yet this awareness did not stop her. She kept going in circles, sticking needles into her wounds.

Penny felt that she could not leave these men because she feared losing her father's goodness. Yet they left her, or kept her dangling, which she associated with his death. So he died repeatedly in the midst of her love. She came to see that her mother's depression played an enormous role in her need for such men, for they were essentially unavailable. They vanished emotionally when she reached for them, so that her initial excitement was followed by vacancy. She was left in an emotional vacuum, which is what she dreaded with her mother.

These men aroused Penny's admiration, idealization, excitement, anticipation, then tormented her with coming and going, culminating in preponderance of emptiness over nourishment. Penny had ended an earlier marriage when it became clear to her she lost more than she gained, that her husband, who had begun more like her lively father had ended more like her emotionally dead mother. These relationships could go on for years. They tied her life in knots. By the time she saw me, her childbearing years were on the threshold of ending, and she was still going in and out of university, putting her life and studies and work on hold for long periods in the service of men who were not there for her, sometimes lovers, imaginary mates or partners.

Penny was convinced that if she had had the chance to interact with her father, through and past adolescence, she could have placed limits on relationships that ate life away—not getting into them so often, not staying with them so long. She would have incorporated a better blend of nourishment and limits. As it was, she had a real capacity for fun and enjoyment. But she did not fully appreciate the hold of her addiction to nothing—not only to goodness lost, but a ghastly, vacuous, boundless, pain-filled demand where an able mother might have been. She had lost her father's lively protectiveness at a crucial moment, but she failed to have an alive-enough mother almost from the beginning, when roots of self were forming.

She had known, as a teenager, that with no father to protect her, she had to intensify her fight against falling into the pit of her mother's depression. But she did not realize how much of her mother she had incorporated into her self, without wanting to. Penny did not become psychotically depressed, but her mother's depression cast a long shadow. Penny went through long periods alone, keeping herself alive with solitary fantasies. Eventually fantasy loses power, withdrawal starts to feed on itself. "I don't want to withdraw. Once I start I get worse and cannot get out of it. Time goes by and I can't do anything and don't get anything out of not doing anything." It also scares her when fantasy *does* work and she spends endless time enjoying it in an unreal sort of way. For when she emerges from a bout of withdrawal—fantasy or no fantasy, rich or empty—time has passed, she is older, and her life is still waiting.

As long as she could link not having and not being to her father's death, she could pit the heritage of his real warmth and aliveness against a hole in life she fought off. His presence somewhat compensated for her mother's swamp, but she failed to realize how much of the latter permeated her, stamped her. She held on to his aliveness for dear life, and he fanned hers. Somehow or other, with this mutual affirmation of aliveness, she fought her mother's deadness, but not completely. The latter tugged at her each time she tried to build a life. In one way or another, whenever she began to make something of herself, she stumbled, her life underwent semi-collapse, whatever she built disappeared in sand. It was not merely prohibition against success that stopped her, but crucial lack of support, partly dating to missing support when her personality was forming.

Her problem involved more than guilty dread of leaving the bad and becoming her own person. It was, also, that when she tried becoming her own person, she crumbled into a weakness that antedated and undermined her determination to realize an active, desirous self. Her father was not able to save her from the swamp mother, although he helped a good deal. She would, finally, have to face the swamp in her own being or keep falling victim to it.

Her father could not save her from herself. For years, she used the good from him to ward off the bad from mother, but the time was coming when she would have to meet the boundless swamp in her own self. She could not milk the good feeling between father and herself in order to postpone herself indefinitely. Perhaps all along she had been waiting for him to come back and save her, before she could let herself live. But even if he returned and did his best, he could not forever substitute for what was infirm in her foundation.

Goodbye–hello

It might not be surprising to learn that Penny was a bit flighty when it came to therapy. She had run through two therapy relationships just before I saw her. She seemed frightened, yet proud, that her last therapist became miffed and moralistic about her leaving. Very like her mother, he warned that she had a deep problem she was running away from and she should stay with him (the primitive unconscious communication felt like, "Be with me or damnation."). Also, à la mother, she feared suffocation, slavery, being submerged. She wanted to feel she could come and go and come again. He laid down his version of the law, which to her seemed arbitrary and self-serving: follow the rules like a good patient, or never come back. She liked the idea that she got to him (miffed him), even if she lost out. She needed to feel that someone was there, even if it caused difficulty.

It did not take long for her to test me also. Just when I thought we were connecting, she wondered whether she should not see a woman analyst. I was the good father, but she really needed to work something out with the bad mother. On the one hand, like her previous analyst, I saw that she had to be in and out, that she was unable to commit herself, that really being in therapy with me was akin to dying (like the men she picked must feel with a woman). On the other hand, working with a woman therapist could be a good thing. I opted to stay with what felt most comfortable to me: not knowing and openness. How dare I know what was best?

I told her I was with her whatever she wanted to do, that she probably could get something either way, abundance of riches. I shared what I could about my feelings. "I'd feel a loss if you left me. But I'd be happy if things worked out for you. Sort of like my kids. I feel bad if they break a date with me to do something else, but I'm happy if they live their lives." I really meant it.

We explored her feelings about seeing a woman therapist, why she never did, the benefits it might bring. She came up with the idea of seeing me while she looked around, and I agreed. She had an interview with an excellent woman analyst, and I shared my appreciation. I felt as surprised when she decided to stay with me, as I felt when she wanted to leave. In the back of my mind I could sense that she could reverse herself at any time, perhaps *must* reverse herself (if only to see whether she could).

It occurred to me that the feeling of "surprise" she evoked might be important. The surprise of leaving has a little rip, the surprise of returning contains delight. Perhaps she leaves in order to return. One puts up with rips to feel happiness. Perhaps that is a stuck point: her returns have not paid off, have not led somewhere. In her life, leaving–returning becomes the same old thing. In therapy, it can be different. Something more or different can happen.

Such leaving–returning . . . the rupture of her father's death, the black hole of her mother's depression . . . the loss of father's aliveness, too much of mother's clinging, guilt-provoking, demanding deadness . . . in adult life, the stream of jobs, men, therapists, starts and stops at university: I began to feel we were drawn together so that she could create/find the give-and-take her life needed to move past rupture and despair, so that she could be the "more" she felt she was. Of course, one does not "cure" rupture and despair, indelible as they are. But it is possible to enter the living stream of a relationship that grows with rupture–return, that makes room for despair, so that rupture/despair do not have the last word.

For periods, I would feel my being, self, psyche mould itself around whatever state Penny brought in. It happened effortlessly, unpremeditatedly. We are amazingly permeable beings. If she was caught in panic, hysteria, rage, grief, frozen and blocked, or excited by joy—my inner being shaped itself around her state. What happened was wordless and imageless but can be partly reconstructed by words and images. It was as if percipient, loving waves of feeling supported, touched, licked, washed, cleansed, healed parts of her wounds—as if invisible, immaterial psychic substance went in and out of pores and ventricles of clogged and ragged self that needed to feel the caring permeability of another's self-substance.

At the same time, our personalities kept their usual shapes, and we spoke about whatever concern engaged Penny at the moment. We were two people speaking with each other, supported by sub-vocal intimacy, two people growing out of a common core yet unique centres of subjectivity. At other moments, we seemed to have nothing in common. Learning to tolerate "nothing in common" made us freer. At times we pushed against barriers to find each other. We pushed away from or towards each other, as the moment dictated. Our sense of separation–connection evolved through nasty upheavals and lovely times.

The therapy relationship is not free of insidious mixtures of toxins and nourishment—no relationship is. However, the therapist *knows* this, knows it with her or his whole being. The therapist may not know, at any given moment, how he or she is poisoning the patient, but, in principle, knows that no one is a

"pure" or "innocent" agent of change. Virtually all human interactions are compromised in one way or another. The miracle is
that grace works in our real lives, our real persons, as we really
are—toxins and all.

Perhaps what makes the therapist seem omniscient is knowing
that therapy is doomed to failure in some ways but may succeed
in others (was it Pound who said you never succeed in writing
poems, you only fail better?). No therapist can know ahead of
time how the work will succeed–fail, but one proceeds with a
modicum of faith in the bit of success that may be possible. Any
little success can make a big difference in a person's life. The certainty that one's own psychic viruses are affecting the patient,
even if they are invisible when one searches for them, enforces a
necessary modesty. There is always the possibility that one is
wrong when one imagines oneself right or right when one feels
wrong.

Nevertheless, therapy is a place where one can discover and
rehearse blends of nourishment–toxins one lives on and try new
blends and variations that better support life. Penny, for example,
could go over ways she poisoned as she nourished herself, owing,
partly, to the mixtures she had grown up on. Although her father
symbolized life and her mother death, there were ways in which
her mother's depression and father's aliveness fused, became
compressed—a primal inner couple at the core of her bring in
which aliveness–deadness were all mixed up. There were areas in
her being in which aliveness and deadness were distinct and areas in which they were indistinguishable.

This is complicated by the fact that her mother had nourished
her as a baby, even as depression overcame her. If her mother
was a first life symbol, she was also a carrier of darkness. Thus
aliveness and depression melded into each other, perhaps from
the outset. The father raised life from the dead, saw to it that the
life thread wove on. The father saw to it that aliveness did not
succumb to deadness prematurely, even if the two were partly
fused, even when one could not tell the difference between them.

The difficulty was compounded by Penny's father's death just
as adolescence was rising. The unconscious learning and dread
was that aliveness equalled deadness. To be too alive meant that
one would die. Her mother, the dead one, lived (and is still liv-

ing). Her father, the alive one, died. Nourishment dies. Poison lives. The intertwining of aliveness–deadness, nourishment–poison intensified, since aliveness and nourishment were associated with loss of life.

Penny feared being too alive, lest she die like her father. At the same time, her aliveness lacked the support he might have given it. She had to support herself any way she could, including making use of whatever deadness and toxins were available. Thus her unconscious learning included the following dreadful presentiments: (1) aliveness is dangerous—too much aliveness can kill you; (2) nourishment is dangerous—to be too nourishing equals dying; (3) nourishment can be poisonous—lethally so; (4) poison can (must) be nourishing—paralysingly so; (5) deadness can be life-preserving.

At the same time, life keeps flowing, toxins, blocks and all. The therapy relationship absorbs bitter mixtures of death and life, nourishment and self-poisoning processes, and helps the heart keep opening. Therapist and patient keep coming back for more, are not satisfied, desire new areas of experiencing, and find ways (eventually) to make room for whatever the patient needs to bring in. The patient feels life reshaping, remaking, resetting itself through the problems that plague therapy, some of them intractable.

Penny's having a father who could accept her as a partner in aliveness mitigated her plight, barely lifting her over the abyss. Not only did he mirror and confirm the realness of aliveness, he also recognized that she was like him and he like her, at the same time appreciating their sexual and generational differences. For he affirmed her as a valuable person (including latency pal, budding and pre-budding female), as one who would pursue her own destiny, one who had every capability. She knew herself as a light in life, no matter how down she was for periods, no matter how invaded she was by lasting shame and self-doubt. Her father affirmed her vital spark, her very being, although she will probably always have to deal with ominous counter-currents.

In a transitional way, Penny gets from me (and portions of the therapy field) the sense of being affirmed, of being like me (us)—since she is realizing her wish to become a therapist on her own terms. But more, she feels affirmed in her difference from me. She is pursuing her interest in feminist psychoanalysis in creative ways and reading literature I have only heard about. We are like and not like each other in many ways. She is the next generation, and I feel honoured to be given a role in supporting her creative development. She sought me, partly, because she felt a kinship of spirit—and this kind of kinship traverses sexual and generational lines. It even traverses the similarities and differences of our earthly personalities.

CHAPTER SEVEN

Self-nulling

A good deal of my adult life has been spent helping people who feel badly about themselves. This lack of self-worth may vary—from feeling irredeemably evil, to needing to be treated like shit or garbage, to doubt about one's worth allied with vacillating self-esteem. Variations are myriad.

For some, the bad self is so consuming, there is little room for living. One spends one's time staring at the badness that drags one down. Many find ways to rationalize the bad feeling, put it aside, push beyond it, emphasize "the winner within". Many of these individuals live more-or-less full lives this way. Some land in my office when depression or anxiety or destructive behaviour breaks through. Such a person may not know what to make of this condition. "I've always been an active, confident person. Nothing like this has happened to me before. Everything frightens me. I can't go out. I cry all the time. I'm afraid I'll smash my children."

Most of my patients know the bad self only too well. It is no surprise to them. It is more surprising when they feel good or do something good for themselves, when there is some break in the black winter and sunlight warms and brightens them.

Zero logic

Jean

Once one is in the habit of being nothing, zero, absolute shit–garbage, the mind finds ways to keep one there.[1] For example, Jean was horribly abused by an uncle in childhood. She early learned to keep her mouth shut about sucking him off, about his mutilating her vagina with sharp objects, about him making her feel that it was her fault he was doing this, and that she would destroy life around her if she said anything about it. A sense of reverse causality made her feel evil for the evil done to her.

Jean was an extremely sensitive and multi-talented person, wondrously (originally, I made a typo and wrote "woundrously") efficient when it came to helping others. She painted, wrote, created computer programs for many kinds of needs, set up care-taking structures for ill people, helped people administer businesses. She lived for others. Her remuneration was slim. She barely took care of herself. People were used to expecting much from her in return for little. And whatever they expected, she gave more.

For years, she tottered on the edge of suicide, mutilating herself physically and psychologically. Not surprisingly, if she conceived a desire, it was unrealizable. For example, she wanted to be friends with one of the people she helped. To be friends meant total sharing—no privacy. The other, Ginger (one of many "Gingers"), kept rebuffing her, refusing this kind of "sharing". At the same time, Ginger had no scruples about having Jean do things for her. Jean gave as totally in business, as she wanted in friendship.

Jean insisted that Ginger's rejection of friendship proved that she, Jean, was evil. In actuality, it was unclear what Ginger re-

---

[1] For additional writings on null or zero logic and self-states see Matte-Blanco (1975, 1988) and Grotstein (1981).

jected or resisted. Was it Jean's demand for total penetration, absorption, total availability for perusal of secrets, submission to
soul-scanning? Jean insisted she would never hurt another person. But she needed the other's inner landscape to be defenceless
so that she could plunder it if she wanted to, although she was
convinced that she would never ever do such a thing. She felt that
she would always ennoble and support the other's inner world,
as she aided the other's external affairs.

Of course, Jean was not only exploited but often degraded. It
took years of therapeutic work just to begin minimizing the degree
of degradation that hounded her. People used her and her products
and equipment to enhance themselves at her expense. It seemed as
if one could not resist taking advantage of her, and some did so
gleefully and maximally. Every fresh bout of degradation confirmed that she was evil. It was as if she wanted someone like
Ginger to grant total soul access as proof that she, Jean, was not
evil. Only total surrender by the other meant that Jean was good.

Of course, such total defencelessness was not realistic. Yet it
mirrored the defencelessness Jean in reality lived with her uncle.
Only if the other turned to butter could she claim her own innocent malleability, which was so abused. She wanted the other to
be in a state of total helplessness at her hands, so that she could
refrain from inflicting the tormenting abuse she received. She
would thus constitute a lived paradigm of vulnerability, coupled
with restraint, respect, and caring, as alternative–antidote to the
abuse of vulnerability that ruined her life.

Something always went wrong with her idea of cure, her
fantasy. No one gave herself over to her as tenderly as she was
brutally taken from herself. Yet she could not stop wanting someone's beatific surrender to match and make up for her grisly violation. *She wanted a love as perfect as the violation, a good as good as
the bad was bad.* Her childhood addicted her to extremes.

Let me lay my cards on the table immediately. If someone says
they are evil, I have no reason to doubt it. I am more interested in
how evil operates than in whether or not it does. I do not know
anyone who lives in an evil-free environment or evil-free psyche.
It seems to me a dangerous waste of time to make believe that
one is much better than one is. Yet that is what we do to get by.
Some of us do the opposite, to keep the balance. Sometimes we

make believe we are worse than we are—and really mean it. Jean unconsciously deceived herself into thinking she was as bad as her uncle perversely tried to twist her into thinking he was good.

Yes, Jean may, indeed, be evil, and perhaps only God can fathom how. But she is not evil because Ginger does not want to be her friend. Would she be good if Ginger accepted her? Here, at least, is a flaw in cognitive functioning that can be pulled on, and it seems to be a fairly widespread tendency.

If you love me, it must mean that I am not all bad. But if you happen to be a devil, your love may be contingent on my being bad enough to earn it. In Jean's case, her soul was ensorcelled by a devil who substituted injury for joy. She could not break free of her uncle. He was part of her body sensations. Any hint of sexual or pleasurable sensations immediately triggered the feeling of him commandeering her body, her horror, dread, degradation. Where was her rage?

She must be bad, if God could do this to her. It was as if God created certain people, like Jean, to specialize in excruciating, chronic states of torment. She received some momentary relief by cutting herself and other circumscribed self-destructive acts. Suicide seemed the only viable relief. It would take her out of God's plan. It would force God's hand. Could he do worse in the next plane? Was it her evolutionary task to stay with tormenting consciousness until the end?—to live torment until she or it burnt out, until the next thing happened? Would there ever be a next thing? Did she exist to show greedy society that torment was real, that celebration of fame, fortune, and power was constructed by modular units of suffering behind the scenes?

Why were the Gingers of the world signifiers of God's grace and bounty? If Ginger will be her friend, Jean is good. If Ginger will not be her friend, Jean is evil. In reality, Ginger will exploit her. However, there are people who are friendly here and there. Indeed, there have been people in her life who could have been friends. Jean is an amazing person. She could be a magnet for other talented people or, at least, sometimes connect with other eccentric, gifted souls. But others like her are not Gingers—they are not exploiters. It comes down to needing an exploiter to be her friend. She requires someone who hates her to love her. She needs a hater to be a lover. Null logic is precise and uncanny.

Jean wants to be wanted by a hater. What is worse, she wants to be wanted intrinsically, for herself alone, fully, unconditionally. As stated above, she wants as perfect a love as she was perfectly violated. But she wants this beatific love from someone who hates. If God were perfect Love, he would not do, unless he were perfect Hate. A mixture of love–hate is beside the point. A perfect hater must show perfect love. But perfect love, if it exists, would not do the trick. It would lack demonic charisma.

To untangle Jean, God must jump through hoops. He must jump through all the knots of her being. Nothing less would do. God would have to go through a process similar to Jean's before she could relent. In Christian terms, Jesus must extend himself to include miseries he missed. Jean is way out there in the vanguard of suffering. She needs to feel that Jesus can catch up to her before he can embrace her. She cannot let herself be embraced by a God who cannot keep up with her.

At the same time as she is totally outside God's world, she wonders whether she is not a suffering part of God—a kind of pseudopod or antenna of God, an outreach or ganglion devoted to agony. Perhaps she is a bit of the suffering God, a bit of God's suffering in herself. Consolation from such thoughts is short-lived, since she is pressed beyond limits of endurance.

What is a poor therapist going to do? After all, the therapist is presumably a person interested in Jean. Neither perfect hate nor love, and therefore irrelevant—not a hater desiring friendship. In therapy, Jean is in the odd position of needing to make use of someone who, she feels, is irrelevant. At the same time, she clings to therapy for dear life, barely. Therapy offers nutriment she needs but cannot use but cannot stop trying to use. Perhaps if she tries long enough, the ability to use help will develop. She perceives that therapy may have something to offer, behind a screen, darkly. I firmly believe—and long experience has taught me—that the Jeans of this world need therapists with long-range vision, endurance, patience, persistence: caring therapists to hang in there as long as it takes for struggling individuals to grow the capacity to grow.

Therapists share many—probably all—of Jean's feelings, in one or another form. A difference might be the practised faith that neither desire nor rejection proves good or evil. All the desire in the world will not make self or other good or bad. Nor can any particular rejection be a general criterion of worth.

We hear a great deal today about the exploitative therapist. But in a case like Jean's, therapy may feel unreal if the therapist is not exploitative enough. Can therapist and patient eventually find each other through their unreality? Must a therapist be nulled if she or he is not quite exploitative/hating enough for love to have value?

A particular difficulty in an abuse case like Jean's is the certainty that surrounds manifest atrocity. Jean was a victim of evil, and she felt evil. This sense of evil at the core of her life and personality was clear, distinct, insistent. Jean knew evil first-hand, and the sense of evil knowledge poisoned her life-feeling. She could not shake her conviction that she was basically evil because she had experienced basic evil. Only a basically evil person knew basic evil. What was done to one *is* one—such is self-nulling logic in sub-zero worlds where innocence is degraded, invaded, polluted, if not lost.

Her certainty surrounding evil made the investigation of evil impossible. She clung to her sense of evil, since that was reality for her. To lose evil would mean loss of "sanity". She *knew* what she was about, and she was bad. Her tenacious fidelity to the worst that happened worked against opening herself to other aspects of experience, especially to new possibilities in the present. Nor could she let herself learn anything more about how evil works. She knew enough already. Still, she comes for help.

Food–shit fusion

Self-nulling tendencies are both expressed and maintained by processes that surface in dreams. In this section, I wish to emphasize a fairly common top–bottom mix-up where bad self-feelings are concerned. Many people dream of shitting through their mouth, and some also dream of defecating food, suggesting some fusion of mouth–anus, eating–defecating. Some imagine eating or otherwise taking in (sucking, drinking, absorbing) with the anus. An important variation is the fusion of respiration–digestion, as breathing through the anus, which passes wind. There are many phrases in common speech that suggest top–bottom inversions and fusions, usually derogatory.[2]

Louis

Louis dreamt of shitting sausages in marinara sauce. He feared shitting blood, which had occurred in his life, requiring hospitalization (his illness was not life-threatening, and he made a good recovery). He was relieved to see food, not blood, in his dream, although he worried about it. He began feeling proud of shitting food, linking it with creativity, although he was somewhat mystified.

Louis spoke about Freud's association of anal "making" with creativity, but his tone left me feeling this was not the whole story. I heard something desperate, anxious, tainted, as if he were trying to convince himself that shitting food was good. He was trying to make his dream image a signifier of something good—a sign that *he* was good. "See, it wasn't a catastrophe. It wasn't blood. It was food, something good. Something good came out of my bottom, a good baby. I'm not bad. I'm good."

There is such an undertow of bad self-feeling—we keep trying to convince ourselves we are good, we are not as bad as we fear.

In recent sessions Louis had been speaking of work and family difficulties. He wished whatever he did would be terrific. He did not want to work hard at anything. Things should come easily and be great. He also spoke of wishing marriage were easier. Trying to hold back his rage at his wife and children was too difficult. He felt right in his rages most of the time. In his fury he

---

[2] I have written about anus–mouth, food–faeces, digestion–respiration fusions in earlier works (Eigen, 1986, 1993). Now I wish to emphasize their role in degradation–inflation states, particularly nulling oneself. Other authors who have studied related amalgams of body parts and functions include Meltzer (1973), Milner (1957), Klein (1946), Ehrenzweig (1971), Bion (1965), Freud (1911), Matte-Blanco (1988). Such fusions/confusions have been a persistent object of thought in psychoanalysis, particularly with reference to building our body-image and sense of self.

meant to set others straight. He tried to convince his wife and children that his rage was nourishing.

Louis's face seemed twisted, his body tense. He was trying to convince himself, me, others, that his shit was nourishing, good enough to eat. The common phrase, "Eat shit!", is packed with meaning.

He became a bit more reflective. "I sit down to write a screenplay and picture everyone watching it, all the millions I'll make. I think of writing a show, and it's already a Broadway hit. I never go over anything. I don't rework it. I don't sweat over it. Fantasy is as good as reality. Except I'm furious I do not get the reality. I expect it to come like shitting. Want some good food? Just stick your mouth near my ass."

The sarcastic self-mockery was part of what I heard from the beginning, tinged with panic, hysteria. A kind of grandiose god creating the food of life via anal birth. On the one hand, this means the anus is good, holy (like a sweet baby's ass). On the other, it suggests food that is soiled. There is something wrong with nourishment that comes out the ass-hole. Things are "ass backwards". We put good things in our mouths, shit out waste.

Louis went back and forth between inflation–degradation. On the one hand he was the baby god whose shit is (or should be) terrific. He really did expect every little thing he did to be amazing. On the other, he was the soiler–spoiler, inches from catastrophe, messing up his own and others' lives. To expect his droppings to be eatable short-circuits the hard work that goes into respecting the needs of others.

To get nourishment from his parents, Louis had to take in a lot of shit. He had to swallow their shit and his own as well. They both denigrated and idealized what they put into him, and he did too.

At one point, Louis weepingly confessed, "I have a horror of my upbringing. I can't face the fear that it permanently damaged me. From an early age I've had a fantasy of things easier, better, more OK than they are."

He continued, "My parents couldn't deal with bad things, realities. Anything that went wrong was the end of the world. Once I needed crutches for an injured leg, and my father wouldn't talk to me. He thought it the worst thing in the world that I hurt myself. He blamed me and held it against me. When I tried to tell him what I felt, he threatened to slam me with a hammer.

"He would rage, and my mother would scream. At the same time, she thought I was too good for everyone, too good for the world. She did everything for me. I guess I expected things to come easily—the world would do whatever I asked, as she did. Yet her giving was mixed with screaming, attacks, put-downs. Her giving was assaultive.

"My parents were out of control with us. Parents are supposed to help, regulate. Mine went wild, hysterical. I cannot take defeats. There was no one to support me in trying times, no one to say, 'It's OK, you'll be fine'. I have gone through life hoping for a better world than my parents. Now I'm struggling to get by, just to make a living. I'm angry life is so hard, such a struggle. It's not what I pictured it to be. When things go wrong, I can't support myself emotionally. There's no inner support."

What began with Louis's glorification of anal food (his gift to the world) turned into a confession of disability, filled in (overstuffed) with inflation. The fusion of nourishment with faeces and eating with defecation expressed terrible facts of his emotional life. He had to eat his parents' shit and live on what nourishment it provided. The fusion of nourishment with excreta polluted his emotional life. He expected others to eat his shit as well and find it supremely nourishing.

He was lucky in having a wife and children who loved him, but they balked at putting up with his shit, much less eating it. He felt the horror of his upbringing and wished to go beyond it. He loved his wife and children and did not want to lose them. Moreover, he *knew* he did not want to be like his parents, even if he could not help himself. He kept coming to therapy, hoping to find ways to make life better, to make himself better.

Such deeply set patterns are virtually intractable. They are set deeply in our beings, our psyches, our bodies. They permeate the imagery that governs us. Attitudes and patterns of feeling are codified in unconscious imagery that act as a kind of circuitry, a subway system taking us places we would rather not visit. Imagery reflects our basic realities, but it also moulds and perpetuates them. It can, also, change them. A new image can give voice to and stimulate new possibilities of living.

Louis's image of shitting food summarized a pattern that cursed his life. In the sessions, he progressed from an overestimation of himself and his products to grief over lacking strength and skills for fuller living. He did not want to be the kind of person who expected everyone to eat his shit and think it great. To some extent, he was able to dis-identify from the unconscious idea that shit was food, his the best food of all. After grief came desire and inspiration to be different, to do better, to keep trying.

One difference between psychotherapy and other help modalities is the emphasis on something more than will, desire, inspiration, trying. In addition to these, therapy spends a good deal of time focusing on what holds one back—barriers to living, self-nulling tendencies. It helps give people a somewhat better idea about what they are up against. Reality is more complex and different from what we imagine. Even when we have a fixed, clear idea of what went wrong, our very rightness and definiteness can work against change.

For example, in the case of Louis's shitting food image, as important as what this image might really mean (will we ever know?) is its function in a session. Therapy enabled Louis not only to dream this image but to remember it, talk about it, turn it around in his mind, use it. The image became a reference-point, a summary of tendencies, marker of ambiguities. As it was focused on, it took on different values, first triggering pride in self, then deeper self-recognition and something resembling repentance and rededication. At first the image absorbed Louis's ego into itself, then it was re-situated and re-absorbed in a larger context.

Louis moved from being taken in by it to somewhat transcending it, placing it in a larger frame of reference.

Nevertheless, tendencies encoded in such an image persevere. To use current physiological imagery, they are linked with an autonomic fright–rage and subcortical emotionality that is not readily modifiable. The emotional atmosphere that nourished–poisoned us remains part of the air we breathe, part of our body and souls. It is not a skin we can simply step out of. To use older language, the atmosphere we grew up in seeps into us, becomes steadfast, as if translated into reflexes, tropisms. To counter the latter requires work, insight, vision, time. It is the work of a lifetime, never completely successful, but even a little change goes a long way.

In a way, Louis's dream image was a thought waiting to be born. In an instant, major currents in his life came together. The image spoke to everything he had been through, everything that was wrong with him, everything he incorporated, choked on, and tried to make others swallow. At the same time, the image opened mysteries, reveries, thoughts about life. It pointed to transformation processes that were stillborn, frozen, impacted, but not totally out of reach.

The association between food and faeces is part of a larger symbolic flow, optimally involving fluid movement between in–out, top–bottom, nourishment–evacuation. Reversals and inversions are spontaneous parts of this natural "circuitry" (Freud referred to nodal or navel or switch points and tracks of meaning). If things go well enough, certain organizing dominants occur, like food being primarily food, waste primarily waste. But I doubt that the psyche is ever free of mix-up, confusion, contamination, spill-over.

Food and shit get their symbolic power partly through unspoken crosscurrents and countertendencies. It is always possible for one to become the other. The mind delights in reversals, especially fundamental ones. Something is always itself and something else, often its opposite or counter-pole. Our body provides the mind with plenteous material for confabulation and rearranging (perhaps, too, our mind has asked for and been given the sort of body that feeds imaginative thinking).

Unfortunately, the symbolic flow of meaning can harden and rigidify. The bad things in a life can absorb the good, as well as the reverse. In a life overly pulverized by trauma, the meanings of nourishment and excrement can undergo permanent reversal—top–bottom permanent inversion, more or less. Shit can become the organizing structure for nourishment, so that nourishment becomes shitty and shit nourishing. Images are soul windows. Chronic and congealed reversal of meaning reflect a mangled psyche. Degraded–degrading images reflect and reinforce degraded psychic states. It is necessary to acknowledge the latter, not base one's life on them.

Once the dream machinery gets stuck, something more or different from will, desire, and inspiration may be needed. One needs to glimpse the work of the dream factory itself, get some inkling of mix-ups that drag one down. In Louis's case, absorption of nourishment by shit threatened whatever he tried to build up, made it difficult to build up anything of value. The support and slant he got from therapy enabled him to visualize and face forces that nagged and nulled him. He worked hard to live a life more nourishing than shitty. Nevertheless, the human being he laboured to be would never be in the clear.

The cynical, self-aggrandizing, self-pitying, self-hating side of personality keeps reducing life to shit. Life *is* shitty, if also glorious. The bully tries to convince others his or her shit is good. Once shit–feeding/shit–eating kicks into gear and becomes dominant, it is nearly impossible to get out of. Some part of the self remains addicted forever, but perhaps not entirely. If someone starts therapy, I assume there is something that wants something else and more. Therapy throws its weight behind that mustard seed.

A person comes in and wants to be saved from the shit he or she is drowning in. Yet once work starts, the individual may jump into the undertow, as if relieved of the responsibility of holding out any longer. The kindling of therapeutic desire is necessary, but not enough. Real work on the dream machinery must go on as well. Dreams grow out of the undertow.

It is unfair

The unfairness of life lends itself to self-nulling thinking. Someone stuck in the undertow can always say, "Life is unfair." That is one way of always being right. One of the great strengths of self-nulling thinking is its rightness. It is *never* wrong. If someone in an extreme state of unworthiness and wipe-out moans, "I'm always wrong", there is secret pleasure in being right about that.

One of the great self-reinforcing "gratifiers" that keeps one running a negative maze is the sense of being right about how bad one is or how bad life is. I recall experiments of rats starving to death when allowed to keep turning on electrodes placed in the brain's pleasure centre. People do something like this with attitudes and behaviour linked to the "rightness" centre. They do not let themselves make full enough use of the complexities within and outside them.

A particular form of unfairness that taunts the psychological initiate involves run-ins with people mindlessly and guiltlessly enjoying bad traits one desperately is trying to overcome. It is absolutely galling to be confronted with someone freely displaying behaviour one is working so hard to subdue and transcend.

Gary

My client, Gary, was a music teacher. He worked very hard in therapy to modify his temper and bossiness with his students. He came to the point of recoiling from his rages while leading the middle-school band. As he got better, a colleague's impatience and irritability increasingly bothered him.

The time came when Gary could not bear his colleague's bullying tactics any longer. Confrontation was inevitable. Gary knew he was looking into a mirror and what he despised out there were aspects of himself, but that made things worse. "How can he act that way!" Gary shouted to me. "Here I'm doing the best I can not to be that way, and he doesn't care how he comes on. He goes on spewing on the kids, taking advantage of them. It's not fair."

It was not fair to the children. It was not fair to Gary. Perhaps his colleague was doing himself an injustice as well. Using students as outlets for hostility is unlikely to promote anyone's growth, least of all the perpetrator's. Should Gary bully the bully? He pictured losing his temper, shouting at his colleague. They would fight each other. Students would have to separate them. No, the students were likely to cheer them on. More probably, other teachers or the school's custodian would intervene. It would be embarrassing and not even satisfying, since neither would beat the other, and nothing would change.

Anyway, Gary was working on not being like the bully, even with a bully. But do not bullies only respect bigger bullies? Is it not stupid to turn the other cheek? Are there no other alternatives? Putting one's feelings into words? Gary tried to say what he felt, as openly and sincerely and firmly as possible. He tried to say how he felt his colleague was affecting the children, and he tried to encourage alternative possibilities.

It did not work. There was no magic in putting feelings into words. His colleague politely told him to butt out. He had his way, Gary had his. He heard Gary out, and then he raised his voice and lectured Gary on why his way was what the children needed. He justified himself. He kept order, got the students to listen, to do better.

"I used to be like you", Gary was dying to say. But deep down he was thinking he was still very much like his colleague, very much indeed. "Can't he see it!" screamed Gary's insides. What he meant was, "It's unfair. I see it, and he refuses to. He gets away with murder." The other gets away with what I want to/used to get away with. Gary's psychological conscience was growing, depriving him of gratifications others enjoy.

It had taken years to reach this point. For a long time Gary refused to grow, if growth meant suffering unfairness. He consented to grow in places where there was no unfairness, which left out a lot of life. Why should he grow if people around him stayed the same or got worse? Why should he become less destructive if he had to deal with those who indulged their destructiveness?

He broke up with a number of girlfriends and vice versa when relationships reached the point of requiring sacrifice of rightness in all things. "Why should I change, if she doesn't? It's not fair." For years Gary kept himself in stalemates out of fear of making the first move or a genuine reparative gesture.

Little by little, his taste for growth grew. As time went on, Gary felt keenly how making comparisons held him back. He tried to tell himself that not growing was a loss in itself. If he grew and the other did not, the other lost out. There are many stories one can tell oneself to jump-start movement. Gary began to understand that going through the experience of someone not going through what he was going through was part of the journey, a tantalizingly agonizing part of the initiation.

He vaguely intuited that there would come a time when people who bothered him now would not be so meaningful. If he really became a less bossy, angry person, his bossy, angry colleague might not be so annoying—at least, not the way he is now. Something or someone else might be troublesome: new growth markers. He must make room in his life for troublesome, obnoxious, unfair others. There will always be people he rubs the wrong way and vice versa.

Gary's predicament implies two ways of nulling self. The self-nulling, "I won't budge if you won't." You = current other = business as usual = world = life. This predicament is all too true in the world of politics as well as in individual lives. But there is also the nulling of this self-nulling, summed up in the prayer, "God, take us deeper into life". There will always be obnoxious people, you and I among them. But sometimes we see it and do not like it and want more and other—our little bundle of self, house of horrors, stream of sweet delights: more than enough to keep us busy, plenty to do.

CHAPTER EIGHT

Empty and violent nourishment

Coreen

Coreen's mother bathed her in wealth and the promise of more wealth: "When I die, you'll have everything." Coreen had heard these words ever since she could remember. They mystified her. They made her feel that she *ought* to have everything, that everything was possible, and that one day she *would* have it all.

At the same time, Coreen was told she already had everything. She had every advantage material wealth could bring. She lived in a mansion with her own suite of rooms. She had housekeepers, tutors, activities, playmates. The message she received was that she had no lacks.

Someday she would have everything, and she had everything now. One conclusion Coreen drew was that her life was filled with everything, that she went from less of everything to more of everything, and someday she would find most of everything.

"I walked around, my head filled with everythings, lots of everythings, all animated. Animations of everythings. Lesser and greater everythings of all kinds. I would meet people and classify them as this or that everything. Likewise activities. This activity would be that kind of everything, that activity this kind. Everything was some type of everything. I couldn't do or find anything that wouldn't be one sort of everything or another."

With so much everything, could there be room for anything? Could there be room for Coreen or, perhaps, which is the same thing, too much room? In another session, Coreen said, "I wandered the halls alone, in spite of all the help. I felt too tiny in a space too big. I bled to death in the huge arteries of a house I couldn't fill. I bled to death in a life I couldn't fill."

Coreen spontaneously used an image that appeared in Bion, whom she had not read. Bion (1970, p. 12) wrote of surgical shock, bleeding to death in one's own arteries because of capillary dilation. In analogical fashion, he depicts a mental space so vast that emotion cannot be felt. I believe Coreen when she says that she bled to death in a life (and house) too immense for her to occupy. Her adult life since university has been a slowly accelerating contraction. Her life has grown smaller and smaller, perhaps in an attempt to feel herself.

Coreen was once very busy, her life bustling with people, activities and plans, a carrying-over of her activity-crammed childhood. As the years wore on, she did less and less. By the time she reached 50, there were few people in her life, and she could no longer work. She did little but watch television. She recalled the worthy projects she had participated in, the wider world of personalities she had once taken for granted, and imagined that golden times would be around the corner again. It took many years to realize that her life was on a downward slide. By the time she sought help, the momentum towards dissolution was well established.

Coreen's attitude towards her plight was variable. She could be brutally honest in tracking her stripped-down condition. At times, her speech reached a poetry of denudation. She possessed aesthetic appreciation of her wasteland, while ruefully enduring it. At other times, bitterness left no room for beauty. The ghastliness of her plight was overwhelming, and she watched in horror as her life slipped into oblivion. Yet there were moments, too poisonous and many, in which she still fancied life full and glory imminent.

The sense that life bathed in Everything contrasted acutely with the all-consuming barrenness. "The barrenness was always there, but I tried not to notice. I'd look the other way. There were enough everythings to distract me. The truth is I felt the hole, the nothingness, too. I felt empty even if I did not want to. I knew it was there. Nothing eats everything, and everything fills nothing. Now nothing is where everything was. Yet Everything still whispers, promises, tells me nothing really is not—nothing is everything. Pain is too much. Nothing is real, everything lies. Everything is real, nothing lies. *I am* eaten up between them. *I am* vanishing. Pain keeps me from vanishing, but pain is too much, it obliterates everything–nothing and me."

Coreen grew smaller and smaller inside a contracting core that threatened to reach a vanishing point. Nothing and Everything were too big. She could not be small and condensed enough. Nothing and Everything fed off each other, and she was lost between them. "My life turned inside out. There used to be a lot of everything and a little nothing. Now it's the reverse. Nothing is everything and everything nothing."

Coreen found pleasure, even ecstasy, in reporting the moment-to-moment everything–nothing balance, her psychospiritual pulse. She did this in the midst of mounting, unbearable pain. It was, in a way, the last thing left to her. She did not "work" in therapy. She came to tell about her waxing–waning, overall fading state. It seemed as if she was nearly haphazardly thrown up on the shores of therapy by alarming obliteration waves. Once she had established a beachhead (a place to talk or spill herself out), she seemed content just to come. Each day she showed up was one more day of being somewhere, such as it was.

What could someone who was everything becoming nothing want from therapy? What did therapy offer? For one thing, coming and sharing nothing day after day eventually enabled Coreen to realize that her nothing was no mere nothing. It was nothing with a sting. Nor was her sharing merely sharing. It was sharing with a sting. Coreen was, among other things, an angry, spiteful, stinging person.

In one session, Coreen became aware that she spat her words out. She was spitting at sharing, spitting at therapy, spitting at life. Her everything spat at nothing and nothing spat at everything. Spitting was a kind of stinging and vice versa. Spitting was her way of trying to sting the enemy. She felt too helpless really to sting. Spitting was something babies can do. When you are tied down and helpless, you can still spit, if there is no adhesive on your mouth.

Spit and stinging spite—a spitting image: Coreen was better and worse than a spitting image of her mother. She was not as powerful a figure as her mother. Coreen did not dominate other lives. But her mother's sting lived in her. She organized herself around her mother's sting, grew around a stinging core. When she was younger, Coreen tried to be overly sweet to mute the sting. But she gradually became more acerbic. Coreen's conscience was severe, and she stopped being a school-teacher for fear of stinging children with her words and disposition. She became an efficient, unpleasant, but not really injurious administrator.

Coreen mostly hurt herself. The more she contracted, the more she felt the sting. She squeezed herself around it. Over the years she lost weight and became tinier. One almost expected arrows or broken glass to burst out of her skin. "Mother put her stinging self into me, and I contracted more and more to have a pure bit of my own self. So much me seemed not-me. I put more and more me outside me. Now it's collapsing in. I try to keep it out but it's too much. The way to handle it is become a collapsing nowhere. But nothing nowhere is not me either. My mother was nothing nowhere and everything everywhere. She showed up, gave orders, then was gone. She lived her own busy life most of the time, which did not include me. There's a hole of a mother, a sting of a mother."

Mother is emptiness. Mother is pain. Where is the beautiful mother, mother of plenitude? Coreen loved art and literature, but her relationship to it was largely critical. She was a great critic, but not overly generous. Something of what must have been beautiful, rich, and full survives several times removed, as critic of beauty. Even after she stopped working, holed up with the television, she managed to get to movies and art exhibitions. She was managing to keep herself alive—barely—with some kind of nourishment from somewhere. Would the residue of beauty be enough?

Coreen was becoming a residue herself—a residue of mother parts, but also of herself, a residue of the person she might have been. She was becoming a residue of life. "I'm a pale version of mother's sting and void. I moulded around them, fought them, fused them. I'm a watered-down stinging void. She invaded and left, and I developed antibodies against her and against my feelings for her. Now I *am* an antibody, set to attack whatever remains of me, if anything's left to attack."

Coreen faded more and more out of existence. Her life recoiled on itself. She lost herself in childhood, possibly infancy, although the loss took a long time to catch up with her and she with it. She fought against collapsing into stinging loss, while the latter gained power. So much of her life was not she, it was difficult to find some bit of life that *was* she.

If we are lucky, life blends self–other mixtures in spontaneously workable ways. Self–other feed each other, even in opposition. We do not always have to search for islands of self unpolluted by otherness. In Coreen's case, noxious elements in primal otherness were too intense to be disregarded or put up with indefinitely. She coasted on innate life energy and what nourishment she extracted from poisons, until the poisons became too much for her. They probably always were too much, but Coreen was carried along by life until corrosive forces reached a critical mass.

To turn inward was akin to throwing herself on bayonets or perishing in blankness. To some extent, she nourished herself with art. The world is more than mother and filled with influences and things to do. But interests and cares held her above the stinging void only so long. Little by little, she was drawn into the latter.

Although Coreen's collapse gradually increased over the course of adult life, it gained impetus after her mother died. She had been very tied to her mother. It is not exactly that her mother provided support. But her dominant nature tended to sweep Coreen along. As Coreen grew older, her mother was someone to fight, to be nasty with, to take care of. Her mother did not seem to care about nastiness, as other people did. As long as Coreen had her mother, she had someone who could not understand her, someone to push against, bounce off, to curse and nurse. The strong energy between them kept Coreen somewhat afloat.

Other ingredients mixed in the brew: (1) Coreen was waiting for her mother to die. She imagined that getting rid of mother would mean getting rid of her own problems. Coreen would also get plenty of money, which she associated with freedom, power, ability, calling the shots. (2) After mother's death there was the usual guilt, dread of power, sense of loss, need to join the mother. But the over-riding factor was that the glue that held Coreen together was gone.

Coreen did not guess that her mother's death would open a trap door, a hole in her psyche. She thought she would be liberated. She was taken by surprise by the loss of self that accompanied loss of her mother. She had no idea how much of herself was carried by her mother or was in her mother or was her mother. It was almost as if loss of mother equalled loss of self. There was not much left without the toxic glue that nourished her. Whether there was enough for therapy to build on remained to be seen.

A mug of beer

The problem of nourishment (what it is, how to recognize, secure, and use it) is highlighted in Bion's discussion of lying. Bion writes that truth nourishes, lies poison. Yet lying is ubiquitous, and possibly so is hunger for truth. But how does one recognize a lie, and what does one do with it?

In an introduction to issues concerning lying, Bion (1965, pp. 2–4) provides a semi-clinical example to think about:

"The patient says, 'Suddenly, just as I finished lunch he threw a mug of beer in my face without any warning. I kept my head and showed no resentment at all remembering what you had said about psycho-analysis. So I passed it off without anyone noticing.'"

We do not know whether the patient is relating what happened, lying, mixing lies–truths, hallucinating, and so on. Nor are we sure how to evaluate his tale. What is he communicating or trying not to communicate?

The vignette begins with a statement concerning nourishment. He finished lunch (leave aside, for the moment, whether imaginary or real lunch). In the beginning, there was nourishment. No, in the beginning there was, "suddenly", a surprising impact, just as lunch was ending. First, the language of impact: "suddenly", "just as"—drama, surprise, suspense, the rug pulled from under one, some kind of blow. Just as one might have completed a peaceful lunch, trouble happens: "He threw a mug of beer in my face without any warning." The patient appears to be communicating a disturbance.

The vignette presents violence before nourishment, even if the latter occurred first. Already in the act of nourishment the sudden blow is on the way, the ever expected unexpected blow. Notice of trauma gets placed first, as if trauma is an inevitable part of nourishment. No lunch is complete without a dose of trauma.

What is primary? Temporally, nourishment (lunch, good breast). Linguistically, trauma (suddenly, just as). It is as if nourishment and trauma provide a context for each other. Trauma feeds on nourishment, but nourishment cannot escape trauma. *Primary statements:*

1. In the beginning there is nourishment.
2. In the beginning (almost) there is trauma.
3. In the beginning there is nourishment–trauma.

The patient mentions nourishment in an account of trauma, almost in passing, as if nourishment were an occasion for trauma. Nourishment is tainted by disturbance. Disturbance takes precedence. Many patients feel that nourishment is ruined by disturbance. The constant conjunction of nourishment–trauma can be turned various ways, including asking what traumatic nourishment and nourishing trauma may mean?

Is the patient throwing words or emotions in the analyst's face?—Refusing to?—Both? What would analytic mugs of beer be? The patient's statement has a semi-hysterical tone with its *suddenly, just as, without any warning.* Does he mean to excite or worry the analyst?—Get the latter interested, alarmed, draw him in?

Not to worry. Just in case someone might be alarmed or sympathetic, just as one might begin to feel, "Good God, man, did that happen to you!?", the patient turns all emotion off. He kept his head, showed no emotion (resentment), passed (evacuated) it off. No one noticed him passing it off, none noticed the throw, no one noticed the foolishness, violence, emotion, or shutting down. He caricatures the analyst, keeper of heads, Mr. No-Show-Emotion. A further step would be Mr. No-Emotion-At-All.

A caricature of a cool head *vis à vis* excitable emotionality emerges, in which little is drawn out of either. But that is the point: little is drawn out of whatever happens or does not happen. Instead of rich emotion and reflection, we have movement towards shut-down.

Bion often spoke about maintaining the ability to think clearly in the face of emotional pressures—a concern that drew on his experience as a young tank-commander on the battlefield. Bion's war experience was an especially intense instance of difficulties besetting relationships. Near the end of his life he wrote:

> Since strong emotions undermine the capacity to think clearly, it would seem logical to suppose that a doctor, a psychiatrist, a psycho-analyst, should achieve and retain a capacity for clear thinking, and help the analysand to achieve and maintain a similar atmosphere of calm deliberation.
>
> How? My ability to do so is tested every moment of my life, not only in the course of professional duty but in the day-to-day frustrations and happenings. I am still as far away from achieving success in this endeavor as I ever was. I do not think I and my analysands are exceptional in this. What *is* exceptional is that the attempt is now being made to develop such a capacity through psycho-analysis. [1992, p. 365]

What *are* we to make of the mug-of-beer example? Is Bion making it up? Is he selecting it from his practice? Is he trimming it to suit his need? To what extent does it function as a parable of a ghastly reality many face? Is Bion's work a contemporary *Pilgrim's Progress* depicting vicissitudes of emotional truth in our day, *sub specie aeternis*?

The patient may be portraying part of his developmental history: violent feed followed by abandonment of tension, going into head, shutting down, no longer noticing emotional realities. One gives up noticing emotional realities if one is unable to achieve anything fruitful by noticing them. Yet these realities exert pressure. In this case, they emerge in the patient's account of an event that may not have happened but in an emotional sense (perhaps in some psychosomatic Atlantis) is always happening.

The patient may find pleasure in dangling an account of injury in a way that remains difficult to touch. There is an almost fiendish pleasure in tantalizing the analyst with a "funny" shock, a bizarre transposition of something very serious. The analyst gets a taste of and bears witness to a twist the patient has undergone. The sequence—violent feed, loss of psychosomatic circulation, going into head, shutting down feeling/perception/attention—is compressed into something dense and indecipherable, a knot that affects muscles, nerves, and veins.

The knot exerts centripetal–centrifugal force. Insofar as it is in the psychic body, it can be anywhere, now more in head or stomach or chest or back (pain travels) or in travelling anxieties. At the same time the individual is bound to the knot, he is catapulted far from it and undergoes a twist, a mutation. He is in danger of being drawn into the knot and vanishing, yet thrown so far away that he becomes ghostly.

While the head may be mocking, contemptuous of ordinary feelings and people, the individual may also be loving, the heart a lonely hunter. Many schizophrenic individuals are warm-hearted, not simply contemptuous or indirectly hostile. They are dying to be touched and often form difficult attachments. Their bristles cut both ways. They cause pain to those close to them but also to themselves. They are constantly scratching and cutting themselves inside, as if trying to open the knot, get inside it, get outside it, somehow scratch the pain away. But the twist they have undergone makes it impossible to find what is bothering them or to do anything about it.

The analyst may or may not be able to help. At the very least, he can offer to share helplessness. Shared helplessness in the face of the knot-and-twist can be devastating, but it can also bring relief. I sometimes admire the knot-and-twist's canny productions. "Amazing", I might say under my breath and trace the intricate web it spins, adrift from the core agony, often a ploy or mask or diversionary shell, a disguised invitation. What the twist spins around the knot can be breathtaking in grisly impact, like a once-magnificent snake that has forgotten how to swallow, wasting away, still somewhat glistening, poignant.

Freud's notion of symptoms as disguised libido-aggression has a broader application. In the mug-of-beer incident, the whole person is a disguise. A disguise for what? For the person he might have been, wishes to be, a less twisted self. The self lost in the twist longs to undo the twist. The twisted self with a warm spot longs to be less twisted. Even if the individual becomes the twist and the disguise becomes real, there is still an ache for the really real.

Big bang

The coupling or mixture of nourishment/violence/shutting-off recurs in Bion's work, and nowhere more dramatically than in his use of the big bang image (1970, pp. 12–14; Eigen, 1998). He depicts a state of mind (or mindlessness) in which tolerance for frustration is so limited that mental space cannot function as a container, nor even be represented at all. An individual's explosive projection would have nowhere to go in a space too immense to have a containing function.

Bion (1970, p. 12) suggests that such an explosion is so violent and fearful that "the patient may express it by sudden and complete silence (as if to go to an extreme as far from a devastating explosion as possible)." The extremes—explosion and silence—become one.

Bion conveys an immensity in which emotion is lost. As an aside, he mentions surgical shock (an image spontaneously used by Coreen, above), in which a patient may bleed to death in his own tissues if the expanded space becomes too great for circulation.

In containerless space, the individual's mental content (thoughts, images, words) lose genuine communicative value and deform into quasi-mindless flotsam–jetsam, "debris, remnants or scraps of imitated speech and histrionic synthetic emotion, floating in space so vast that its confines, temporal as well as spatial, are without definition" (1970, p. 13).

In one of Bion's examples, he depicts a nourishing element (expressed in a patient's reference to ice cream), saturated by waves of destruction. Something agonizing happens, and what started as nourishment becomes a scream. The scream eventually stops. One may refuse to scream (negativism), or be unable to (flooding), or the scream may fade or die in nothingness. One may lose interest in screaming and go on to something else, but in the present case, the result is terrible. Nourishment, scream, no-scream become fused.

In some individuals, screaming replaces nourishment, or is felt to be nourishing, or linked to nourishment. Screamers vary, from the silent scream in schizophrenic symptoms, the annoying whining of chronic blamers–complainers, to the strident bossiness of bullies. Others may link silence with nourishment, whether linked to self-suppression or happy satisfaction. It seems a contradiction to think of obliteration as a form of nourishment but in some individuals it becomes a substitute or stand-in for nourishment. One keeps imagining that if one obliterates oneself long and hard enough, the nourishing thing will happen again. One can enter the nourishment/scream/no-scream fusion at any point, so that any term signifies the others.

It is as if a vast explosion occurred at the point of nourishment. Something went wrong. "An intense catastrophic emotional explosion O has occurred (elements of personality, link, and second personality having been instantaneously expelled to vast distances from their point of origin and from each other)" (1970, p. 14). The explosion may be expressed by a scream becoming lost in space, so that the scream can go on forever but not be felt or heard. It loses its function as a scream (meant to link self and other), congeals, becomes diffuse, becomes a no-scream, a void. We find Coreen in a void, hurtling into ever greater emptiness, partly fuelled by the unconscious conviction that emptiness and nourishment are one. Her nightmares are fuelled by explosions she no longer feels.

Judd

From his earliest years, Judd felt that something was off—how badly off depended on the moment of the day, who he was with, where he was. One afternoon, staring from his window, he saw a field ablaze with fire. He knew he was seeing things and closed his eyes. The fire blazed on the back of his closed eyelids. He opened his eyes, and the fire threatened to leap in the window. "There's something wrong with me." The words formed by themselves. He half-whispered, half-listened. There was no one to tell. His mother or father would comfort him, talk him out of it. "You're seeing things", they might say fondly or frightenedly. The experience subsided, and the next thing would happen. Always the next thing would happen.

As Judd grew older, there were moments of no next thing. Suddenly, inexplicably, everything ended. He dropped into horrifying silence, unable to speak. It might happen in a class, at a party, or when he was by himself. At first he thought the clamp came when he had to perform socially or at school. But the moments spread and severed him from his own solitude. At times he closed his eyes and saw on the back of his eyelids a blackness–redness that tinged everything when his eyes opened. The blackness–redness was more-or-less formless, amorphous, akin to the texture of a brick wall or concrete pavement, but not hard, more like a closed curtain before or after a show.

As a young man he had recognized his fire and blackness–redness in the thick, deep textures of Rembrandt and the swirls of Van Gogh. He knew immediately that these were colours not found on earth but in the mind. They were mental colours and, possibly, also, colours of mindlessness.

By his late twenties, amorphous blackness–redness alternated with rapidly changing geometric patterns. He closed his eyes and wished he could paint what he saw, and he realized that he had tapped into a basic ordering process. The mind spontaneously organized itself. The quasi-geometric forms were alive, akin to those of Miró or Klee.

The formless, amorphous textural world of blackness–redness and the ever-transforming world of geometric patternings were real, basic raw materials that soothed and enlivened him. They entranced him and made life feel inherently good and fascinating. They stood in contrast with stormy, painful moments.

"Shut up or I'll give you something to cry about", his father shouted. "I'll kill you." Judd shut up. His fury melded with his father's rage. He imagined his father beating him—felt it, although the beating was almost always verbal. He felt rage course through his father's body, veins swelling, face reddening. Judd's anger pulsed, then froze. Fear paralysed him. Everything inside him stopped. He breathed lightly, afraid to make a sound.

At some point he became aware that he was crying. His chest was heaving. He cried into his pillow soundlessly, stifling his heaving chest's agony. The blackout passed. Rage returned. Through his tears, he thought, "Someday he'll be sorry. I'll show him." There was a picture in his mind of growing up and being someone. His father would be awed, silenced. Judd would be like the biblical Joseph—a greater solar body lesser ones paid homage to.

Tears and rage went into this mental image, which took on a life of its own, suffusing his body with power. Even as he lay motionless, he felt a rush, the fuel of revenge. At the same time, fists of mind that housed the "someday" image, split off and flew upwards, so that human warmth would not weaken them: heart knot, brain knot, a knot within, a knot above—dense cores of self guiding him from secret places.

Another part of silence was listening in the night. Judd would be as still as possible to hear what his parents were saying or doing. He listened for the sounds of sex, but also for what they might tell each other behind his back. When he heard sex sounds, he stopped breathing. When his parents moved, he became motionless. When they spoke, he strained to hear their words. His muscles squeezed and tensed, as if the more vice-like they became, the quieter it would be, the better he would hear. He stared into blackness. The redness must be sex.

Judd became a listening presence in life, as if the main part of life went on behind his back. He listened and watched, straining to decipher what he could not quite see or hear.

Where were words? There was a gap between word and emotion. By the time the words Judd said reached someone else, he was already somewhere else. Judd was often puzzled by responses to what he said, since they rarely anticipated shifts he underwent since speaking. By the time someone heard him, processed his meaning, and replied, the stream of life was in another place. Human communication (or the lack of it) was akin to telling what changes a star is undergoing now on the basis of light transmitted long ago.

Judd became a quiet person. He was comfortable being quiet, but he noticed that his quietness could cause discomfort in others. At times, too, his quietness bothered him, especially when he wanted to speak but could not. His quiet then was loaded with anxiety. He developed a habit of not speaking, so that speaking caused him difficulty. Old emotions associated with silence (rage, sexual curiosity, tantalizing secrets, self-squeezing, tensing, tears) compacted into blank anxiousness. He could not open his mouth and speak in such a state of paralysis.

At such moments, words dropped out of his psychic universe, yet he did not stop searching for words. The more he lost the capacity to speak, the more intense became his struggle to find language. If he could not reach words through speech, he would reach them through writing. He fought madly to link words with states of being, and eventually, without planning to, Judd became a writer.

At first, poetry: Knots dissolved into streams of images, waves of words. Words came in the depths of solitude, as a paralysed person freely moves in water. Knots in his being were cocoons, out of which words crawled, slithered, flew, burst—dense, compacted, fists of feeling awaiting words to be released, to thaw.

And endless reading: Judd read for hours, day after day, his soul lifted by words. Words gave birth to him over and over. Words healed him, made him whole. Reading enabled him to touch the flow that swells within, as it pressed into words of its own. Reading was an adjunct to writing, although it worked both ways. He used words to open life. The squashed, sour life within found openings in words. The bitterness and joy that had no place found a place in words.

Writing was life. Writing gave access to streams of sensations, feelings, states of being. It provided being with special voices. That God said: let there be, and there was, refers to the power of the living Word. It is not that God created the universe (and us) with speech, but speech lifted creation (and us) to another dimension. Life is less and more than words. But there is no substitute for the openings that words provide. For one thing, the biblical creation myth refers to new possibilities of meaning inherent in all things, once speech and writing begins. Through language, all things are created anew.

For Judd, the gap between speaking and writing deepened. He could not get from one to the other without extreme difficulty, except when speaking with himself. But speaking to himself could only take him so far. As much as writing nourished him, he could not live on it alone, no matter how hard he tried. He knew that writing not only opened life but was a substitute for it. It gave him a safe haven, a place life could not invade—up to a point. Safety was illusory. Writing recoiled on itself. Even when alone, his voice began to sound farther and farther away.

He began to be preoccupied with a spirit sensation. His spirit lodged slightly off his body boundaries, somewhat inside–outside his skin. His spirit was a bit like rubber. It could stretch various ways. Sometimes it became a head above his head or a leg besides his leg. It could be high above and below and extended on the sides, or very near his body contours. He spent a great deal of time watching and sensing the rubbery shadow spirit take different shapes. He could feel the pull in different directions and worried lest it/he snap. Walking felt funny. It was odd to coordinate his actual body with his spirit body. He became unsure where to step. He watched himself come apart, as terror overwhelmed him.

Judd washed ashore in my office after several months in a hospital. We were quiet for a long time; I do not remember how speaking started.

"I can't be alone any more"—his voice cracked.

"Who can?"

He cried. "I don't think I can make it."

"Let's not worry about that now."

"I live in terror. I mean—terror is what there is, and I'm in it."

"Yes, terror is nearly everywhere."

"But there *are* spots without it, aren't there? Only, not for long, not for *me*."

"*Me* is very special."

"Yes, yes. Even if I can't make it, is not that true?"

"Yes, even if you can't make it."

Judd closed his eyes for a moment: a breath of peace. *Me* had uttered some words to me.

Empty and violent nourishment

Emptiness and violence can get so mixed up with nourishment that they can come to substitute for it. In a way, Freud (1937) conveyed this by asserting that every psychic act combines life and death work. If life and death drives fuse, death might seem nourishing because of its fusion with life (as life might be frightening because of its fusion with death).

If libido is part of every psychic act, everything is infused with some degree of pleasure. This can be horrifying, as the most ghastly destruction can have pleasurable elements.

Freud scandalized reason by suggesting that people clung to illness because it was secretly gratifying. People became ill because of something amiss with love and stayed ill because of hidden sources of love illness tapped.

Freud's view too easily degenerates into pre-Freudian moralism. The patient does not want to get better. The patient is a shirker, lazy, a malingerer, afraid of hard work, afraid of life. To what extent is one's desire on the side of life or death? If you want life, go for it: It is up to you. Such thinking is less than a step away from a control psychology: you can be in control, master of your ship—the very stance Freud ambivalently questioned.

Freud's challenge is more multilayered and difficult. We are in conflict with our life and death drives, which are partly antagonistic–cooperative with each other. Aliveness gets us in trouble. Fear, shame, guilt, caring tone us down. Sometimes we tone down too much. Death becomes more powerful than life prematurely. Once this process gathers momentum, crossing over from death to life can be nearly impossible. Nevertheless, the fact that death feeds on life can provide some ground for hope. It is always possible that life can find a helping hand, whatever the odds against it.

However, death processes can become so advanced that nourishing life elements become minimal. It can happen that death
begins feeding on death, once life asymptotically reaches a vanishing point. This approaches Bion's (1965, p. 101; Eigen, 1996)
formulation of a force that goes on working after existence, time,
and space have been destroyed. That is, destruction continues in
subzero dimensions, off the grid, after life is eaten away. Even in
such circumstances, help is sometimes possible.

The following diagram is meant as a visual aid rather than as
a model or anything formal. It brings home difficulties met in
working with empty violence and violent emptiness. It may have
some value as a shorthand summary of a personality nulling itself.

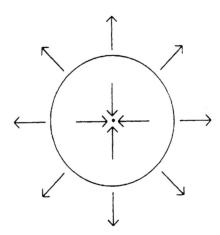

Vacuum–Evacuation Diagram

The arrows pointing away from the personality's perimeter
represent a centrifugal evacuative force. Anything that might
stimulate, support, or add to the richness of experience is evacuated before it gets in or before the core is touched. This includes
anything outside or inside the circumference that might increase
the appreciation of reality.

The arrows pointing towards the centre represent a centripetal
movement towards or into vacuum. Whatever escapes evacuative
tendencies gets whisked into the vacuum–void. The point at the
centre expresses "contradictory" possibilities. It is the vanishing

point, emotional minimum, maximum denudation, a singularity in the black hole.

One can imagine times in which the entire circle (personality)—including all evacuative tendencies—is sucked into the point at the centre. The entire personality or self vanishes. Imagine self as a collapsing star, forming a black hole, drawn into its singularity, nothing left but a naked singularity, disappearing in a luminous flash.

To speak of time is poetic license, since time–space become infinitely distorted in the formation of the black hole and even more so as the hole is pulled into its singularity. One may disappear through the point and emerge in other universes, into less or more inimical space–time possibilities. One may explode into nothing, "create" a new universe, mutate into who knows what, fizz out as infinite density and diffusion become indistinguishable. All of these are expressive of what people go through.

The point may be infinitely sensitive and/or infinitely numb, and *the person is trapped outside and inside himself: outside the circle, and inside the point.*

Coreen was trapped outside herself. She had a point of consciousness far outside the boundaries of her personality, dissociated from herself. At the same time her personality kept collapsing, emptying, and she was trapped inside the vanishing point, the centre of the black hole. She contracted to a point of infinite density, ever on the verge of infinite diffusion.

There were times when she travelled through her vanishing point, surfacing in other worlds. She intermittently found new circumstances and started life over. But it did not take long for each situation to collapse–explode.

New groups she joined asked her to leave because she became so difficult. She degenerated into a sort of singularity tolerating no space around or within.

A few seconds with her seemed forever, so intense was the pressure her personality exerted—compressed control . . . demand . . . accusation . . . angry need . . . massive deprivation. One feared not only being swallowed up, but being caught in a warp, bent out of shape, swirling in a breakdown with never-ending twists. Whatever one offered became part of the vacuum.

Judd's longing was more accessible, his breakdown more private. He was able to use others as support in the face of breakdown. His tone and touch lacked the barbed-wire element of Coreen's, although he ripped himself inside. He seemed less interested in controlling others than in being touched by them. His longing for heart-to-heart contact was closer to the surface, although that could be controlling too.

Judd, too, vanished outside and inside himself, but a heart-point remained—a more naked, unprotected desire, tinged with kindliness (a very selfish kindliness, perhaps). Once gripped by words, like Narcissus by liquid reflection, a mutation occurs. Words open alternate realities that may be disastrously alienating, but they may also preserve the feelings they mute and mask. Judd clung to words as a substitute for people and experienced madness. But his words grew out of feelings and, partly, led back to them in altered form. Judd's breakdown led him to help, where words can function as a bridge and extend the range of feelings, not merely propel him to outer space. Once words and psychosis take their bite, one can never be the same. But if help is possible, enough riches lie ahead to make the journey worth while.

Judd's family life almost caricatured the traditional family. His father's love was harsh and mushy—quasi-violent outbursts mingled with self-pitying appeals for confessions of boundless love. His mother was patient, soft, covertly anxious, a relatively soothing presence compared to his father.

Still, his mother had worked when Judd was young, and the piercing pain of her morning good-byes never left him. He pretended to be a big boy, not to care, but he cared immensely. He was less lonely when she was at home, but by the time he was in his teens his loneliness became acute. Nothing filled it, except for moments. Odd to say, her basic goodness supported his loneliness—that is, she was good enough to enable his loneliness to bloom.

Rageful outbursts (father) and patient soothing (mother) mixed in the palette of his emotional substratum. Both parents were devoted in their ways, although Judd was stung and paralysed by paternal egocentricity and maternal selflessness. Without realizing it, he grew up loved but unseen. His father justified his outbursts by appeals to his limitless love. His mother made Judd feel she understood him, when in fact she substituted her loving image of her good son for the nasty/ok reality he was gradually losing. As time went on, he mainly knew himself when he was quiet, when he was not there enough to be fused with the imaginary son of their devotion. His mother worried that he thought too much, when he was simply emptying himself in a place her love could not find.

Judd's detour to find himself was a long, hard one, through colour, forms, words, breakdown. In the end, the warm longing that drove him mad saved him, for it made him accessible. He was floridly psychotic, with a heart that longed for life. Coreen was too wry and scorching to allow simple, dumb longing to surface. There was nowhere for it to incubate in childhood. Perhaps she mocked it from the outset. Perhaps her mother was too icy and cutting to stimulate and support it. She knew emptiness and loneliness, of course. But that warm stretching from the soul's fingertips did not have a chance.

Judd's parents lived from the heart, in limited, injurious ways, Coreen's more from the head, critical, stabbing, self-servingly objective. Coreen began with a bigger map of the world than Judd, but Judd inhabited his little bit of life more fully. Coreen's existence shrank in astronomical inversion of her mind's picture of what *her* life ought to be, while Judd expanded to fill the bushel he feared beyond his reach.

CHAPTER NINE

Shadows of agony *X*

George

George is dead, anxious, and intensely alive. He is all of these at once. He wants help because he cannot bear being so dead and anxious. He is unable to speak in public. He goes through agonies trying to open his mouth and make sounds come out: "I feel I have something to say. Something forms in me, builds. I believe in it. It is my truth. But as I try to speak my truth in a group, I go blank, numb with panic, nothing comes out. It's humiliating. I can't move. My tongue is frozen. It's like making in my pants as a child, sitting in invisible humiliation. Can't people see the panic?"

He does not have much trouble speaking with me. He describes paralysis well. But I see signs of it in his face, which seems semi-immobilized with tension, gripped too tightly, something in his head contracted like tight sphincters. He is lean, tight, tense.

His father was a successful writer and lecturer, his mother a chaotic therapist. His father was orderly, warm, but away much of the time and personally distant. His was the warmth that self-contained, reflective people sometimes have—real but measured, not wild or bubbly. His mother was wild but cold, domineering, pressing. She came at him with the full force of her being—chaotic, wilful, demanding, clawing at him with diffuse, insistent needs.

When George came to therapy, he associated his deadness with a brother who had died in childhood. Although his brother had died of an illness that had nothing to do with George, he identified with his dead brother, felt guilty for living, that he ought to be dead, he mimicked deadness. The survivor's guilt is very real. I suspect all of us have survivor's guilt, aware of those who did not make it, of aspects of ourselves that died as well.

George grapples with the survivor's guilt that scars him, but he has gone back to earlier, harder-to-reach sources of agony too. In today's session he finds a breast stuffing him with suffocation. "It's more than not being able to breathe at the breast. The breast itself fed me suffocation. It's difficult to imagine my mother just offering me her milk, letting her milk be something I could get. Her milk was something she had to put into me, stuff into me, choke me with. She needed to put herself into me, stuff herself into me. She couldn't leave room for me. She didn't know what it might be like to let me have my fill, to let me drink for myself with her help. It wouldn't be enough to support my need for a good feed, to help me do it. What was most important was not my getting milk from her, but her putting stuff into me. She somehow felt confirmed by trying to stuff me with herself. I was drowning at the breast."

George repeated the last phrase. I could feel the drowning. His whole body, face, mouth seemed to me a compressed asshole mouth—tight, rigid, partly suffocating, but also very tight to keep out the suffocation. It was as if he tightened his mouth, the skin on his face, his entire being, to fight off the suffocation. His being contracted to a point that could not drown.

"My mother had energy, noise. I couldn't hear myself with her. My voice got drowned out. Now I feel I couldn't hear my own screaming. My screams got drowned out by her noise, her invasion. My thoughts get drowned out in the inside world. Nothing can build if everything keeps drowning, suffocating. The only thing that survives is visceral, touch, fluttering heart feelings, visceral anxiety storms—they survive. The rest is momentary, gone as soon as I engage in it."

On the one hand, a hole the mind vanishes through; on the other, a teat stuffing it with suffocation and drowning: vanishing–stuffing, emotional storms, gasping, stiffening ... rigid funnel mouth, hard shell of teat, cavity breast—everything gets lost. Such is the situation George finds in the session today. He follows the thread of agony to this moment, this hell. Is it a construction, fantasy, something he made up? Whatever it is, it is real. In one form or another, it haunts his life on a daily, hourly basis. He has never quite expressed his hell this way before, but the feelings are familiar. They've tormented him since the birth of memory, as if the agony awaited his birth, needing him to slip into it.

George has a fairly successful life. His work is meaningful, he writes, he loves his wife and children, he shares intense moments with friends. He is in love with creativity and feels most free writing, immersed in currents of language, struggling with life's mysteries. He rarely feels merely dead or anxious then. Even when dealing with dread and deadness in his work, creativity lifts him beyond them. Creative work brings him to a place that is meaningful and alive, not imprisoned by the lifelessness and the numbing panic that so readily oppress him. He writes in private what he dare not speak in public—what he cannot think in public.

Even when not writing, George has many alive, meaningful moments. His friends move him. Literature moves him. His children open his heart to new levels of being. He is deeply connected with his wife. He is alive to the flow of daily events—a joyful or poignant moment with his children, a fleeting contact at a party, a chance remark by his wife, a face that rivets him. Moments of heightened reality in everyday life touch him. His complaint is that they vanish as if they did not happen, almost. They leave him virtually the same as before—empty, tense, panicky, blank.

He feels it ought not to be this way. He ought to be able to speak, think, build more than he has. He ought to be able to make more of an impact. Blankness tortures him. The fact that he has built a family, profession, a way of life fail to impress him. He feels as if he has failed to build himself—that something in himself has remained mute, stillborn, rigid, vacant. In spite of his capacity for intense feeling and love of language, there is some devastating way he fails to feel himself. He slips away from himself, cannot feel his impact on himself or others.

"In therapy I go into the water. But I don't get baptized, reworked. I stay under. I'm underwater, and then I leave. I suppose it's some kind of Buddhist state, and I don't even know it. Psychotherapy is throwing water on a drowning man. Sometimes I think you have something up your sleeve, an incantation, mouth-to-mouth resuscitation. I think you'll find some way to offset the despair, hopelessness—because I'm totally lost. With Zen there's some kind of freedom through the nothing. This nothing doesn't offer that kind of thing. Are you afraid of talking against that background of nothing? You're afraid of saying anything, because you can't say anything that helps?"

For a moment, I was not sure whether George was speaking about himself or me. Was I too quiet? Did he take my silence as a token of despair? It came to me to say: "You said you became this blank inversion of nothing to save yourself from your mother's everything."

"So it's not the genes? I don't have a gene for this kind of nothing?"

Was he being sarcastic? Mordant? Making fun of me?—"A nothingness gene". Why speak at all, if it comes down to a nothingness gene. But even nothing needs development.

Even if it is a gene, the *living* of whatever is possible is up to us.

"Foolish heart words, beginnings of something. Flood washes them out, heart drowns", he mumbles: mother's flood, blank heart fluttering, visceral fright—blank with fright. His blank emotionality mimics the mother flood, a version of her in him, coupled with toxic paralysis, partial soul rupture. He values the flood that infuriates him, that blanks him out. Without this ghastly feed, there might be a worse nothing, although his nothing is bad enough, plenty to torture him for a lifetime. His nothing keeps him alive in a blank state, a dead, panicky state.

Near the end of the session George partly rises out of this state by mocking it. Something happens that allows him to vent his bitterness in a semi-superficial way. My office is on the first floor. The window is slightly open to let in air. George hears someone

sneeze outside and blow his nose. I did not hear it but fully believe him.

"That was great!" he exclaims. "Someone just blew their nose.
That says it all. It had a nice sound to it. Sums it up." (Pause.)

"Sucking a breast with a stuffed nose", I say.

"That's how I feel when I try to speak and can't. Not being
able to breathe while I suck at the teat of thought. It's a form of
speech. Gasping is a form of speech. The stuffed nose gets into
your cells. You get trained, repeated stuffedness. You stay stuffed
everywhere and can't find it."

Gasping substitutes for speech, holding back instead of letting
out, a kind of frozen shock (an eternal inhale or stoppage of
breathing) pre-empts spontaneous in–out flow. For a moment
George imagines what it feels like not to be stuffed. There *are*
moments when one breathes easily. How good those moments
are! How rare they seem to George! He almost always feels
stuffed, rarely breathes freely. I wonder how many people are
suffocating without knowing it.

I think of Frank McCourt's (1996, p. 103) description of his
father sucking the snot out of baby Michael's nose, so the child
can breathe. The family had already lost three children. An ill
baby brought death near. For the moment, the drunken father
freed the family from death—a moment all can breathe. George's
psyche, mind, soul—clogged, needing a father to suck it clear:
Was I up to the task? He was waiting.

The next week one of George's friends killed himself, after
having been on the brink of suicide many years. His friend's family was riddled with mental illness, addiction, and recent parental
deaths. Yet his friend had always been a voice for life. His friend
had no trouble speaking out, siding with underdogs, trying to
make life better for those he touched. He seemed to have boundless energy and ability in the face of fathomless depression.
George often spoke with admiration about his friend's dedication,
assertiveness, faith. His friend was an inspiring presence.

As the session went on, I found myself wondering why one
person survives and another does not. Surely, the pain of many
who live is no less than that of many who do not. Was George's
pain less than his friend's—was mine? I do not think so. I doubt,
too, that his friend's tolerance for pain was less, since he had

tolerated excruciating pain for many years. Nor was it a difference of ability to metabolize pain, since the psychic pain George
complained about was stuck, imponderable, immovable. Finally, I
asked George why he thought he lived and his friend died. What
he said surprised me.

"Playing guns as a kid. Running around shooting, getting
shot. Killing, getting killed. It was great. We couldn't get enough
of it." He went on to add that years of sports took up where guns
left off. Playing, playing, playing—hard and long. Using his body,
using everything he had to the limit, beyond the limit, total exer-
tion, competition, body on body. It gave him an enduring sense of
pleasure and power outside the pain, a full, abiding joy outside
the depressive pull. As long as he could use himself, he would
not drown forever.

Something in his body and body soul gave George pleasure
and satisfaction. His cells knew pleasurable aliveness, intense
aliveness, not only nothingness and suffocation. At the same time,
I wondered whether George might not be more outside himself,
more detached than his friend. George possessed a certain distance from himself and his experience, even in the midst of pain.
He made his distress an object of observation and found words to
describe it. To see and speak or write his pain was second nature
by now. He almost automatically created a circuit from pain to
printed page, from vacant, piercing pain to me, his wife, his
friends, his journal.

George complained about seeing himself and his pain from
the other end of a telescope, even when drowning. He lost imme-
diacy as fast as it came, a chronic out-of-body viewing of self that
was maddening. He was intensely inside and outside himself at
the same time. George could be cut off–immersed, alive–numb
together. This capacity tormented him but, I suspect, also provided checks and balances, albeit painfully.

His friend relied more on drugs than words to work with his
feelings, although he was good with words when it came to helping others. He worked at getting others to incorporate and move
past what bothered them. He tried to do for others what he could
not do for himself. In fact, he did not work with his own feelings
so much as try to mute or dampen or get away from them. In
spite of his competence and ability to speak, he remained pro-

foundly resourceless in his solitude. He found no bearings in the nest of self. Whatever was wrong with George in public, he had a feast of self in private. He transcended the flood, undertow, and tormenting suffocation in solitary reverie. George's torments became raw material for his work.

Thus George had resources inside and outside his lived body, beyond the depressive pull. The immense pleasure of playing at killing and being killed as a child, followed by years of sports, left a residue of strength and heightened élan that depressive pain could not take away. At the same time the pleasures as well as the agonies of detachment mingled with immersion to keep the potato-chip quality of life going. Pain could not kill curiosity and wonder—including ghastly wonder at this condition.

Years of overmedication and drugs took a toll on George's friend, blunting the hunger an agonized consciousness has for life. George's hunger for life was keen as ever, in spite of his mind's hole and incessant frustration. Perhaps the hole that caused pain provided an outlet as well—since pain vanished in its source, like everything else. The very vanishing George could not stand provided some protection. If his friend had a hole that let pain in and out, it was saturated with drugs and medicines. There was no place his friend could vanish psychically. The area of disappearance was filled with drug states. There was no place to go but out. It is important to be able to disappear in the midst of pain, even if disappearance is painful too.

Agony X

Winnicott (1989, pp. 119–129) writes that we seek our madness as well as our normalcy—that, in fact, we seek our madness in order to be normal. Our trying to be normal is plagued with a sense of underlying madness or madness at the borders. If we fail to address deep madness, life may feel unreal.

Winnicott doubts that the original madness can ever be reached. It would be too painful to bear and, in fact, we lack the equipment to bear it. We were unable to bear it when it happened, and we are unable to bear it now. We simply have not evolved the capacity to experience the worst—not fully, unabatedly. As infants we try to avert our gaze when we do not like what we see or when we have had too much. All through our lives also we avert our inner gaze when confronted with too much to bear.

A primal response to too much pain or horror is to scream and lose consciousness. One screams in response to pain, but as screaming goes on it blots pain out. If screaming goes on overly long, it can substitute for pain. One screams and screams and screams until agony, rage, panic become a blur. At first, feeling and screaming are one. Feeling translates into screaming and sometimes vice versa: one screams what one feels and feels what one screams. Screaming may bring a loved one or care-taker, someone who tries to help. But sometimes it fails to do so. If it chronically fails to do so, screaming becomes empty. It does not meet with confirmation. It is a scream in the void. The scream becomes a void. It becomes a way of voiding feeling. Eventually, screaming substitutes for feeling.

In one or another form, one can go on screaming all one's life as a substitute for feeling. But it also is possible that screaming dies out. A person's capacity for feeling may die out with it (Bion, 1970, pp. 12–15; Eigen, 1998, chapter 3).

One may scream oneself into a stupor or loss of consciousness. Or, to a variable extent, one may lose consciousness in the face of unbearable agonies with or without screaming. In an earlier work (Eigen, 1986, Chapter 3) I described states of numbing, stupor, and blanking out in response to ghastly agonies. In literature, sleep is often portrayed as a response to pain (e.g. Faust's merciful sleep after provoking Marguerite's suicide, in Goethe's *Faust*). Many suspect that the sleepiness of analysts in sessions attempts to diminish the impact of painful experiences and is not only a consequence of having to remain physically inactive.

One becomes scarred not only by pain, but by one's response to the latter. If one's scream becomes meaningless, one's response to what bothers one becomes meaningless. If one chronically suffers loss of consciousness in the face of unrelievable agony, the capacity to respond to what bothers one can suffer grave lacunae or even fail to develop.

As time goes on, we respond to unexperienceable madness by nibbling at its corners. We experience bits of agony X in muted forms. Winnicott lists a number of abbreviated psychotic anxieties, such as disintegration, unreality feelings, falling forever, lack of relatedness, depersonalization or lack of psychosomatic cohesion, to name a few (1989, pp. 127–128). Through partial or derivative psychotic anxieties we get a glimpse or hint or taste of what originary madness might be like. If we see God through a glass darkly, we also see original madness through shadow dreads.

In order to experience original madness as such, we would have to be defenceless, yet aware. We would have to be strong enough to endure pure horror without distorting our experience of the latter by defending ourselves against it. We would have to experience what deforms us without being deformed: we would have to experience what we cannot experience.

It may be that original madness is an hypothesis of a pure state, like Galileo's hypothesis of a vacuum. It guides us in our thinking about reality, without necessarily being real itself. Imaginative hypotheses of ideal states may help us actually see what *is* there. Nevertheless, the hypothesized original madness—whatever it is—*may* be real, all too real. Winnicott believes it functions as a background reality that exerts claims on our attention, whatever our foreground reality may be.

Therapy provides a chance to dip into original madness in manageable doses. Winnicott (1989, pp. 128–129) envisions going through bits of madness and repeatedly making spontaneous recoveries. It is crucial that the therapist does not try to "push" the patient into "sanity" and disrupt what needs to happen. The therapist needs to help the individual find his own rhythm and way of going in and out of what bothers him.

George's inability to speak in groups and blank anxiety were frozen agonies he could communicate. The more he got into them, the more they led to agonies he could not communicate—unspeakable agonies. The first steps in therapy were relatively easy, painful as they were. First, George spoke of a circumscribed deadness alternating with intense aliveness. It did not take long for him to associate deadness with the death of a sibling. His tongue was a tombstone; his dead brother was the deadness within. As he went into *that* agony (agonizing deadness associated with dead brother), more global, inchoate agonies appeared.

Emotional storms precipitated by invasive maternal chaos turned into a permanent blank, panicky paralysis.

A stiffness and tightness frequently characterized George's physiognomy, skin tone, posture. He was stiff and tight not only because he was his brother's corpse. He chronically stiffened in the face of mother's emotional storms. He was not simply dead in the midst of these storms. He was petrified. As therapy went on, what had first appeared as deadness became blank terror. George felt fringes of an icy chaos that once were arms that held him, nipples he sucked, air he breathed. It was difficult enough to stay with frozen chaos connected with envisioned maternal storms. Still, the terrifying mother he grabbed on to with his mind was but a portion of the unbounded, unimaginable agony that at one time was his world.

Mother was not always terrifying. She could be terribly gratifying as well. She had calm, loving, caring, softer moods. George was not one thing. He had a varied emotional world. So did his mother. But the X that brought him to therapy was an unrelenting agony connected with somewhat definable distant agonies, fading into boundless agony beyond conception.

What is the point of dipping into and staying with tributaries of agony X? Results of this work sometimes seem slim. One problem is that understanding—even genuine emotional understanding—does not do the trick. Understanding has its uses. It helps provide provisional frames of reference so that the individual may feel somewhat more oriented in his emotional universe. This may help a person to get his bearings in the ins and outs of daily life. But this very orientation can be a source of frustration if it promises more than it can deliver. Very often a person understands the reasons for his deadness or anxiety while remaining dead and anxious. He can function better given his disability, but paralysis or lack of feeling torments him still.

George's early complaint of deadness shifted. He was not dead—he was paralysed. "Part of me is so paralysed, frozen. Another part is so intense, exuberant." The shift came about, partly, by repeated focusing on his state, getting into the agony, staying with it over time. As he stayed with it, it began to shift. It remained an agony, but with a shade of difference. In therapy, he maintained as much contact with it as he could take. He kept describing it, speaking from it, letting it speak. He had twin emotional states: intense aliveness–intense paralysis.

The time came when I mistakenly called the paralysed part a dead part, and he corrected me. "It's not dead. It's still a feeling, a crippled state, not a dead state. You can't speak but have a beehive of thoughts going on in your brain, and it causes incredible stress on your body. My body's defeated most of the time, struggling to do something about it, get past it, pushing at it. I am like a stone someone's trying to talk to, but not a dead stone. My body's caught between animate–inanimate. My brain is caught between animate–inanimate. I'd like to be able to break out of the shell that forms at those moments, but it's too powerful, like an infection I don't have antibodies for, a virus in my brain."

Slim progress for over five years' work? George's life was going fairly well, whatever his problems: rich marriage, family, work, friendships. He was leading a good life, a decent life, a full life. It is likely that without therapy George's life would have contracted, if not capsized. It would almost surely have been more severely embattled from the incessant inner strain he supported. Therapy gave him a place he could talk his guts out, give voice to the ghastly agony he lived with, without fear of being talked out of it, or causing damage, or overburdening a relationship. Therapy did not undo his suffering but helped hold his place while he struggled with his pain. It helped him find strength and ability to keep at it and live to the best of his ability.

There were moments the veil lifted. Sadly, his friend's funeral was one of them. George spoke strongly, movingly, well. He said what was in his heart, his mind. His problem was never about having heart and mind. It was about expressing them in public. I suspect wrestling with his agony in sessions prior to the memorial service played a role in his speaking.

"At the memorial talk some vague sense of Barry's [his dead friend] spirit gave me courage. This is the least I could do, given the torture he went through. For two days I was obsessed, fearful about speaking up, but if I didn't do it I couldn't live with myself. People said I spoke with great eloquence and deep feelings. It surprised me."

"Death drove you to it", I said.

"Death drove me to it", George repeated softly. "I knew there was an expectation that people who knew Barry would say something. I was one of the first. If I waited too long, the endometriosis of my brain would do its strangling thing. I thought out what I wanted to say, went over it in my mind a few times. But the actual saying of it—I didn't know if or how the speaking would happen. I could open my mouth and there would be nothing or incoherent stammering or awkward jumbles. So often my mouth tries to open and there are only chaotic knots. But words came as I felt them. Thoughts and feelings spoke themselves. Now Barry's like a dream. A short time in the grave, and he's like a dream. I thought I heard his voice the other day when I was working. Maybe I'm breaking down. Maybe I can collect disability and spend my days listening to music, reading, writing. I don't know. Maybe something *is* happening. Yet I feel I'm barely keeping it together."

Was the fruit of five years of agonizing therapy that went nowhere a terrific ten-minute talk at a memorial service? Would he have made the same terrific talk without therapy? Was therapy worth the time, if it dropped through the hole George could not climb out of? Would feeling agony get anywhere other than feeling agony?

George's thoughts and feelings might keep disappearing through the hole in his agony. But some of the fury, chaos, controllingness, and emotional noise loosened its grip. There were moments, both in therapy and in public, when his voice rang out like a bell—few and far between, perhaps, but not non-existent, not insignificant. They were reference-point moments, moments of possibility. Together, they challenged the choked, stuffed, strangled state. Staying close to the agony had its own kind of purity. The agony cut a path through suffocation, pierced him, kept piercing him. Breath goes through the opening, in and out. The joy of speaking through the agony makes a very special sound.

CHAPTER TEN

Soundproof sanity and fear of madness

Winnicott (1965, 1974) suggests that fear of breakdown draws on breakdowns suffered by the individual before the latter could process or remember them. The breakdown feared already happened. Winnicott depicts the infant as overwhelmed by states too much for it. The infant's environment cannot protect it from overstrain, and the person carries the imprint of being broken in infancy.

Although the original breakdown occurred too early to be processed and remembered, it can, partly, be recaptured in current dreads of breakdown or in semi-breakdown experiences that beset life. It can also be relived in psychotherapy in semi-tolerable doses.

In a somewhat later formulation (1989, pp. 119–129), Winnicott takes this theme further and writes that the breakdown occurred before it could be experienced; he goes on to suggest that it can never be fully experienced. He postulates a madness that always remains somewhat out of reach, but which we cannot stop trying to reach. His locution shifts from fear of breakdown to fear of madness (although both phrases are used).

In an especially telling passage (in an especially telling essay), Winnicott (1989, p. 128) wonders whether it would not be useful to use the symbol X to suggest the madness at issue. A possible scenario is that faulty environmental functioning allowed an external factor to impinge on the infant before the infant could manage it. In a way, this is a very sketchy, inadequate notion, since all of us live through so much that is unmanageable. Nevertheless, Winnicott focuses on a particular moment in the face of the unmanageable, a moment in which the individual is threatened with going under and does go under. What is uncanny about this loss of mind, psyche, self is that the "experience" involves a loss of the capacity to experience. The individual cannot experience the loss of experience because the capacity to sustain such experiencing has not yet developed.

The core of madness is not encompassed by even the most ghastly nameable agonies. For Winnicott, the madness he points to is so much worse because it occurred while the personality was beginning to form, a time too early to organize, hold, and experience what was or was not happening. As one grows, defences organize around this point of madness, which one sometimes glimpses in disorganizing moments. One of Winnicott's most striking remarks is that the madness that cannot be experienced is what is most personal to the individual: "What is absolutely personal to the individual is X" (1989, p. 128).

Life and therapy provide momentary glimpses of X, but only for split-seconds, since defences quickly organize around such openings or pulsations:

> In the simplest possible case there was therefore a split second in which the threat of madness was experienced, but anxiety at this level is unthinkable. Its intensity is beyond description and new defenses are organized immediately so that in fact madness was not experienced. Yet on the other hand madness was potentially a fact. [1989, p. 127]

Some of Bion's (1970) evocations of nameless dread hover over Winnicott's unthinkable agonies, associated with madness X, a most personal potential fact. Winnicott lists a number of ghastly states available to us, which point to the original madness as pale reflections. Included in his list are disintegration, unreality feelings, lack of relatedness, depersonalization, lack of psychosomatic cohesion, split-off intellectual functioning, falling forever. He includes, also, the experience of ECT with generalized panic. He might have added the horrible screaming when fear of dying (loss of psychosomatic being) is one with the loss of consciousness in insulin coma therapy, as the individual fades in and out of consciousness (aliveness). Any of us can add our favourite horrors.

Winnicott lists these as hints of what the original breakdown or madness or X might be like, if we could experience it. They are images seen in a glass darkly, shadows on the cave, derivatives, muted intimations, terrible as they are. In one or another way, they—or agonies like them—are facts we organize ourselves around or against, but, in one form or another, they make themselves known or felt, and we live in fear of them.

An individual who is not too badly broken can go through life dealing with X innuendoes well enough much of the time. Nevertheless, a reliable sub-population in clinical work involves individuals who have gone through life confidently only to begin suffering enormous panic or obsessive ideas or paranoid anxieties, to the point of near-paralysis. Such people often say, "I've always been the strong one, the one others relied on. I've never had problems like this before." X is totally alien, has no meaning. Another reliable sub-population bathes in some version of X. Self-assurance or X-free moments are inconceivable. These individuals are used to hellish torment. For them, it is difficult to attribute meaning to anything but profiles of X.

In either case, Winnicott suggests some spontaneous rhythm of dipping in and out of X has been lost or never established. In his recommendations for clinical technique, Winnicott warns against trying to get the patient to be sane or short-circuiting tastes of X. He, rather, envisions an attitude that allows the madness to be undergone in such a way that spontaneous recovery is possible. As this happens, one gets a sense or "feel" for going in and out of X offshoots naturally, as part of life. This is different from the prevailing attitude that madness X ought not be part of life, and that one should be able to find a way of living without it. It also differs from the belief of some in touch with agony X that life outside it must be phoney.

To summarize a movement in Winnicott's thinking about fear of breakdown/madness:

1. Fear of breakdown refers to a breakdown that happened long ago, in infancy. It can be experienced but not remembered. It is recoverable by experiencing breakdown moments in therapy. It is not a matter of recovering repressed memories, but living in the present bits of what could not be organized enough to be repressed.

2. Since breakdown occurred while personality was forming, one did not have capacity even to experience what was happening. One lacked ability or equipment to undergo original madness as it occurred. One could not be present at one's undoing. The intensity was too much to bear. One would have to experience breakdown of life, mind, self, psyche before one could be there long enough to experience it. Yet an underlying sense of what one dare not, could not tolerate experiencing remains as a defining fact, all the more powerful as a potential fact.

3. What is absolutely personal to the individual (original madness X) is always out of reach. This astonishing statement has at least two parts: (a) what is most personal is originary madness, X; (b) X is always out of reach somewhat. One might envision X akin to a Platonic form, instead of or in addition to ideal Goodness, ideal Madness. Or one may imagine X as Galileo postulates an ideal vacuum in which to measure the rate of falling bodies. For Winnicott, it was a defining potential fact, very real, possibly the most real and personal X about an individual.

Madness became central to Winnicott's thinking as his work evolved (1989, pp. 482–492; 1971, pp. 73–77, 87). He risked remarks he feared made him seem mad to patients (and himself?), and he felt good about winning a measure of useable madness. He suggested that therapy could ward off the feared madness and still achieve benefits, but a deep sense of something wrong or off might be missed. He had the ability to immerse himself in the reality he was trying to "describe", "find", "create" during the period of writing. His essays bear the imprint of this immersion, so that the deep reality of moment becomes a central, defining fact.

Madness is a theme he returns to repeatedly, its central significance gathering momentum over time, until unknowable X (original madness) becomes pivotal—what is absolutely personal to a psychoanalyst who was always concerned with the roots of the personal.

One wonders what relationship unknowable X may have to Winnicott's formulations concerning the "incommunicado self", the most personal core of an individual that must not be violated, the point of no compromise. I do not believe that Winnicott explicitly linked and developed these themes in his published writings. The term, "private madness" (used by Khan and Green in various ways), takes on added import when linked with Winnicott's assertion that original, unknowable, unexperienceable madness, X, is what is absolutely personal in an individual.

In good psychoanalytic fashion and in practical, clinical terms, Winnicott portrays a double movement in development and therapy. He writes that a compulsion to get to X arises out of "some basic urge . . . towards becoming normal" (1989, p. 126). The need to move towards X "is slightly more powerful than the need to get away from it. The individual is forever caught up between the fear of madness and the need to be mad." For Winnicott it is important not just to analyse defences, but to taste the madness anxiety the latter cluster around and try to bind. Moreover, he asserts that there is a drive or compulsion or urge to get to the unexperienceable X, as well as fearful movement away from it. The individual eventually may become more adept at working with and making room for both tendencies. Becoming a partner with this double capacity is not forced, since growth of a spontaneous rhythm is at stake.

Winnicott (1989, p. 126) writes that cure only comes if the person "reaches to the original state of breakdown", the core anxiety around which defences are organized and reorganized. This is an ambiguous statement, and for present purposes I am tentatively taking it as written—reaching to, not reaching. The individual moves in dual directions, towards–away, incessantly, forever. Winnicott places greater weight on "towards" as a motor in therapy and life, but both are heavily weighted. One somehow feels what health would be like if going through original madness were possible. One settles for towards, but there is something in reaching towards that tastes of life in the goal region.

Note that Winnicott asserts that the individual reaches for what is absolutely personal, original madness, X—which, I sense, must somehow be related to the precious, sacred core of self, the incommunicado, inviolable core. Winnicott advocates a necessary reaching towards original madness at the roots of the personal. He advocates this as part of a therapy relationship, just as the madness originally arose within a relationship at the beginning. The madness we ran away from near the outset we gingerly reach towards through therapy, both tendencies omnipresent. I believe we exist to support and aid development of the personal, inviolable core, so interfused with X that we would be kidding ourselves to think we live outside the latter.

A clinical implication and a partial truth for living is that we need to be in touch with original madness in order to feel real. One of Winnicott's primary clinical preoccupations involved discovering–creating conditions that enabled individuals to feel more real and alive. In his fear of breakdown/fear of madness papers, written towards the end of his life, he suggests that reaching towards X is part of what makes one feel more alive and real.

It is part of Winnicott's creative ambiguity that we need a touch of madness to feel alive. Yet part of our mad core, an unreachable X we are driven to try to reach, is the result of unfathomable devastation that hit as we were forming, a traumatic state that can leave us feeling dead and damaged.

X and toxic nourishment

We do not know what X is. We can neither experience nor know it. We postulate it as a potential fact, yet also as a reality we grow around, with, through. It may be viewed as an ideal pole or limit, like total chaos or nothingness. It determines a vector of experience, a sense of something breaking through, something collapsing, associated with unbearable, unthinkable agonies. So it is not simply a blank state, but heavily valenced with terror. While functioning always as a potential or virtual reality, it is clear that for Winnicott it is a fact of life—terribly real, a basic fact that permeates and shapes experience.

X and one's ways of relating to X may be terrible facts that can become more or less malignant and poisonous, a deforming state of affairs. Let us say, a meteor from outer space lands and causes a black winter of the soul, so that proper nourishment is not available. Suppose meteors land repeatedly, smashing different parts of the psyche. The craters are deep and lasting, but they are the least of the damage. Suppose these deforming meteors are chronic parts of the atmosphere we grow in, parts of everyday expectations that inform the colour and tone of awareness. Suppose a major portion of these impacts arise from those who care for us most, so that what deforms us is part of the atmosphere of intimacy. In such an instance, the crash that leads to loss of sunlight and food is also the source that sustains us, providing whatever nourishment is possible.

Intimacy simultaneously nourishes and poisons personality. Those closest to us, who support our growth, wound and warp us with deformations in their lives, personalities, selves. Toxins and nourishment are inextricably mixed in nearly all deep interactions. Yet no one would grow without intimacy. That we are nourished by a state of affairs that deforms and poisons is a difficult paradox of our existence. X is part of this state of affairs. X feeds and poisons the personality. One feeds off what one most dreads. This state of affairs can be more or less exaggerated and extreme. In many instances, the pressure of X and the conditions associated with the latter can lead to personalities that are mangled, suffocated, contracted, meanly or chaotically impulsive. Common language refers to someone being bent out of shape.

The pressure exerted by X and the damage resulting from unbearable, relentless X-impacts may intrude on an individual's awareness, so that a person actually *sees* horrifying twists and warps of self. There are individuals who can tell you they are poisoned–poisonous and, from moment to moment, tell you something about what the poison is doing, as lucidly as Socrates reports the progressive numbing of the hemlock. However, these individuals are not merely numbed by poisons—they are in ghastly pain and distress over their condition. It is pain and distress they have had to live with from an early age, and while they long to be rid of it, it is part of the milk of life. The madness they fear and fight and long to be rid of can disappear only if life disappears.

A taboo secret that stains human life is that madness is nourishing. Our question is not whether or not we will be mad or nourished by madness, but whether our dreaded, sought-for nourishment can be less lethal to us as individuals and groups. Is it possible to be less poisoned by what nourishes us? Is it possible to become less poisonous madmen–madwomen? Does our madness have to be poisoned–poisonous? To what extent, in what ways, can we achieve a measure of workable madness, a relationship with ourselves that is at once inspiring, supportive, a bit wise (not merely sane, which is also too destructive).

Soundproof rooms, steel plates: premature sanity

Wanda

Wanda had grown up in luxury, bathed with the good things of life. She was beautiful, ebullient, honest, had many friends, made a decent marriage, raised a family, loved her work. What bothered her?

She had a nagging feeling that she was missing something in life. The nagging feeling that something was off or missing took a long time to gather strength enough to compel attention. It followed her over the years and transiently bobbed up in the midst of pleasures, sorrows, joys. She shrugged it off, and it asked little of her. When I met her, it had become more of an irritant, but she found ways around it.

Therapy was supposed to be one of those ways. She would enter therapy, find what bothered her, emote, speak freely, and it would be gone. Unfortunately, therapy rarely works that way. It is a characteristic of the beast that the more one experiences in therapy, the more there *is* to experience. The capacity to experience grows, and with it, what *can* be experienced grows as well.

I suspect that Wanda was able to come in because the X that was off focused on her work. Therapy was palatable because the spotlight was not on her, but out there somewhat—a problem with working. Wanda was a writer but unhappy with herself as a writer. She did not become the writer she had hoped to be. She had thought she would be more creative. She imagined her writing deeper, fuller, more intense and telling that it was. She was best at light, casual pieces, smart and perky, for women's magazines and trendy issues.

For many years, success blinded her to her difficulty. She enjoyed the glitter, praise, ease. From time to time she would attempt something substantial, and she researched serious issues that mattered to her. But when she sat down to write, the quick-paced, bright, smart tone won out. The fact that people read and liked her work blunted the distress she felt because her work seemed superficial to her.

In therapy, she expressed her frustration at not being deeply creative. No matter how she tried, she could not break through. She felt a barrier like a steel plate inside her. She did enjoy being superficially creative. Writing came easily, if she did not try to go past the steel plate. Her writing flowed on the surface of the plate. It sparkled in its way. If she tried to go deeper, she crashed against steel.

Why not be satisfied with what she *could* do? Hers was not such a bad lot. She appreciated creativity, including her own. One participates in creative life as one is able. We are all at different levels, given gifts of various degrees and kinds. What is wrong with using, as best we can, what we *can* use? Many learn to work with materials they are able to work with and make the best of it. We cannot all be Saul Bellows or Sigmund Freuds.

Yes, but this is precisely what galled Wanda. She was not Emily Dickinson, not even Erica Jong. "Did you see Mary Gordon's piece on her mother this Sunday—in the *Times* magazine section?" Wanda said. "Now that's writing. I'd give anything to write like that. She made you feel something about life, something that matters." Yes, I had seen it. It grew from a world of feeling beneath the steel plate. How does one make experience–word connections in the flow beneath the steel plate?

Was the limit Wanda complained about final? Could she push its edges, open more? Would Wanda's pushing–opening simply make her better in the world above the plate, or would it take her to places she imagines she would like to go? Something was closed to Wanda and would not budge, but she could recognize the wished-for X in others.

Wanda's wealth and success brought her into contact with some of the creative people she admired. Her admiration had many edges. In some amusing or cutely fighting way, she would bring out lacks of those she looked up to, tearing them down as she praised them. Wanda was fun to be with up to a point, but if she looked up to you, watch out! You were liable to find yourself the butt of jokes in her articles, if not jabbed on the spot.

Wanda had a fighting manner of speaking, as if she pushed past a barrier to get the words out. Whom or what was she fighting? Was it only anger at limitations, fury at who she was not? Even her anger seemed small, as if her frame could not amplify it. At her worst, she did not get very scary. She was the cutely tight-fisted one, railing against something she could not fathom. She paced through emotions like a little soldier in a strange land threatening to swallow her up.

I took her feelings seriously—very much so—but felt that she expressed them in ways that others might not take so seriously. The sensation began growing in me that Wanda did not take herself seriously in some important way. She was a little girl fighting to be taken seriously, yet she failed to do so herself.

After Wanda conveyed her frustrations as a writer, she waded into difficulties with her family, focusing on an older brother. She recalled a scene in which her brother had tried to kill her. He had placed her in a dangerous situation, then walked away and watched. She saw him smile triumphantly as she struggled. His wicked expression cut her still. Someone helped her in time, but she was imprinted with a sense of helpless struggle in the face of death—a feeling she fought against. Part of the steel plate was a residue of frozen fighting against danger that transcended her.

She had gone through childhood playing and fighting with someone stronger than herself who wanted to kill her. This was her explanation for her insecurities, anger, over-readiness to fight.

She was determined not to give in to being small and powerless. In group situations, she often was unabashedly rivalrous and competitive, refusing to take a back seat. She enjoyed her triumphs, but she realized, as time went on, that she often silenced more talented group members and closed subtle developmental possibilities.

"I'm always shutting my brother up, refusing to give in to him, refusing to be weak. I'm not going to let him do me in. I'm not going to let his bullying get me down. I'm going to push past his wish to beat me. Sometimes I see myself being this way with people who aren't like my brother. It carries over. I get sharp, pushy, testy, brittle. I tell myself, Wanda, take it easy. You're with a nice person, someone you want to get closer to, someone with something to offer. Don't step on her. Don't squash her. I get sharp-edged and can't calm down. I can't help myself." At such moments, Wanda was cut short by her own personality, helpless in the face of herself. Enough of her survived to build a fine life. But she could not stop fighting to live, so that she could not let life support her.

She did not like to talk about her parents. She easily talked about her brother through angry tears. Her parents seemed more like craters, empty spots, although not, by any means, simply so. She had a hard time locating deep or intense feelings for her parents. She described her mother as a benign presence who went to charity affairs, helped the local library, and saw to it that things ran smoothly. "My mother was tall, lean, birdlike. She didn't fly but bounced from activity to activity, pecking here, there, never biting more than she could chew—a well-mannered bird with an eye for little things. She rarely tired. She wasn't a mother you could hold on to or who could hold you very long. She had quick, nervous energy, always finding things to do."

Her father spent his time overseeing the family fortune. He was polite, soft-spoken, kindly. He was not withdrawn or aloof so much as conscious of his power and authority and conscientious about its use. He preferred understatement to exuberance. His contact with the children took the form of family dinners and boat trips on vacations. Wanda enjoyed these trips. Her father loved his boat and shared his pleasure with family and friends.

On the boat, her father was relaxed, humorous, un-rushed, and the family felt his warmth in a more concentrated way. Yet even as Wanda spoke gratefully of intermittent good moments, she made it clear that neither parent offered much sustained contact—goodly people with much to do.

Wanda learned to make do with the warmth and good will her parents offered, but she was basically on her own. Her father was not around enough, and her mother could not sit still. No one had the time or the ability to listen carefully to her difficulties or even to notice them. Her parents provided a good shell and setting, with every advantage, and the children used it as they pleased or were able. There was plenty of help in the household to attend to the needs of the day.

She looked forward to her father's intermittent infusions of warmth and knew her mother took care of what needed taking care of. She learned from them to stay with the flow of the day, and things would take care of themselves. Be helpful and active. Her brother got somewhat more attention from father, in the hope that he would take over administration of the family estate someday. But this did little to offset the general brittleness and emptiness of their upbringing. In spite of her brother's show of strength, Wanda sensed that he was in trouble and that they were both in need.

As she grew, she felt herself becoming birdlike like her mother, warm like her father, but neither warmth nor activity was enough to offset the anxious anger that kept pressing through. It was difficult for Wanda to admit what she did not get from her parents, because they were kindly and helpful. They provided a good shell, but something at the centre was missing.

To some extent, their approach to children reflected an ideology. Parenting provided the chance to foster a child's sense of independence and responsibility. It was not that listening, warmth, or intense interactiveness was excluded—but it was secondary—not the point. The point was becoming good citizens, helpful people. The fierce inner contact needed for the writing Wanda wanted to do was not part of the universe she knew, nor did she find it in herself. Her parents did not seem to have an inkling how mad the real world of childhood was, and Wanda

SOUNDPROOF SANITY AND FEAR OF MADNESS 183

had a hard time finding categories for her mad experiences. Her parents' tolerant attitude suggested that whatever she felt was something that would pass. Childhood, after all, was a fleeting affair, a small affair, not to be taken too seriously. Someday she would be old enough to do as her parents and take her place in the world.

Childhood was something to be lived through on the way to becoming an independent, responsible adult. Not that childhood was to be got through as quickly as possible, or that there were no childhood pleasures—and not that childhood was only pleasurable. But the pain and difficulties of childhood would pass, and one would move on to what life was really about. While Wanda lived her childhood, she had already partly transcended it. Wanda developed a sense of independence from her childhood as she went through it. She could not simply be a child, as there was no one to simply be a child for.

Simply being a child plunged her into madness—the madness of life with her brother without adequate protection. The madness of life with her own private self, with no one to link up with. No one took her insecurities and anger seriously. The things that bothered her did not get a genuine hearing. They were to be transcended without much fuss, so that what was really important in life could be reached. Wanda was left with a private universe that had no intimate support, while her external life had more support than it needed. Her parents' warmth and concern lifted her up, while excluding *her* at the same time.

Wanda was in danger of excluding herself from her own life. Yes, she fought her brother, but she ended up fighting against childhood madness that had nowhere to go. She fought to be included everywhere. She could not take feeling unseen. She fought for visibility. But all the fighting made it difficult for the missing madness to become visible. It began to dawn on her that her life as a whole, successful as it was, was somehow mad. As much as she gained by fighting, a precious X eluded her. Something she longed for was lost.

How odd to long for madness—what a relief, to make it through childhood madness to adult sanity. Wanda grew up and survived her brother and their secret dangers. She survived feelings that had nowhere to go. She survived madness that had no markers. But the very act of survival left her with a sense of loss, something undone. Not until therapy, did her missing madness begin to find a voice.

Wanda did not act like a walled-off person, one living in a shell. She was involved with people, groups, activities. She was very alive—she loved life. But there was a shell within, and after much successful living it gradually caught up with her. She was walled off from herself, in spite of all the feelings she expressed. The time came when she could not stop sensing the wall, the shell, the steel plate, no matter where she was or what she did. No matter how happy, sad, angry—she saw the crater.

Everything she had did not make up for what she could not have—sustained emotional contact at the birth of life with those who loved her most. She found an inner place born in a barren crater, in spite of all evidence to the contrary, in spite of the genuine caring and warmth. Part of the madness of her upbringing was her parents' sanity. They were too sane for a child. Her craziness had nowhere to go. She lived it out with friends, with her brother, although he threw her back on herself. She developed "normally". But inside there was an unknown soundproof room in which emotions did not resonate, in which she could not hear or feel herself—so soundproof and invisible that she could not see or hear it. She did not know it was there and was not compelled to find it, until it began to void her life.

It was precisely by being successful that she began to feel she could not achieve the "right" success—she could not be successful in the way she really wanted. She must remain a superficial person if her deeper self disappeared in a soundproof room she could not enter, sealed in a seamless steel plate. She stared at her dropping-off point, the crater she grew up in. She began to feel that all her life an inner ear was quietly listening for echoes in the crater but she failed to hear the listening or, rather, failed to attend to it. It was like discovering an anti-universe or anti-life as a mirror image to the one she lived. To what extent could she sustain her embryonic double vision of the life she had and the life that did not have a chance. Could she hear the tuning fork in the soundproof room?

Hyacinth

In trying to convey his sense of reaching towards madness X—a potential fact, not experienced, but absolutely personal— Winnicott (1989, p. 127) thinks of the wonderful smell locked in a newly planted hyacinth bulb. No dissection of the bulb will convey the scent. Only the flower opening will eventually reveal it. So may a person open to the smell of madness. The original madness, if experienced, would be *indescribably painful*. As the flower of madness opens and as we open to it, we smell what we can of it. We taste what agony we bear, at times crossing the line of the bearable. It is a line we must cross many times and fall back to what is barely bearable. We taste and smell somewhat lesser agonies, which, reminders or portents, intimate ungraspable X.

Winnicott offers a kind of mirror of Plato's account of building capacity for the Good. We taste sensuous pleasures and grow into emotional, intellectual, and spiritual ones. We ascend from pleasure to the Idea of the Good Itself. With Winnicott's Agony X, we taste lesser agonies, build awareness of greater ones, reaching towards Original Madness: X itself. Did Winnicott unconsciously associate the smell of hyacinth madness with Baudelaire's flowers, with Hawthorne's poison tree?

Did Wanda suffer from invisible developmental failure—a sense of growing up without anyone smelling her unknown madness, leaving what was *absolutely personal* locked up?

There are many reasons to live, many ways to come alive. Smelling the madness in each other as we open and close is a crucial part of feeling alive—a little like flies on faeces, dogs smelling each others' rears. It is often difficult to know what is or is not nourishing. Certain forms and uses of "sanity" can be sterile. There are ways that madness can feed life as well as ruin it. A good deal of Wanda's therapy will involve recovery/discovery of the madness that she could not live, partly because of parental push to premature sanity, partly because life revealed bits of madness in unbearable, indigestible ways. She did not know what to do with the worst life had to offer, so she was not able to make fullest use of the best.

CHAPTER ELEVEN

Angling in

The problem of being nourished by poisons seems fathom-less when confronted by cases in which a person's sense of "well-being and vitality spring from the same characteris-tics which give trouble" (Bion, 1965, p. 144). Bion has in mind mental illness so persistent that it is often attributed to inborn physical pathology. He wonders whether it might not be better to understand the individual's difficulties as arising from a "*normal* physical state and to spring from the very health and virility of the patient's endowment of ambition, intolerance of frustration, envy, aggression and his belief that there is, or ought to be, or will be (even if it has to be created by himself) an ideal object that exists to fulfil itself."

The very traits that are part of illness are, in some way, part of health: ambition, frustration, intolerance, envy, aggression, be-lief in a compelling ideal object. Is illness/health a matter of too much/too little, right or wrong use of such ingredients, warped ways of structuring them, varied ways of relating to warps?

A clinical point is that in attempting to remove illness, one may damage what is most alive and creative in the individual.

This is an old theme in psychoanalysis. Rilke sounded it when he feared losing his angels if his devils were tampered with. It takes many forms, not least among analysts themselves.

There are many jokes about analysts developing a language only they can understand, although even members of particular schools are at war with each other. There are many popular portrayals of loss of vitality consequent on psychoanalytic maturation, although both maturation and vitality tend to be idealized. The best customers in the therapy field might be therapists themselves. But the problems therapists face are not very different from those of other professionals—and ultimately the difficulties professionals face are not very different from the rest of the population.

In psychoanalysis, an individual may fear loss of self if he cooperates with the analyst. He fears loss of individuality or self-substance if the analysis proceeds. A question at stake is what kind of cooperation is possible? Are there threads of different kinds of cooperation? What of the complex relationships between varieties of cooperation, compliance, and slavery? Will the patient be frightened more by the analyst's need or refusal to enslave the patient? How honest can an analyst be about what he does to make a living? In what ways can what kinds of honesty help or harm particular cases at particular times? And what of the analyst's dread of loss of self? What of the dangers to a person in attempting to be or not to be a therapist? What are the poisons that nourish? What can psychoanalysis do if difficulty is inborn?

Bion writes of a "crux" that is reached if analysis progresses. The individual reaches a point where recognition of conflict between alternative methods of meeting personal problems becomes possible. Bion (1965, p. 142) calls these alternative methods "transformations in hallucinosis" and "transformations in analysis". Both capacities exist in various degrees, kinds, and relationships in individuals; now one, now the other dominates. They feed as well as oppose each other. Both have assets and liabilities. Both have ancient histories.

We are endowed with hallucinatory–analytic capacity, each contributing to survival, integrity, richness of living. Either can run amok—for example, hyper-hypotrophy of either or both. At the particular crux Bion (1965, pp. 142–143) has in mind, what is at stake is hallucinatory "solutions" to difficulties based on surplus envy, rivalry, hate, superiority versus analytic solutions based on cooperation, compassion, generosity, complementation.

A kind of morality play evolves: hate versus love, superiority versus cooperation, envy versus generosity. In this scenario, the former grouping is associated with hallucinatory solutions, the latter with analytic. Both war in individuals. Either capacity can contribute in positive–negative ways depending on situation and use (e.g. hallucinatory aspects of love, aggressive aspects of analysis). In tracing the significance of psychic movements, we have only our own analytic–hallucinatory processes to fall back on.

I have seen work on the "analytic" side cause damage, partly from prohibition of hallucinatory nourishment in the analytic couple. In each case, the analyst thought he was doing the right analytic thing but lacked a "feel" for life being destroyed by analysis. Such analysis is often the analyst's hallucination. Nothing can replace a "feel" for the life of an individual, whether at any one moment one leans more or less towards hallucination-analysis. Of course, to point out the dangers of analysis is not to praise hallucinatory outcomes. Wisdom keeps an eye on both capacities.

Bion contrasts two kinds of patients at the crux: one for whom reliance on hostile hallucinosis is secondary and one for whom it is primary (part of inborn disposition and character). In the former, Bion feels it possible to reconstruct the disturbed state and hallucinatory solution, so that the individual can find more adequate solutions. In such an outcome, analysis may lead to a restoration of the patient's personality so that "he will approximate to being the person he was when his development became compromised" (1965, p. 144).

If hostile use of hallucinosis ("coating of lies", 1965, p. 129) is secondary, the patient can rework personality through mutual cooperation rather than remaining sealed in mistrust. What is critical at the crux is "the character of cooperation between two people", not "the problem for which the cooperation is required" (1965, p. 144). Improvement—within a certain range—does not so much hinge on the problem presented as on the quality of cooperation achieved. The individual not born into a personality sealed by hostile superiority may be more able to take a chance on a mutuality that taps dormant faith in living.

But what of difficulties when problems are part of inborn disposition and character? Bion states a kind of conditional law: the more the problem is part of the individual's inborn nature, the harder it is for him to modulate allegiance to hallucinosis as "*the* superior approach" (1965, p. 144). Here it is not a matter of oscillating allegiance—the back-and-forth testing that spontaneously evolves when dipping in and out of hallucinosis-and-analysis in ways that take growth forward. The difficult case Bion has in mind is tightly gripped by and tightly gripping "*the* superior approach"—hallucinatory solutions driven by "an inborn need to be on top."

Bion does not say such cases are impossible—but that difficulty increases. Whether or not the difficulty is primary or secondary, the individual in analysis reaches the crux. The question is what happens at the crux. There are those who respond to the faith underlying analysis, begin to view life more truthfully, and try to extend the horizon of possible solutions and those who fall back on the status quo and try to remain inured to the call of the more or the other. In either case, there are dreadful premonitions, acute fears.

The sense that the loss of bad parts of the personality "is inseparable from loss of that part in which all his mental health resides, contributes to the acuity of the patient's fears" (1965, p. 144).

The sense of superiority embedded in hallucinatory solutions draws on the sense of might in the person. Ambition, envy, aggression, demand, idealization contribute to aliveness, even if they attack the latter. One reason superiority–inferiority, might–weakness are so fused is the surge one gets attacking aliveness. One feels alive attacking aliveness. A ghastly outcome is that this way of being alive promotes a sense of deadness—and deadness becomes a way of living (Eigen, 1996).

Many patients in this position feel super-real and super-fraudulent, simultaneously overestimating–undermining the self. They are mighty ones beating down inferior elements, even as they go under in depressive fatigue. To stop beating oneself up is to abandon the most reliable rush of might-and-fright one knows.

Alice

In such a state, an individual may not recognize or appreciate a genuinely healthy moment. Alice (chapters 1 and 4) could scarcely tell the difference between health and illness. After years of work and many gains, moments outside illness quickly drown. One day Alice came in feeling destitute and injured: her personality injured her. She recounted mistakes that caused her bad karma. It reached the point where the wrong thought would make bad karma worse. She could not avoid damaging soul, damaging cosmos. She would never be a person whose good thoughts and deeds lead to better karma, better cosmos. She was grinding herself down.

As I listened, I thought of an orthodox Jewish woman I know who is very superstitious. She fears that death or disease will come to her children if she does not follow laws and customs as prescribed. Any failure of intent and practice can be catastrophic. Alice has a friend like this woman. Alice can objectify some of this kind of thinking when she sees her friend. I found myself saying, "If a woman fails to light Sabbath candles, she will miscarry. Her babies die at birth. . . . If she doesn't go to the ritual bath, she becomes mortally ill. . . . If you allow cut fingernails to fall on the ground, a pregnant woman may miscarry if she steps on them. . . ."

East and West have no monopoly on power to inflict pain on oneself. There is a horrible intensity in stabbing oneself, ugly as one feels. There is astounding strength in the stubborn tenacity and persistence of self-hate. Spiritual ambition is transformed into chronic self-reproach. Aggression is hideously released in the only space one dares—nuclear reactions in deep sea or underground inhabited only by oneself. In Alice's case, envy scarcely has time to surface, she is so busy counting failures. There is ideal goodness somewhere in the nature of things, but she is on the wrong side of life and does not reach it. She judges herself by the goodness she fails to reach. This is the daily bread she lives on.

Is there not enormous strength in such weakness? The weak inherit the earth because they are the only ones strong enough to endure the depths of humiliation. The so-called strong would kill themselves rather than get used to abysmal degradation. The weak persevere under such conditions. They strengthen themselves by feeding on poisons.

After I called attention to how her Buddhist thinking was like her Jewish orthodox friend's, Alice told me about some hours with her cat. She had a delightful time throwing him a cloth ball, watching him pounce and pummel it and absent-mindedly hit it back to her. They did this all evening. She loved it. Here was a moment of freedom, grace, clearing.

If only life could be re-centred on the openings these moments provide. She could let me know of this moment only after making sure I saw her living suicide. Here is another sort of health, not based on rivalry, ambition, aggression, envy, intolerance, or even idealization. It was an earthy taste of heaven, a beatific bit as real as the awesome intensity of self-hate: an alternative infinity. In time, such moments link across years, friendship deepening between them, if given half a chance.

Denise

Denise lived in a semi-shared hell (Alice's was more private). She surrounded herself with people who functioned as care-takers. Her husband took care of business and living arrangements and generally acted as a protective buffer between Denise and whatever needed to be done. Her friends provided for emotional needs. One or another was ready, day or night, to manage desperation calls. They checked in periodically to see how she was doing. If necessary, they came over in minutes, even at three o'clock in the morning. Denise did not feel she could survive without the support system she had assembled over the years.

She wondered why so many people did so much for her, especially her husband. What did they get from it? She was a basketcase with practically nothing left over for others. Yet she could rely on people being drawn to her.

She spent a long time in sessions saying little, yet she was quite expressive. In ten minutes her face could go through a range of fear states, each nuance projecting enormous change. I doubt most people would notice such changes or make much of them. But I found them striking and could feel why she might develop a loyal following among those who tuned in.

I could feel myself hanging on her expressions as she created cradles of unforgettable slides of emotional states that I might not access without her. I felt almost privileged to mould myself around her in order to taste her inner world. I easily saw how being with Denise could be addictive: soul potato crisps. Each mini-shift of expression revealed a new facet of fear, which, once seen, seemed imperative to know—as if she were filling gaps in one's sense of self.

To some extent Denise was oblivious to the effect of her own intensity (a little like a woman only semi-aware of her erotic impact). She was sure she made a bad impression. She feared people thought little of her, she was so fearful, held back. In her mind's eye she did not act or look like someone people could think highly of. She had long hair and let it fall over her face, to hide herself. For many months she was certain I would not recognize her if we met on the street. She feared I would not know who she was when she came to sessions. Her halting speaking style made her feel stupid in other peoples' eyes.

Yet Denise filled out and came alive when she played the piano. She was a successful pianist and managed to play well in front of groups. She found this a major paradox in her life—so shy and retiring generally, she was a fish in water on the concert stage. There were times when she became anxious playing in public, now and then paralysingly so. But usually the playing carried her. In her apartment, she played for hours. The image came to her of a crippled person feeling free in water, although she not only swam, she flew.

It is possible that music is the true medium of life (see also chapter 4). What is outside music is something else, akin to dead skin perhaps (dust to dust), awaiting musical breath to infuse it. For Denise, no music . . . no oxygen: Life outside music is downtime or worse. Her personality disintegrates without it, as a body dies without air. If Denise is not playing, one finds her in a more or less disintegrating state.

People are poor substitutes for music. But life must be lived with people—one cannot play piano all the time. It is too bad that one cannot play people like a piano. To some extent we *are* musical instruments responding to each other. A therapist can be like a piano the patient plays. At times the players vanish, and the music plays itself. But a good deal of the time players obtrude, disturbing the music that lives through them and that they live through.

Denise sought therapy in part in order to find a way of plugging in when she was not playing the piano. If only being with people could be like making music. People provide insufficient support, but if she did not find ways of making being with people work, there would be no support at all. She tried medication, but she rejected it. She did not like the way it made her feel. It did lift her out of depressive fears to variable degrees, but she could feel it lifting her and did not like the feeling of being lifted. It put a thin coating around her insides. She needed access to her insides, even if she felt dreadful and did not want to feel dreadful.

She turned to me as she might to medication, as she might to music. I could not do what her husband and friends did. They provided 24-hour coverage. They were always there, helping her between playing times. I pictured Baudelaire's mother holding him while he wrote. He could not hold himself together by himself. Denise had an elaborate network of mothers. What might I offer?

She was past talking. She had had many therapists—cognitive, behavioural, psychodynamic, interpersonal, transpersonal, gestalt. She had tried psychoanalysis twice, on the couch, five times a week. She had tried body therapies. Therapy and analysis had helped, but not enough—they did not touch the core. Perhaps nothing could. Not that she was never moved, or did not feel connected with some who tried to help her. But somehow the work passed through her, and disintegration continued.

In early phases of work she spoke about her youthful desires. She wanted to be famous, and she did achieve a certain amount of fame. To do that, she had worked hard, climbed steps, mobilized forces. She idealized work in the sense that music made heaven on earth. Heaven was natural, more natural than anything outside it. Denise did not "get" the point of life outside heaven. Heaven was reality, most real reality. Ordinary life was unnatural, less real. For Denise, music was the primary state. Earth existed as a setting for heaven, as a place for heaven to be. Everything outside heaven was more or less lifeless, disintegration-prone.

For a good part of her life she worked hard to make heaven possible. She was an achiever—a "have" rather than a "have-not". She harnessed ambition–aggression in service of ideal feeling. She was not especially given to envy. The music of others added to hers. To be part of any increase of music in the world increased herself. She was not small about the success of others, her heavenly partners.

It was as if the sum of ambition–aggression in her personality decomposed when she was not immersed in musical life. If she was at dinner, tired, going to a show, spending time with a friend, buying clothes, taking a cab—whatever held her together loosened its grip. She came unglued, she unravelled—spinning, reeling. Outside heaven, everything died.

I have been doing therapy for over 30 years and have few illusions about helping people no one has helped. (When I was younger, it was another story.) I do have a few odd strong points. One of them is fear: I have been afraid all my life. I have been afraid of people and lots of things. I have endured a myriad nuances of terror, dread, gradations of fear. Often I shut them out and am insensitive. I cannot live only in fear. But I am aware of fear infinities, and they register on my face, they resonate in my being.

Denise can plug her fear modem into mine. The problem with this sort of transmission is that it is transient. Like e-mail that has been read, it becomes unavailable or disappears as time goes by. Nevertheless, it makes her feel something real with another person for a time—not exactly heaven, but some kind of link. She feels relief—a minor relief in the scale of things—feeling her fear in mine, mine in hers. She had never met anyone who matched her range of fear and let it show.

Another strong point is my belief in heaven now. I believe in heavenly moments. The notion that "a thing of beauty is a joy forever" is more than a credo. It is a living fact. These joy moments connect and radiate and give life meaning. It may not be possible to live without them. Religious people often tell us that quality of will is more important than affect, and I would not want to argue. But if will fails to be nourished by wonder, it becomes poisoned–poisonous. In any case, I do not do very well without heaven. I can live outside heaven for longer periods better than Denise can, but only because I sense heaven in the background, heavenly undercurrents, and I am not convinced that much exists outside them.

A problem for Denise is not that heaven is real for her or that she accesses it through music, but that so much of life outside it does not feel alive at all. After years of bouncing from one therapist to another, the die rolled her into one living in heaven and fear. Our heavens, as well as our fears, connected. It took only a micro-moment. We felt an instantaneous jolt of recognition. Elements of experience that are real for me resonated with kindred elements that were real for her, and vice versa.

I saw her surprise, disbelief, relief, and a smile spread through us. It was as if she thought, "Ah, another strange one, a mutant, someone from somewhere else, more at home in heaven than earth, afraid of worldly life." Did we seek refuge in heaven because life was too scary, or was life too scary because we were too attached to heaven? Whatever bias, I realized an event had taken place that extended Denise's range of being and might extend it more. She saw aspects of her secret self in another face. More, the heavenly, fearful impulse that drove her, her idiosyncratic mixture of hellish heaven and heavenly hell, not only found *simpatico* reverberations, but seeped into another's emotional field. For moments, at least, often longer, we were mutely awash in a psychic blender that mixed what we poured into it, creating new psychic tastes.

I was not like others in her support system, because I was not, in principle, available whenever she wanted me. She could not reach me at any time. I did not exist to make her feel better. Of course, I responded to her calls, and sometimes she felt better, sometimes worse. Feeling better–worse was not the main thing that happened between us. Among the significant things that

happened were new ways we felt together, nuances of states created by our being together.

Her husband protected and sheltered her, but Denise felt that
she could not communicate with him. He was a good man, a
practical, confident soul, at ease in the world. She could not imagine surviving without him. But, she insisted, there was no real
contact between them. She was hopeless about their relationship
yet would never give it up.

"Why is he with you, if he doesn't know you?" I wondered.

"I do his suffering for him. I do his ecstasy for him."

"You access heaven and hell for him?

"That's my function, like a diva."

Is that what I do too?—access psychic areas people prefer to
learn about several times removed, if at all (as in art, writing—let
others do it), a sort of sage of psychic garbage dumps, junk-
yards? Heaven is dangerous too, if it stops one from living, spoils
life.

Denise and her husband have their division of labour. It
works, up to a point. Perhaps their lack of deeper communication
enables them to stay together. If he opened to her inner being,
they might sink together. Others try to help her, but they are not
in a position to sit quietly, say nothing, comment freely as the
spirit moves them, attend to nearly imperceptible shifts of being.
A therapist is for 45 minutes in the luxurious position of letting
twists and turns of feelings wax and wane, savouring worlds individuals evoke, finding responses through savouring. Therapist
and patient experience their impacts on each other, create new
impacts together, discover how to grow through impact and response.

At our initial point of meeting, fears and heavens reverberated
between us. Once contact had been established, we could vary,
amplify, extend it. By including me in her life, Denise's range of
heavenly–fearful experiencing grew. Her world stretched to include me. Since I was part of her world, part of her, she adapted
to my idiosyncrasies, as I did to hers. If she wanted me in her life,
she would have to make room for me—someone not at her beck
and call, someone interested in creative responding. I, too, had to
learn the secret of how to wait for Denise and let her know I was

waiting and find ways to find her. It was not that she eventually tolerated and made use of more that was outside heaven, although this was so. It was more that heaven gradually grew to include possibilities that had once seemed beyond it. For a long time I functioned as a kind of medium between heaven and the world, between heaven and fear.

Seamless seams

Over the long haul, Denise and I suffered many breaks and battles. What I need to emphasize is that without the taste of heaven at the outset, our relationship would not have survived our disappointing ways. It is crucial that no early judgement was made about the health–illness of our contact. Our fear–heaven circuit simply *was*. Relationships do not always work this way. Sometimes people begin in heaven and end in hell. Relationships short-circuit and break when disillusionment comes. On the other hand, there are relationships that begin in hell and move towards heaven. Some start with a good deal of noxia that has to be suffered before something decent happens (Eigen, 1993, pp. 25–42). Many combine these patterns in changing ways. What is real between people may change for better or worse. One rarely knows ahead of time what a particular heaven or hell may contribute to a growing sense of reality.

With Alice, a good deal of obvious aggression against the self had to be tolerated. Self-hate was palpable, dense, thick. If one was not at home with self-disgust and grim self-attack processes, one could not be with Alice long enough for something to happen. Denise and I plugged into each other through heaven–fear. Alice and I through shared self-hate. What was common between the two was that we liked each other and accepted each other immediately, from the first moment of contact. I could see that Denise and Alice felt my liking as I felt theirs, and we liked our liking of each other. It is akin to people who rarely feel found, finding one another—mutual finding of the eternally unfound. I am not sure how this works, but that it happens is a fact of my experience.

Alice failed to realize her ambitions as early and fully as Denise. No one supported her. Her parents attacked every positive move she made. Whatever she achieved was with immense pain, struggle. She struggled for decades to begin to approach the place where many people start. To get close to starting was an immense achievement. Without a therapist she could be with, self-hate would have devoured her. She appreciated her hard-won gains in ways that seemed beyond Denise. Denise took more for granted.

Envy took an invisible, insidious form for Alice. She was down to begin with, but she put herself down even more by comparing herself with others. The success of others did not provoke overt envy so much as make her feel not viable all the more. The world was a merry-go-round spinning too fast for her to get on. The whirling blur nauseated her as she sank further into paralysis. The idea of a heaven she feared leaving was foreign to her. Heaven was something for others. It was enough for her to get through her daily hell.

Yet Alice seemed to have more capacity for gratitude than Denise. She appreciated breaks in hell, tastes of heaven here and there. Denise expected more, and little bits of goodness had less impact.

Alice began working with me when she was younger, and her world expanded little by little over the years. She grew into better friendships, a profession, and life circumstances. Denise began past the half-way mark. Her life had been shrinking for years. We spent a great deal of time riding out the contraction before growth began anew. Her early rise to fame did not provide a good model for the living needed now.

Another patient who had weathered grisly self-attack processes for decades, recently provided her own model for something therapy gave her. It has some relevance for Denise and Alice too. We met after a therapy she had been in for many years turned destructive. She was aware of the good she found in therapy before it soured. I was able to build on good work that had been done, as well as start anew in the wake of the bad end. Apparently I was less dogmatic than her last therapist. We spoke of serious things but also of whatever bubbled up between us.

She felt my touch lighter than her past therapist, and we laughed more.

One day, after we had been working for nearly six years (a drop in the bucket), she gave me a present before our summer break. Psychoanalysts are trained not to take presents but investigate the purpose or psychological underpinnings of the gift. Every practitioner has to find his or her way with new moments. So much depends on the tone, feel, or meaning of the day. Freud, I recall, thought a patient's gift near the end of analysis had a liberating effect for the giver. In any case, I did not stand on ceremony and immediately sensed that something good was happening, thanked her, and waited. The fact is that I felt a sense of wonder that we had come so far.

She said, "I want to tell you what I have gotten from you. I want you to know. When I came here, I wanted an umbilical cord. I thought we would form a symbiotic connection, and you'd tune me into life. But something else happened. Just your being you brought me out of the hole I was in. I couldn't use you the way I imagined, but found a kind of relief I didn't have much of before. Instead of umbilical symbiosis, I got something I couldn't anticipate. At some point, I realized a raft was forming underneath me. I would sink, but a raft I didn't know about lifted me up. It was freeing, not the symbiotic ocean I thought I longed for. Something would rescue me, hold me up, I wouldn't drown forever. So much of my life I have been suffocating under water. Now I can breathe. When I am with you I feel we're both supported by life. It's not just a sea or ocean underneath, but life itself. You've helped put a raft under me or helped me find it, and the raft is life itself."

Therapy as life support is supported by life. Therapy as a life form is a small part of living processes that support and alter it. One hopes that therapy mediates contact with life in less debilitating ways, leading to fuller, better living. It is not one thing that is said or done so much as interpenetrating affect–attitude fields in which different "feels" for life reshape each other (Eigen, 1995).

Sometimes it *is* a remark or two. I think of sessions I had with Wilfred R. Bion in 1978. He told me to break away from my analyst and get married. It is difficult to convey the impact of his words, they are so tied up with the impact of his person. I do not want this to sound very idealizing, because what happened was very real. As it turned out, I saw him the year before he died. We spoke of many things in a short time. A number of our interests overlapped, and he did not hesitate sharing thoughts.

I did not find him forbidding, but he was not informal in the American sense. He seemed familiar to me—somehow lowly like me, not someone above—yet very determined, persistent, if flexible. A deep inner resolve was part of his person, not without humour, but not "funny". He unhesitatingly affirmed what he thought to be currents of aliveness in what I told him, whether or not they seemed pleasant. He did not pick apart healthy–unhealthy aspects of aliveness, but he highlighted aliveness itself, warts and all. The long-range result was that, like my patient, I unexpectedly found that my life-raft was in my own living.

A little bit of contact goes a long way.

I have since learned how central a fact marriage was for Bion (1994, pp. 222–223) and that he spoke to me from the core of what was real for him, what made him real. He spoke from his living being to help a floundering soul. The transmission was immediate—impact and response—yet unimposing. And the marriage he helped release me into has made all the difference.

I last saw Bion at a party in his honour before he left New York. I went up to him, and he began reciting Milton. Someone asked him why he acted in ways to arouse hostility among professionals. His presentations evoked hostile, even scornful questioning by some. He said he noticed that happens and was astonished. He claimed he did not understand it. I was astonished by his astonishment. Was he feigning naïveté? Bion has investigated more regions of hell than any psychoanalyst I have read (Eigen, 1998).

But I suspect many professionals are afraid of heaven even more than of hell. One reason may be a healthy mistrust of heaven, since it is often misused: think of all the slaughter for the sake of heaven or using one's hell to support another's heaven. Individuals cling to versions of heaven in enslaved–enslaving ways. Children are abused for the sake of heaven. Hope of heaven steals lives away.

Yet heaven is no less real for the abuses it serves. It plays an enormous role in human affairs, for better or worse. One cannot

cancel heaven because one does not like its difficulties or consequences. Tastes of heaven make life worth while.

Our days are uplifted by heaven, shattered by hell. We keep
trying to work with both. Psychoanalysis tends to be biased
against heaven. Heaven is associated with infantile omnipotence,
hallucinatory wish-fulfilment, pleasure principle. Individuals
need help living in the real world, getting along with real people,
making a real living, raising real families, making real discover-
ies. To do this, they need to deal with pain, frustration, difference,
the difficulties of living. Wisdom literature from ancient times
counsels finding the middle way—not being overly attached to
pain–pleasure, success–failure. Psychoanalysis shares something
of this vision.

Yet heaven and hell are recurrent facts of daily life. They cannot be wished away by analysis. All too often, I have met individuals who have had their heavens–hells analytically abused.
Analysts tend to fashion interpretations that emphasize the pain
of being a separate individual, in the face of the wish for unrealistic gratifications. There are therapists who infantilize patients by
providing too much gratification or foster the illusion of oneness
in the hope of providing nourishment the patient missed. When
the bubble breaks, the hells are ghastly. But there are therapists
who cannot bear the build-up of heaven, any more than the patient can stand the build-up of pain (not that analysts are too
good about pain either). Too much is relegated to the realm of the
"unrealistic", and the patient is pushed towards a vision of adulthood the personality cannot support.

Realities looking for contact are not tolerable. The analyst de-
flects them, tries to squeeze or channel them through interpretive
filters the analyst believes in. One side of the personality gets
played off against the other (infant–adult–parent, pleasure–reality, real–ideal), ritualizing divisions. Many patients get help in
consolidating the war against infantile or destructive elements.
But there are also patients who are wounded by this attempt and
fall back. They fail to vault the wall into "adulthood". For them,
any push into "adult" living seems premature.

An individual's heaven or hell may be more real than the facts
of daily life. For many, heaven–hell is the salient fact of life. For
them, analysis must not only be a place where heaven–hell find

voices, but where they are enabled to evolve as living realities. They need their passports validated in order to find entry into life (or they devour and are devoured by life). Heaven–hell undergo transformations as individuals grow. What we face in therapy is the result of transformations that failed to happen, aborted evolution, and the deformations that have taken their place.

The problem is that these so-called deformations are life itself—mixtures of ambition, aggression, rivalry, envy, ugliness, beauty, cruelty, love, passion, wonder, hate, beatific surges, bitterness, openness, rigidity, resolve, vacillation. Writers of the past several hundred years have tried to capture profiles of this mixup: will, power, imagination, drive, boredom, apathy, helplessness—an explosive–entropic universe . . . a mechanical, dynamic, uncertain one . . . plasticity and limits . . . evolving or changing visions. Individuals are caught up in the vortex of visions, of unfathomable forces. The blender throws some up on the psychopathic, impulsive side, others who are more self-effacing, under the heel—all kinds of shifting mixtures.

A therapist cannot do more than his personality allows. Yet we are called upon to try to do more. We are called to keep stretching, if we can—if we can take it. Often we break, splatter, die out from fatigue, come back, regroup, begin again. Nothing stops us, especially failure, not even the hostility or admiration of patients and colleagues. Our own heavens–hells push us further into reality and keep on pushing.

Mystical visions of heaven on earth offer a challenge. I believe that this is so for many kinds of mysticism that espouse a love of human dignity (hate mysticisms are obviously exclusive). The ethical challenge to individuals in heaven is whether or not heaven is inclusive or exclusive. The contracted individual lives in contracted heavens. To what extent can therapy enrich the flow of heavenly–earthly life, mediate heaven–earth interweaving, while not denigrating heavens that are beyond reach. Perhaps it is the denigrating attitude—earth denigrating heaven, heaven denigrating earth—that keeps the brakes on, whether cynically sour or righteously idealistic. Denigration is a kind of self-irritant through which one keeps a hold on oneself.

Earth does not exhaust heaven, nor heaven earth. Visions of concordance make room for otherness. Prophets and mystics tend to emphasize brotherly–sisterly love, helping one another, respect for sameness–otherness. In actuality, ambitious, aggressive, rival-rous, envious individuals/groups have made ambitious, aggres-sive, rivalrous, envious use of heaven. Heaven becomes a club, banishing rivals or undesirables. In keeping with a visionary–hu-manitarian tradition that values the least of us, Jesus turned things upside down, making heaven for the bottom, not only the top (the top have a tougher time getting into *his* heaven). It did not take long to reverse the reversal, insofar as heaven remains a pawn of domination–submission. That does not nullify heaven or make it less real: It is real all the more.

William Blake envisions heaven as war between all possible voices, in which all enjoy maximum expression and mutual en-hancement. In such a vision, ambition, aggression, rivalry, and heaven work together. Impossible? Yes, of course. But it *does* hap-pen in small doses in therapy and life. And it *may* happen more, if we keep catching on to how heaven–hell–earth work together when they do. And even if we cannot really know how this hap-pens (when it does), we may develop a "feel" for it, a sort of psycho-spiritual "body language", and angle in more than we do now. It is a capacity we do have that can evolve, if we keep touching it and allow it to touch us.

CHAPTER TWELVE

Desire and nourishment

S AGE 1: "Follow your bliss. Be a troubadour, courtly lover, knight. Cut *your* path through the forest. Live your eye–heart connection."[1]

SAGE 2: "Train bliss. School desire. No beginning or end to desire, all sorts of desires, lower, higher. Let desire evolve."

SAGE 3: "Find the Middle Way."

SAGE 4: "Not less than Everything."[2]

"Love God with all your heart, soul, might, mind. Do not kill, steal, covet—which amount to God not being enough. Be God-centred, God-anchored. Live deep in God. Filled with God, you won't keep eyeing your neighbour's stuff. You won't turn aside after your hearts and eyes, which cause you to go astray."

Opening is more than desire.

* * *

---

[1] I have heard Joseph Campbell say things like this, and I have lifted them out of context.

[2] D. W. Winnicott (Phillips, 1988, p. 19) imagined this T. S. Eliot phrase to be a possible title for his autobiography, if he wrote one.

Desires are distracting.

I walk down the street with a two-year-old. He hangs on a gate for 20 minutes, swinging back and forth, falling off, climbing on, getting hurt and crying, swinging and laughing, smiling, very studious. There is nothing more marvellous or challenging than something on hinges. He is scientist, fun-lover, dancer. He does the same things over and over with slight variations. He is an experimenter. His being is tickled and thrilled.

Desires are gateways.

He tries to climb a wall but can't. He wants me to put him on it, and I do. He walks on the wall. I am a little scared and careful, walking by him, my hands ready. He runs, slows, topples almost, likes tipping, back and forth, on top of a world, higher than his body can take him. He is in a higher body. On the ground his body has weight. On the wall he flies, sort of, above his weight. Again, laughter. Being weightless is serious business. How high ought he go? What if he becomes a balloon? Funny thrills. Waves of thrills. Higher than Dad. Look at Dad's smiling, worried face. Happy and worried. What a world! What a life!

We have not walked half a block. Stairs catch his eye. Another 20 minutes walking up and down. He runs at birds, and they fly. He runs after birds again, and they fly again. The birds land near where we started from, and he runs back. He sees an empty stroller [push-chair] and wants to push it. We will never reach the end of the block unless he wants to race ahead of me and have me chase him!

Desires are distractions. Distractions are deliriously alive.

* * *

M1:   "Since menopause my body is dry. I don't want sex. I mean, I want it, but it won't be good. I can't come like I used to. No deep orgasms. It's too much work. It's easier not to do it."

M2:   "I feel bad about myself. I'd rather work out or go to work than have sex. But I love my husband. I love him more now. We do not fight as much. We've found how to be together. Sometimes I start sex because I think it's bad not to have it.

Once we get into it, I like it, sort of. It's good to be together. It's healthier having something than nothing."

* * *

BREAKDOWN 1: "If I had not slept with her, I'd be OK. It blew me away. It was way too much. I kept thinking, 'This never happened to me before. How long can it go on?' We kept doing it, five, six times, all night. I've never felt anything like it. The most of anything. Better than heaven. I thought I made it to the other side. I'd never be afraid again. Then the crash, the panic. I've never felt worse. I couldn't control it. Just terror and more terror and more terror. I have not slept through a night again."

BREAKDOWN 2: "If only someone had sex with me. I was so alone. I felt awful and alone. I couldn't break out of it, and no one reached out to me. If they did, I couldn't find it. Sex would have helped. Sex always helps. Sex makes me feel better. I've had a lot of sex since my breakdown. Sex makes me feel more whole. Sex makes me feel loved."

* * *

Candy: "I've never worked with a man before. I have got to work something through with a man. I want to have a relationship, I want a partner."

Candy is gorgeous. She has many men. In recent years, they tend to sleep with her, treat her badly, break off. Soon she will be 40. She cannot build a career any more than a relationship. She is impatient with work. Her jobs are not interesting. She cannot give herself to anything for long. She is extremely frustrated with herself. She has so much potential.

She shows me a piece of writing she did that is brilliant. She shows me a painting she did that is brilliant. She radiates brilliance. She radiates sexual brilliance and creative brilliance. To use her term, she is very juicy.

She quickly zeros in on her father. He is hypercritical and ignores her feelings. She is part of his ego. He used to show her a photo he called "*My* Candy." It was *his* girl, the version of her he recognized as his: thin boned, angular, underweight, like a model. The inference was that when she failed to fit this image, she was not his girl. She was someone else—or perhaps nothing, banished from the kingdom.

She went off to college, put on weight, and became attached to a Great Man who looked down on everyone—an extremely talented man too good for the world, too good for her, nearly old enough to be her father. With him she had orgasms. With him she was breathless. He opened everything, rolled out the red carpet of the universe. They travelled, marvelled at life. Her role was to be there when he wanted her, support his brilliance, feed him her body (which was a kind of soul), lend her flame to his.

She became less and less to his more and more—nothing to his everything. He treated her worse and worse. Her suffering became unbearable, and, finally, she escaped into another consuming passion with a man who had another woman, a man who became the love of her life. He was the first man who listened to her, who really heard her, who gave her himself. But by the time he chose Candy over the other woman, Candy had become numb, and when they lived together, she turned off. For a time, they awaited her return, but her coldness never left. In the end he was driven out and eventually married someone else.

In the first months that I saw Candy, she had seven affairs, each seeming to last an eternity. Her meetings with men were raw and packed. She analysed the ins and outs of every feeling, as if things were blown up in slow motion. Each had a tone and a life of its own but led nowhere. Sometimes she felt that each experience was its own justification. Yet the impact of so much going on so quickly pummelled her. She was tossed by waves beyond control. On the one hand, these moments enriched her life. On the other, she was left stranded, her life at loose ends. The partner she sought was nowhere.

When I said something about her father in all this, she defended him, making sure I knew how superior he was, how high-quality the two of them were, even if she were in the neglected, inferior position. She judged men as her father judged her. She subjected each moment to the same hypercritical consciousness she was used to being subject to. No man and she survived each other very long. If the exchange of injury was not open and obvious, it went on liminally, but no less effectively. She was always injuring the other in her mind, as well as feeling injured. At the centre of her being, injury was always happening.

After half a year with me, her relationships settled into two main ones. She stumbled on a creative man who listened to her. She was not used to being seen and heard emotionally by someone she liked and felt attracted to. She treasured these moments. At the same time, she became involved with a man who was self-destructive, mirroring her self-defeating elements. She acknowledged that seeing me must have something to do with finding a man who valued and heard her. Could she sustain this kind of contact? She needed outlets for her self-destructive core.

For the first time, Candy spoke of a calm centre. She realized it was in her power to injure both men. Just a few months earlier, she had felt depleted, torn apart, diffused by men who used her. Now she felt important to her men. She could be a genuine centre of their lives, and they hers? Need she choose one? Could she have both? More? Could she give up any?

Candy knew the calmness came from being desired, loved, valued, heard. She had found a man who really cared for her with the emotional intensity she needed. He was not boring. He shared himself and wanted to know *her*. More than that, he was *able* to know her. The catch was that he was younger than she, and Candy dreaded being dumped as she grew older. There were always reasons not to choose. She knew that seeing other men would, sooner or later, sink the relationship.

When I wondered whether it was not her destiny to see lots of men and enjoy them and become rich with experience, she became angry, and felt that I sold her short. She wanted a partner—but could she *be* a partner? She wanted someone to share life with, to enhance life, to share experience. Now that it seemed almost possible, she balked. Had she been fooling herself all these years? She was willing not to be a mother—but not to be, and have, a partner? If I did not understand this about her, I understood nothing. Yet the fact was that she turned off after being with a man for any length of time. She feared turning off. She wanted intensity. Yet so much of what she went through left her depleted and drained. She did not want to go through turning off.

She could not live at a watered-down level, but could a relationship survive her need for intensity? Now the cat was out of the bag. Could she be the partner she had always hoped to find? Could she be what she demanded from others? She never faced the possibility that she might not be able to sustain the sort of relationship she thought she wanted. It was not simply bad luck. It was incapacity or, perhaps, a need to re-visualize what was possible, desirable. The focus shifted from what was wrong with others to a difficulty she was having with her own feelings. She felt claustrophobic with one man, agonizingly confused, guilty, torn apart with more than one.

She told me, nearly from the beginning, that getting in gear with someone physically was easy, but doing so emotionally was the most difficult thing in the world. She hid or felt the other hiding. She let her body do the speaking. The result was that she and her partners never came to know each other. They got along physically, then parted. Any attempt at emotional interchange varied between unsatisfactory and disastrous.

Letting her beauty shine thrilled her. *She* shone through her beauty. *I* felt her mind–soul–spirit consciousness alive in beauty. She felt me see her, to some extent, and we enjoyed some mutually alive spirit tingling. But in her real life she was not used to shining *through* her beauty. Men's eyes tended to stop at the surface, like her father's. In one way or another, she thrilled starring in their photographs. She got off being a great picture, packing visual wallop, seeing men light up and charge after her. The gap between desire and emotional contact was enormous. Desire nourished and emptied her.

A potential value of therapy is that it is an arena in which desire and emotional contact can grow together. Candy and I liked each other. She enjoyed my thinking her beautiful. She felt my desire. Yet she also felt my consciousness touching hers, and hers mine. She could not buy me off for long with beauty. Something more was needed. We had to dig in. We were here to help her find herself, get somewhere. I needed to work with her as a person, not only a body. Not less than being a person would do.

At the outset, she let me know that she did not expect to see me for very long. Therapy was short-term, quick, proactive, problem-directed. She acted as if she could control growth, or that I ought to be able to catalyse the growth she wanted on demand. Nothing could be further from the truth. The fact was that we had to do what she could not do with men. We had to get to know each other. We had to take time to let feelings grow. We had to evolve the capacity to sustain the growth of feelings that had usually been dissipated in sex and were breaking up.

Since it did not look as if we were going to have sex, the only weapon she had was breaking up. Just as she was getting closer to the man who liked her (and to me), she decided to fly overseas to see a man she had met on a plane a year earlier. Or was it the other way around—she began to get closer as she flew away? She wanted me to see her when she returned. She wanted her boyfriend to keep seeing her too. She wanted us to be patient, but she needed to fly away. She found safety in desire, in whims. She wrapped herself in desire as in a protective barrier.

The world was a great juke-box with lots of songs to play. She could not say no to herself, and why should she? I raised problems inherent in selection. We were together for nearly a year—longer than she had anticipated, longer than most of her relationships with men. As long as she saw me, she saw no other therapist. Pick one, miss others. Is loss built into getting something? What would she lose by flying away? What would she gain?

Perhaps one thing she might gain is losing a relationship that rubs her nose in her incapacity to let life build. Ought I see her off at the airport? Ought I be there when she gets back? Can she be with me long enough for desire and contact to mingle? Must mingling kindle flight?

Candy was furious when I said she attracts more men in a week than some of my patients do in a lifetime. "What good is that if they degrade me", she bristled. Ah, but who degrades you now? Perhaps she flies to escape the dreaded degradation, perhaps she flies to reach it.

* * *

BAR 1:   So Marla and the Donald split.

BAR 2:   So? What's new?

BAR 3:   They're a dime a dozen. Dames. You can get as many as you want. You do not need to be rich.

BAR 2:   I am married 30 years. I do not have the dough to split. Anyway, I need my wife. You know, she keeps things going. Without her, I'd only have work to complain about. What fun would coming here be then?

BAR 1:   He could have whoever he wants. Why shouldn't he?

BAR 3:   He bought the Miss America show.

BAR 1:   Wow.[3]

* * *

The best thing that ever happened to me was becoming a father. It brought me out of myself, deeper into myself, deeper into life. It taught me what love is—more about love. By degrees, not easily, with much difficulty, it made me a better husband.

I could imagine saying that becoming a father was the worst thing that happened to me, but this is not true. A baby is an atomic bomb in your life: so much shattering. stretching. Not everyone can take it. A lot run away. Some become violent.

A change happens, and you have to catch up with it. But you may never catch up with it.

* * *

"Dr. Eigen, Dr. Eigen—"

"Yes. Yes. Is something wrong . . . ?"

"Look! Look! The baby is perfect."

The cord was wrapped twice around its neck. It had been in distress. Its face was totally purple. Was it dead? I dropped out of the universe.

---

[3]I have heard people say things like this on WINS radio news (May, 1997).

In a few minutes the baby was on my lap, in tune with every-thing, as if no discontinuity exists between uterus and outside world. He followed a light on the other side of the room. He seemed at one with what is. Was this a taste of the harmony ancients spoke of?

* * *

My feelings for my patients change instantaneously. I see them at the moment of birth, as if I were there. What if my child were the person in my office? How would I want a therapist to treat *my* child? My heart opens. Original Face is everywhere.

It will take a long time to learn how to become a therapist with the changes I am undergoing. It is like starting all over again, and again, and again. Physical birth is definitive, umbilical to post-umbilical. Psychological birth goes on and on. A therapist never stops being born. There are therapy births so protracted, agonized, they seem like dying.

We are born a little at a time. Something dies for every bit born. There is a background sense of not being able to breathe, while our lungs fill with air. We find what we *can* do while embedded in limits. We press against incapacity, as against a window that hides what it shows. Psychological is stranger than physical birth, although both are more or other than we dream.

* * *

A young man seeks help. He is engaging, he smiles a lot. He tells me he is a writer who wants to write about the good things in life, happiness: There is enough writing about hard, awful things. He has had a pretty easy life ... affluence, privilege. He has not had to fight for anything. He loves a beautiful woman who recently moved in with him. They fight all the time.

She feels he is not caring enough. He is angry that she does not give him time to write. She does not do enough. He cannot get out of himself. Both want what the other is not providing. They love each other, but they cannot get along. Neither is prepared for what living with another takes. Neither thinks life should be so painful.

I hint that he is just tasting the edges of suffering. For the relationship to work, he will have to go through much more. He is aghast. He does not think life would be worth living if this were so.

I think of a young couple in the news: They cancelled their wedding and killed themselves instead. A note left behind said something about her drug addiction, and that they were not happy.

* * *

You try to make the world better for your children. You hope they will not have to go through the dreadful things you had to. You feel the pain of not being able to nullify their pain.

Confession: In my life, pain opens new heights. Suffering brings me to new places. I hear of people who live differently. On television I see some people who have much more of "everything". I cannot speak for them *or* my children. For the moment, I speak only for myself.

No one wants a bitter cup. Yet the path of suffering contracts to a radiant point. Yes, radiance! But is radiance enough?

* * *

Ah, the visual–aural pleasures. My heart leaps when I see the stars, sky, colours, water, faces. Cherry Blossom Festival at the Brooklyn Botanical Garden—people, flowers of every size, shape, colour. My younger boy wants to plant the big purple tulips in our garden—and will! The names of herbs and flowers are aural treats. My spine tingles as I mouth them. Japanese drummers and dancers make silence dance and drum. My older boy plays drums. My younger boy plays electric bass. My wife and I started them on other instruments. They found their way to theirs. Pulse beats: How did they know?

Erroll Garner taught himself piano. He could not read a note. Someone asked him how he had done it. He asked, how does a beaver know how to build?

What do you teach yourself? *Really* teach yourself?

Where is your desire and love one?

* * *

For many years sex kept me alive. Many girlfriends. Even when it was bad, it was good. The only really bad thing was me, only it took me a long time to figure this out. My relationships tended to be tortured, for one or another reason. I thought it had to do with the other person, perhaps my choice of the other person. I picked the wrong one, not beautiful enough this way, that way, not scintillating enough, too little this, too much that, whatever.

Only after I was married did it dawn on me with crystalline authority that my relationships had been tortured because *I* was tortured. Yes, *I* was the red thread that ran through my life. What was bothering me was *my* pain, the pain of being alive. Sex soothed it; work soothed it; triumph soothed it. But it continues, a background throb, building like a toothache that leaves room for little else. Is that why I am a therapist? Spending my life doing root-canal work on other people's souls? While my own ache needs the most work of all?

I feel the ache! I feel the ache! The ache I feel is life aching! The ache of always being somewhat born . . . the ache of aliveness.

I sit for hours just feeling it.

Raw joy is a bull in a china-shop—and I love it. But little by little I learn to trust the joy that passes through the ache of aware-ness—the joy another can say "yes" to.

As I write this, I am smiling: sweet aching heart and wild joy couple, not entirely wild, far from tame—something I can say yes to, also.

* * *

Lacan (1977, p. 322) writes that desire acts as a defence against *jouissance*, limits *jouissance*, prohibits the full play of *jouissance*. Desire structures *jouissance*. It functions as barrier, brakes, filter.

How can desire, which is infinite, act as brakes?

Let *jouissance* be originary, boundless. Primordial *Jouissance* is Infinite Immateriality: an infinite of infinites. Not *Ein Soph* as such, but up there. It is, at the same time, radiant orgasmic expe-riencing, a sensation going on forever.

To taste unbounded *jouissance* sets one free from desire.

Desire obtrudes, disturbs unbounded *jouissance*. Desire is partly a lack, a wish for fulfilment, an infinite itch one cannot stop scratching.

Jouissance is infinite fulfilment now.

Where there is desire, there is law. There is drive for every-thing lacking and laws regulating it. Law obscures desire's structuring function. Laws are imposed on desires and desires attract laws. Structure circles structure.

Desire *ruptures jouissance*, dips into it, whets appetite, inflames itself. Desire squeezes *jouissance* into this or that desire. *Jouissance* has been known to consume desire, as those who burn to a crisp seeing God. But *jouissance* may be very pliable and part of any desire.

Some people identify themselves with their desires, and their desires with *jouissance*. It takes some catching on to realize desires are lesser infinities, *jouissance* a greater infinity. Desires are particular takes on *jouissance*. One may or may not be able to grow into a particular funnel over time. It is not *jouissance* one is mistaken about, but one's funnel system.

One's entire personality may be a funnel, an avenue of access or approach to *jouissance*. If something is wrong with personality as a filter, one cannot shake off something wrong with one's relationship to *jouissance*. Many feel something wrong or off with their lives, but fail to realize they may have a stinging stain as long as personality exists.

* * *

It takes some people a lifetime to discover filters that work for them. Not all desires are compatible with (one's) personality. Even more difficult than discovering limits inherent in desire is the task of discovering which desires mediate one's growth at a particular time. Which desires take one closer to or further from *jouissance*, and in what ways?

I am glad I did many things that were bad for me. I am sorry they lasted as long as they did. I am sorry I could not make them last longer. But ways of life I wanted did not work for me.

For example, as a young man I became a beatnik, living in Cape Cod, Mexico, North Beach. Jack Kerouac's *On the Road* was a propelling force; so was Descartes' radical doubt, which I applied to self and society, without quite understanding what he was up to. Everything was subject to radical questioning and stripping away, at the same time one rode currents of whatever came up. I idealized the vagabond, the spontaneous.

I am a failed beatnik. It may have worked for Allen Ginsberg, but it did not work for me. By my mid-twenties, I was quite ill. A waitress who let me stay with her in my feverish state told me she did not think beat life was good for me . . . it is not for everyone. Her words hurt me, but they were real and I had to consider them. What I wanted and what my personality could bear did not match.

I went into therapy and started over. The need for extremes did not leave, but I had a stable hub to whirl around. Whatever I did or did not do, there was therapy to go to. I wanted lots of women and followed desire and opportunity. I gorged on sex and solitude. But I remained raw, torn apart, edgy, until I married. I understand marriage is not for everyone, and it is very difficult for me. But single life was harder.

My therapy hub vanished when my analyst's marriage fell apart and he moved away for some years. When he returned, he was something of a negative model of how I did not want to end up. He was a wondrous enlightenment-seeker, but ravaged by aloneness, which I think played a role in killing him. Not all the people he saw made up for no everyday connection with someone.

I was not able to weave through jewels and rocks and holes of my desires enough to marry until fairly late. I may have become a therapist, partly, to become the hub I lacked. I was just starting as a therapist when my therapist left. It was as if we had lasted long enough for me to begin replacing him. I did not have him, but I had myself, at the centre of a somewhat more stable life than earlier. I was in the same city, doing the same thing, with a roof over my head, whatever the changes. To be a therapist meant, partly, to take care of myself (as my therapist had taken care of me, up to a point?).

But being a therapist to myself did not push me into the next stage of my life. It took a push from the outside, a combination of three therapists. Wilfred Bion told me to get married (in so many words!), and a consultation with André Green, a year later, further cleared the way. I could chase desires for the rest of my life and not get what I wanted. Did I even know what the wanted X was? I already was in my 40s.

Bion was a spokesperson for an inner voice in my youth. I had long wanted to marry and be a father. But I wanted many other things and became absorbed in my analysis instead of marrying.

Women come and go, analysis goes on and on. When my analysis broke down, it was as if a womb had blown up around me, leaving me raw and exposed. More hunting, scavenging, many kinds of wilderness, no manna in the morning—years of hunting for wombs. Was it possible to be real and married? How does one get out of wombs? How does one get into them? Wombs–wounds. One needs to know something about the relationship between nakedness and clothes in order to be with someone else successfully—in order to find the swinging gate between claustrophobia and diffusion.

* * *

"If I am not for myself, who will be? If I am only for myself, what am I? If not now, when?" The now and when in this saying by Hillel can cover many decades. I had to learn that neither analysis nor chasing desires would save me before I dared husband life. By then I knew that marriage and family would not "save" me either. No experience would do or fail to do the trick.

One desire is enemy of another. Beginnings of compassion and sacrifice are dearer than desire. I do not feel I decided anything, just dug in more deeply. Does it all depend on points of time?

* * *

Desires are nourishing, like ocean waves. They can kill you, thrill you, fill your heart with beauty, feel good all over. Freud teaches that we are made of many desires on many levels, often in conflict with each other. We are composed of systems within systems of desires. And most of our desires have laws that go with them. If we picture a Buddha made of infinite teats, we can picture our desires as all the mouths these teats invite. "God opens his hand and satisfies the desire of every living being", the psalmist says.

Since antiquity, desire is portrayed as Janus, or many-faced: good and evil twins, gods, brothers, horses, inclinations, catalogues of desires running through Greek myths. When we are drawn to love God with all our heart, soul, might, this means with all our desires, good and evil. Desires split us—we are divided by desires. Lacan teaches that desire is split and riddled with holes. Platonism and Buddhism portray a ladder of desires, and as we ascend through higher desires, we begin to gain a certain freedom from desire. Desire leads us beyond itself.

In a way, this is true with every pleasure. It is no easy matter for human beings to simply experience pleasure. "Pure pleasure" tends to be an intellectual abstraction, an object of reductive analysis, and not simply because pleasure is mixed with pain or emptiness. Pleasure almost always tends to be more than itself. It is a common and strange quirk of language to speak of things as merely pleasurable.

I recently tried an experiment, asking students to describe something pleasurable. Their descriptions always involved something more than pleasure—hints of ecstasy, bliss, joy, well-being, thrill, beatific bits. Pleasure spread through body and self, so that a good experience confirmed one's sense of self, made one feel better as a person, made one feel better about oneself. Pleasure was associated with the goodness of life. In no case did pleasure mean simply pleasure.

Language leads us into different worlds of experience. If one lets oneself be circumscribed or defined by the language of pleasure, one needs to keep fooling oneself in order to stay within the limits set. Pleasure is a signifier of the bounty of life and is associated with an array of states leading to the ecstatic. In sex, pleasure is often a gateway to ecstasy. In the case of failed ecstasy, pleasure is often ecstasy's stand-in or substitute. One is not after pleasure so much as after what pleasure gives one or where pleasure leads.

* * *

We can be fooled. We can be wrong about anything, especially about things that seem so right. We learn, too, that we can cling to things that seem so wrong. This is especially so when desire is associated with toxic nourishment.

A patient recently described how her parents had attacked and neglected her. Throughout her childhood, parental nourishment had been associated with neglect and attack. She said she became used to breathing bad air, eating bad food, thinking bad thoughts.

Desire tortured as much as nourished her, since she learned to get what nourishment she could from torturous situations.

She tried to think good thoughts, breathe good air, eat good food. But she ended up in situations that contained elements or vestiges of the neglecting–rejecting atmosphere she was brought up in. She invariably confounded emotional toxins with nourishment in a never-ending struggle to find more of the latter. The very root of desire was tainted with poisons that nourished her. Even when she managed to find a relatively decent situation, she drifted towards what might be bad in it, to the point of staging destructive scenes.

One can want what is bad for one as well as good, and these desires can be indistinguishable. In extreme form—only too common—human beings can be nourished by evil desires. It is an ugly realization to find that there are people who are not only addicted to degradation but thrive on it. Unconsciously, they degrade the atmosphere of the world, so they can extract what nourishment they can from poisons they are used to. They may even nourish themselves by inventing new poisons (or more effective variations). Solutions they seek compound the problem. Cultural pollution accelerates, and one hunts in vain for words or images or actions that provide an antidote.

There are dead people who feel relief when desire comes their way. Any desire is better than no desire in such a state, even if desire's wind wreaks havoc in its path. The same may be said for impulsive people overflowing with desires. Can one know when desire will uplift or cut down a life?

Uncertainty concerning desire is one reason Freud placed so much emphasis on talking, together with mental trial and error. I think of the sage who wondered what to do when he was angry. He consulted writings of other sages, and by the time he formed some notion about his state, his anger had ebbed. If one talks oneself out, one might avoid doing bad things. But one might miss out on life as well.

* * *

Sometimes things come together . . . or break apart and come together.

A writer sought help with his life and for nearly a year poured his heart out. He loved his wife, but not passionately. Their love had always been more parental, tender, caring, lacking desire. They were not unhappy. They each pursued careers. They were good friends. They wanted children, but she did not conceive. Tests showed he had a low sperm count. Therapy consisted mostly of listening to endless confessions of guilt over wanting someone he felt sexy with. He and his wife had built a good life. They shared a house, interests, friends. How could he leave? How could he hurt her? What would she do without him and he without her? They had been together for many years. But something was missing. Did he have the courage to try for more? What if he threw away real goodness for a fantasy?

Perhaps medical help would facilitate a pregnancy. Would having children with his wife not be better than starting a family with someone he did not know? Who knows whether medical intervention would work?

When medical aid became a real possibility, he bolted. He wanted to father a child of passion, not jerk off in a bottle. With agony, guilt, anxiety, he left the marriage. Before the end of another year, he had met someone he felt sexually alive with, had found a better mixture of caring and desire, a more physical relationship. His sperm count went up, and his partner became pregnant. They began a family.

He felt grief over leaving his first wife. They remained friendly. He felt deliriously happy about finding desire and starting a family. I received notes from him for many years, telling me of his progress. How did this happen? I have no idea, except that creating an atmosphere where people can hear themselves sometimes does strange and marvellous things.

* * *

Often a projected and attacked damaged self comes to be linked with desire or semblances of desire. A man with an extremely damaged/damaging mother was able to marry. However, he could not sustain sexual arousal with his attractive wife. He wanted her to watch porno movies with him, but she was not inspired by them. She preferred having sex naturally. He was angry at her and judged her defective for not being as aroused as he by porno flicks.

He was at the top of his profession and used to people listening to him, even catering to him. He did not have to give much of himself to others. Yet he performed on a very high level. He was clever and dedicated in his work. In his work, he was intact, at one with himself, potent.

His clients came to him in various states of damage and need of repair. He took up their causes and made the best of them. He was looked up to for being good at helping others. Oddly, his professional life shared something with pornography. In both, he flew over his damaged self. Both work and pornography supported and catered to denial of self-damage.

While immersed in pornography, he felt a sense of imaginary intactness. As in work, he triumphed over his feelings. He reached planes higher than his damaged self, beyond his psychotic mother. Pornographic scenes triumph over feelings. The action is what counts, whatever the actors may (or may not) feel. Sex acts are staged for an observer and sales. The visual impact packs the punch, not a body's feel from the inside. Pornographic sex is visual consumerism, rather than being deeply spontaneous or naturally expressive.

He was, in effect, enraged at his wife for not joining him in making sex into something one is outside of. He was external to himself and could not bear her living from the inside. At the same time, he needed "inferior" inside people (with inside messes), so he could locate his damage in them and attack it (he felt superior to the needy ones he serviced and who serviced him). It vaguely occurred to him that many actors in porno flicks come from abusive backgrounds. There are many ways of flying above damage. What he could not bear was the refusal to act as if the damage were negligible or did not count.

There are many ways to handle connections between damage and desire—fight–flight the most common. In the case above, the damaged self is kept far away, externalized at too great a distance. Movements towards the inside are attacked.

In one case, more extreme than the above, a man could not understand why women did not want to be with him. He could not take in how abrasive he was. He saw himself as brilliant and amazing. Yet women ran away, rather than be warmly awed. The truth was that he could not let a woman live inside him. There was so much damage to his own inner woman that real women were too threatening. There was no place inside him for a real woman. He felt desire, but desire isolated him, since he used it to deny damage. He needed to be coached to stop killing the woman and let her live within him—no small feat.

The opposite is the man who feels so damaged that he cannot say no. He bathes in damage, rather than denying it. He will do anything a woman wants. Sooner or later, his system recoils. He becomes claustrophobic and must escape. He is insufficiently outside himself and feels suffocated. He all too readily identifies with the woman within, particularly the incapacitated or damaged aspects. He is endlessly empathic until the recoil. He needs coaching to kill the woman a little at a time, as he goes along. He needs to listen to signals that the bond is becoming too consuming and create space for himself, even if it means putting the other off for a while. Every relationship has balancing acts between damage and desire that keep one learning.

Epilogue

Fusions of trauma and nourishment mark all lives. Sometimes the balance tips very much to one or the other side. Trauma may be so severe that nourishment becomes less and less possible. Personality becomes so occupied with dealing with wounds that little is left over. Difficulties are even greater when trauma becomes nourishment. Still, there are cases in which deep lines cut by trauma provide access to depths that are otherwise unreachable. In such instances, nourishment follows trauma to new places. We wish things could be otherwise . . . easier. But we have little choice when illumination shines through injury.

Nevertheless, we do nourish each other and continue nourishing each other. Something comes through. We procreate and create, build cities and cultures, and nourish affections and creative efforts. That our nourishing efforts contain social and psychic poisons, that, to varying degrees, we ourselves are toxic, is part of the challenge we find ourselves forced to face. Our faith—ever tested—is that facing this challenge well brings us to places we could not have found otherwise, and that some of these places are very worth the trip.

REFERENCES

Benjamin, J. (1988). *The Bonds of Love: Psychoanalysis, Feminism, and the Problem of Domination.* New York: Pantheon.

Benjamin, J. (1995). *Like Subjects, Love Objects.* New Haven, CY: Yale University Press.

Bion, W. R. (1965). *Transformations.* London: Heinemann.

Bion, W. R. (1967). *Second Thoughts.* Northvale, NJ: Jason Aronson.

Bion, W. R. (1970). *Attention and Interpretation.* London: Tavistock.

Bion, W. R. (1992). *Cogitations.* London: Karnac Books.

Bion, W. R. (1994). *Clinical Seminars and Other Works.* London: Karnac Books.

Bloch, D. (1984). *"So the Witch Won't Eat Me": Fantasy of the Child's Fear of Infanticide.* New York: Grove Press.

Ehrenzweig, A. (1971). *The Hidden Order of Art.* Berkeley, CA: University of California Press.

Eigen, M. (1986). *The Psychotic Core.* Northvale, NJ: Jaron Aronson.

Eigen, M. (1993). *The Electrified Tightrope.* Northvale, NJ: Jason Aronson.

Eigen, M. (1995). *Reshaping the Self.* Madison, CT: Psychosocial Press.

Eigen, M. (1996). *Psychic Deadness.* Northvale, NJ: Jason Aronson.

Eigen, M. (1998). *The Psychoanalytic Mystic*. London: Free Associations Books; Binghamton, NY: Esf Publications.

Fairbairn, W. R. D. (1954). *An Object-Relations Theory of the Personality*. New York: Basic Books.

Freud, S. (1911). Psycho-analytic notes on an autobiographical account of a case of paranoia (dementia paranoides). *Standard Edition, 12*: 3–82.

Freud S. (1937). Analysis terminable and interminable. *Standard Edition, 23*.

Grotstein, J. (1981). *Splitting and Projective Identification*. Northvale, NJ: Jason Aronson.

Kennan, G. (1948). *Policy Planning Study, 23*. In N. Chomsky, *What Uncle Sam Really Wants*. Berkeley, CA: Odonian Press, 1992.

Klein, M. (1946). Notes on some schizoid mechanisms. In: *Developments in Psycho-Analysis*, edited by. M. Klein, P. Heimann, S. Isaacs, & J. Riviere. London: Hogarth Press, 1952.

Lacan, J. (1977). *Ecrits*. Trans. A. Sheridan. New York: Norton.

Lautreamont, le Comte de [Isadore Ducasse]. (1868). *Maldoror*. New York: Penguin, 1978.

Matte-Blanco, I. (1975). *The Unconscious as Infinite Sets*. London: Duckworth. [Reprinted London: Karnac Books, 1998.]

Matte-Blanco, I. (1988). *Thinking, Feeling, and Being*. London: Routledge.

McCourt, F. (1996). *Angela's Ashes*. New York: Scribner.

Meltzer, D. (1973). *Sexual States of Being*. Perthshire: Clunie Press.

Milner, M. (1957). *On Not Being Able to Paint*. New York: International Universities Press.

Milton, J. (1667). *Paradise Lost*. New York: Odyssey Press, 1935.

Phillips, A. (1988). *Winnicott*. London: Fontana.

Winnicott, D. W. (1965). *The Maturational Processes and the Facilitating Environment*. New York: International Universities Press.

Winnicott, D. W. (1971). *Playing and Reality*. New York: Basic Books.

Winnicott, D. W. (1974). Fear of breakdown. *International Review of Psycho-Analysis, 1*: 103–107.

Winnicott, D. W. (1989). *Psychoanalytic Explorations*, edited by C. Winnicott, R. Shepherd, & M. Davis. Cambridge, MA: Harvard University Press.

Young, R. M. (1994). New ideas about the Oedipus complex. *Melanie Klein and Object Relations, 12*: 1–20.

INDEX

adaptation, interpersonal,
    between mother and
    infant, 86
aliveness:
  attack on, 190
  frightening side of, xviii
  sense of, xvii, xviii, 45, 93, 96,
    101, 103, 104, 105, 106, 107,
    108
  and normalcy, 100–108
anxiety(ies):
  control of through medication,
    59
  core, 175
  madness, 175
  paranoid, 173
  psychotic, 167
  unthinkable, 172

babies, time demands of, 69
Baudelaire, C. P., 185

Benjamin, J., 112
Bion, W. R., xx, 48, 60, 79, 129, 140,
    155, 166, 200, 217
  on big bang image, 148–149
  on lying, 144–148
  on marriage, 201
  on nameless dread, 172
  on transformations in
    hallucinosis and
    transformations in
    analysis, 188–191
Blake, W., 204
Bloch, D., 45

child abuse, 124
clinical examples:
  "Alice": poisoned by parental
    self-hate, xv, xvi, 1–12,
    80–82, 191–192, 198,
    199
  "Ben": music subdued, 82–83

hate:
  as poison, xiv, 48
  self-, 1
Hawthorne, N., 185
helplessness, sharing, 147
Hillel, 218
Hitler, A., 14

Jesus, 61
Jong, E., 179
jouissance, 215, 216
  and desire, 215–216
Judas Iscariot, 13

Kennan, G., 17
Kerouac, J., 216
Khan, M., 175
Klee, P., 150
Klein, M., 129

Lacan, J., 215, 219
Lautreamont, le Comte de
  [Isadore Ducasse], 107
loss, layers of [Penny: clinical
  example], 111–116
love, poisoning by, xiv–xv

madness:
  expressed as bugs, 58
  fear of, 171–185
Matte-Blanco, I., 79, 124, 129
McCourt, F., 163
Meltzer, D., 129
Milner, M., 129
Milton, J., 107, 201
Miró, J., 150
miscarriage, 35–55
  prevention of through therapy,
    46–55

nameless dread [Bion], 79, 172
normalcy, 85–108
  primary, 85, 93

sense of, xvii
variations in, 105–108

Oedipus, 45

personalization–depersonalization
  [Winnicott], 87–88
Plato, 61, 185
Pound, E., 119
primary aliveness, 98
primary normalcy, 85, 86, 93, 94,
  96, 97, 105
  and self-hate, 98–100

rage:
  injury, 48
  therapeutic, 6
Rembrandt Van Rijn, 150
Rilke, R. M., 188

seamless seams, 198–204
self-hate, 26, 52, 59, 62, 64, 66, 80,
  99, 191, 192, 198, 199
  maternal, 3, 25, 27
  parental, 1, 93
  and physical deformity, 94
self-nulling, 123–137
Socrates, 61, 177
suicide, 13–34, 60, 124
  of high-school football player,
    14–15, 16, 17

talking cure, therapy as, 46
transformations in analysis vs.
  transformations in
  hallucinosis, 188
trauma, 55, 90, 91, 133, 145,
  225
  and physical deformity, 86

vacuum–evacuation, 155
Van Gogh, V., 150